Economic analysis and moral philosophy shows how understanding moral philosophy can improve economic analysis, and how moral philosophy can benefit by drawing on insights and analytical tools from economics.

Part I focuses on rationality and argues that in defending their model of rationality, economists wind up espousing fragments of a highly contestable moral theory.

Part II deals with methods of evaluating economic outcomes and institutions in terms of their consequences for welfare, such as welfare economics and utilitarianism, and the standard theory of welfare implicit in these evaluations.

Part III is concerned with liberty, rights, equality, and justice, which are also important in evaluating economic policies and institutions. Part III presents alternatives to the questions welfare economists ask and to the terms in which they try to answer them.

Part IV introduces technical work in economics that is guided by ethical concepts and relevant to moral theorizing. It shows that moral philosophers also have a lot to learn from economists. A brief discussion of relevant literature follows at the end of each chapter, and at the end of the book there is a glossary of relevant terms.

Economic analysis and moral philosophy

CAMBRIDGE SURVEYS OF ECONOMIC LITERATURE

Series editor: John Pencavel, Stanford University

The literature of economics is expanding rapidly. Not only are familiar topics being refashioned by research advances but economists are now addressing issues across the range of the social sciences. Cambridge Surveys of Economic Literature are designed to keep students and professional economists abreast of the latest developments. Each book presents an original perspective on the subject, offering an evaluation of the literature and an accessible review of the topic. The books are thus intended to be both teaching tools and authoritative guides to the field for specialists.

Economic analysis and moral philosophy

Daniel M. Hausman
University of Wisconsin-Madison

Michael S. McPherson
Williams College

 CAMBRIDGE
UNIVERSITY PRESS

Published by the Press Syndicate of the University of Cambridge
The Pitt Building, Trumpington Street, Cambridge CB2 1RP
40 West 20th Street, New York, NY 10011–4211 USA
10 Stamford Road, Oakleigh, Melbourne 3166, Australia

First published 1996
Reprinted 1997

Printed in Great Britain at the University Press, Cambridge

A catalogue record for this book is available from the British Library

Library of Congress cataloguing in publication data

Hausman, Daniel M., 1947–
Economic analysis and moral philosophy/Daniel M. Hausman,
Michael S. McPherson.
    p. cm.
ISBN 0 521 55202 8 (hc) – ISBN 0 521 55850 6 (pbk)
1. Economics – Moral and ethical aspects.   I McPherson, Michael
S.   II. Title.
HB72.H355   1996
330–dc20   95-8814   CIP

ISBN 0 521 55202 8 hardback
ISBN 0 521 55850 6 paperback

SE

Contents

Contents

Figures

Acknowledgments

This book arose out of a survey essay, "Taking ethics seriously: economics and contemporary moral philosophy," which we published in the July 1993 issue of the *Journal of Economic Literature*. We would like to thank John Roemer for commissioning that essay and for the detailed criticisms he offered of several drafts. Others who were of tremendous help were Richard Arneson, Henry Bruton, Nancy Cartwright, David Colander, Marc Fleurbaey, John Kautsky, Eric Kramer, Philippe Mongin, John Pencavel, Philip Pettit, Amartya Sen, Julius Sensat, Max Steuer, Hamish Stewart, Alain Trannoy, Gordon Winston, students at Williams College and the London School of Economics, and anonymous referees. Harry Brighouse, Henry Bruton, Lester Hunt, Andrew Levine, Patrick McCartan, Jonathan Riley, David Ruben, Larry Samuelson, and Daniel Wikler read drafts of chapters of this book and offered valuable assistance. The research and writing of this book were supported by a collaborative research grant from the National Endowment for the Humanities, and Hausman also gratefully acknowledges the support of a Vilas Associate award from the University of Wisconsin-Madison.

Introduction

1 Ethics and economics?

Economic analysis and moral philosophy is concerned with economics and ethics, but it is not about how to behave on the shop-floor or in the corporate board room. We prescribe no code of conduct and preach no sermons. (Well, maybe there are just a few sermons.) This book is about the relationships between economics and ethics, not about how to act morally. In *Economic analysis and moral philosophy*, we hope to show how understanding moral philosophy can improve economic analysis and (to a lesser extent) we hope to show how moral philosophy can benefit by drawing on insights and analytical tools from economics. We are writing mainly for those who are interested in economics, and we want to help them in their economic analyses.

This focus may seem a big let-down. Surely it's more important to grapple with life-and-death moral problems! You'll get no argument from us about that. We fully agree, and we're not proposing that people stop asking moral questions. On the contrary, we hope this book will show how important morality is in economic life. But our concern is with economic theory rather than directly with economic life. *Our job will be to show clearly how understanding moral philosophy can improve economic analysis.*

Indeed our focus may seem even more disappointing, for we will argue that the main value of moral theory does *not* lie in prescribing what to do in particular situations. Although moral theories do guide conduct, they are not cookbooks for good behavior. Their main purpose is to give people a theoretically satisfying account of the nature of morality, where it fits into their lives, and why they assign it the importance that they do. Similarly moral theory is important to economists not exclusively, or even principally, as a guidebook to "correct" policies. Rather it helps them to see how to think productively about the moral dimensions of policy problems and helps bolster their confidence in recognizing and dealing with these moral issues. We hope also to show how knowing some ethics can help economists understand how the moral dimensions of people's lives influence their economic behavior.

3

Moral insights will, to be sure, be more important to some parts of economics than others. Moral ideas will not help much in forecasting the price of wheat or in refining theories of exchange rate determination. (Exchange rates and wheat prices do however result from the choices of human beings – not profit-maximizing automatons – and the moral dimensions of their choices might sometimes have some significant impact.) Moral ideas may be more important to economists who are endeavoring to help reconstruct the economic systems of Eastern Europe or who are trying to help citizens think through the trade-offs between environmental protection and economic growth.

1.1 What are moral questions and how can they be answered?

Many people feel uneasy about moral questions. They are not sure how they relate to legal questions or to questions about social standards. And they feel that answers to such questions are "subjective" or "relative." These feelings have some justification. But these qualms do not imply that all answers to moral questions are equally good or that people never have good reasons to regard some answers as better than others.

Consider an example of a genuine moral question facing an individual. A young woman attending college becomes pregnant and is trying to decide whether to have an abortion. Notice first that hers is not a legal problem. Knowing that abortion is legal does not tell her whether she ought to have one, and, more controversially, knowing that it is illegal does not automatically tell her that she ought not to have one. Second, hers is not a question that a sociologist can answer. If she reads that 62.37 percent of her fellow citizens think that an abortion is permissible in circumstances like hers, her problem has not been solved. She still needs to decide whether she ought to have the abortion or not. Nor does it help to say that moral questions are subjective and depend on feelings. For her feelings depend in part on her *judgments* (about, for example, the moral standing of a fetus). It seems that her moral question is real, that some answers to it are better than others, and that it is possible to think rationally about which answers are better and which are worse.

There are genuine moral questions about social policy, too. For example, the question whether abortions *should be* legal cannot be decided by ascertaining what the law *is*. (In the United States, one can also ask whether laws concerning abortion are consistent with the constitution, but questions about what the constitution ought to say are moral, not legal or constitutional questions.) Similarly, one cannot decide whether abortions ought to be legal by taking a poll. A poll can determine what most people believe, but it won't say whether they're right. Those who believe that abortions ought not to be legal cannot be refuted by results of polls showing that most people believe that they should remain legal. One addresses moral questions instead by making arguments.

The view that moral questions have better and worse answers and that arguments can help us find out which answers are better has been criticized in several ways. People have pointed out that moral judgments are *prescriptive* – that they say how things ought to be rather than how they are – and that moral judgments thus cannot possibly be literally true or false. Even if this is correct, it does not follow that all moral judgments are equally good. Some prescriptions are better than others. Others have argued that there is no method of resolving moral disagreements and that consequently all one ever gets in morality is disagreement. But there is a method: one can formulate arguments – that is, one can look for premises that others can agree on and then use logic to try to reach some agreement on the issues in dispute. Obviously moral questions are often hard to answer, and disagreement may persist for decades. But there is lots of agreement in ethics, too. Few people approve of torture for any purpose, and even fewer approve of it for the purposes of entertainment.

A more serious objection often made to the view that there are better or worse answers to moral questions is that morality is *relative*. In one sense morality clearly is relative: what's right depends on (is relative to) what the facts are. Whether it's permissible to knock over a frail old man depends on whether he was about to be run over by a truck (and was thereby saved). But to recognize that one does not have a well-defined moral question until one has specified what the facts are is perfectly consistent with the idea that well-defined moral questions have better and worse answers.

In claiming that morality is relative, people sometimes mean instead that whatever a person (or a society) believes is right is automatically right ("for that person or society"). But when the woman in the example above is trying to decide whether it is morally permissible to have an abortion, she is not trying to find out what her beliefs already are, she is trying to find out what she *should* believe – that is, which answer is actually best. Similarly, when legislators are trying to decide whether abortion should be legal, they are not trying to find out what people in their society believe, but whether abortion should or shouldn't be legal. Furthermore, if whatever people believed about ethics were automatically right, there could be no moral disagreement. Since there is moral disagreement, people's ethical beliefs may be incorrect. Similarly, if a social consensus guaranteed its own correctness, all defenders of unpopular views would automatically be mistaken. But iconoclasts cannot be refuted with polls, and social consensus is not proof of correctness.

Concerns about *tolerance* also motivate the denial that people can be "objectively" wrong about morality. Economists and non-economists alike may fear that there is something dogmatic and intolerant about believing that one has the right answer to a moral question. But people who are genuinely tolerant are not moral skeptics: they believe that tolerance is (non-relativistically) good. To believe that there are better and worse answers to moral questions and to seek them requires a willingness to understand the arguments of others and a recognition of one's own limitations. Such an objective commitment to tolerance is a better remedy for dogmatism than is an impossible skepticism.

So in our view there is nothing suspect or intolerant about believing that some answers to moral questions are better than others and that rational argument can help one to judge which answers are better. These theses are implicit in individual moral judgments and in policy-making, and it is hard to deny them without simply denying that there is any such thing as morality at all.

1.2 How is moral philosophy relevant to economics?

The thought that studying ethics is of relevance to economic analysis may seem far-fetched. Why not consult tarot cards instead? Many people – indeed probably some of you reading these very words – regard moral philosophy as abstruse gobbledygook that cannot help one do *anything* better (except perhaps to spread confusion). If one is seeking clarity, why look in a swamp?

Our hope is that readers of this book will not come away with the impression that argument in moral philosophy is obscure, incoherent or unworldly. It is, to be sure, intellectually demanding, abstract, and often intricate, and we'll not dispel all puzzlement. Like economics, moral theory is loaded with controversies and unresolved issues. We want most of all to show that moral reasoning helps one to get a surer grip on serious problems about how to make our lives and our society better.

But even if moral philosophy clarifies morality, why should it clarify economics? One might object: "Economics is science or engineering. It shows how to arrive at certain goals, but unlike ethics, it does not prescribe what goals one should have. Economics provides technical knowledge that has no more to do with ethics than does geometry or physics. No matter how sensible and well-conceived ethical theories may be, they have nothing to do with economics and cannot possibly help one understand economies."

This whole book is a response to this objection, but we only tackle it head on in the appendix. There we criticize explicitly the "engineering" vision that portrays economics as entirely value-neutral. In the text, on the other hand, we try to be constructive and to show how moral questions do indeed arise in economics. If, after seeing how moral questions arise and why their answers matter, readers are still interested in the arguments purporting to show that economics ought to be value-free, they can see what we have to say in response to such arguments in the appendix.

1.3 Organization of this book

Chapter 2 presents two examples that illustrate ways in which moral questions arise in economics, and our concluding chapter (chapter 14) returns to these examples and applies concepts, distinctions, and principles developed in the chapters in between. Those eleven chapters are divided into four parts.

Part I focuses on *rationality*. Like morality, rationality is normative. One ought to be moral and one ought to be rational. One is wicked if not moral and foolish if not rational. Yet rationality, unlike morality, plays a conspicuous role in contemporary economic theory. Economists usually deny that economic theory presupposes any ethics, but they freely admit that it presupposes a great deal about rationality. However, economists cannot have it both ways. Endorsing their theory of rationality, we will argue, unavoidably commits them to controversial moral principles. In defending their model of rationality, economists wind up espousing fragments of a moral theory.

It also turns out, we shall argue, that exploring the connections between morality and rationality leads to criticisms of economics, because the moral principles implicit in standard views of rationality are implausible. When these principles are stated explicitly, very few people would endorse them. The standard views of rationality also make it hard to understand the rationality of norms and of morality itself. Taking ethics seriously in this case leads (or so we shall argue) to serious theoretical criticisms of basic principles of economics.

Parts II and III then zero in on concepts and theories of economic *evaluation*. Which economic policies and institutions are best? How should they be judged? Part II focuses on methods of evaluating economic outcomes and institutions in terms of their consequences for welfare, such as welfare economics and utilitarianism, and on the standard theory of welfare implicit in these evaluations. We shall criticize the preference-satisfaction view of welfare that economists defend, and we shall argue that welfare is not the only thing that matters ethically. But we do not doubt that welfare is of great moral importance and a major aim of Part II is to clarify its role.

Part III is mainly concerned with four other notions – freedom, rights, equality, and justice. These notions are important in the evaluation of economic policies and institutions, and moral theories have been built around them. When one shifts one's attention away from welfare, new vistas appear. Not only are there new questions and new aspects of economic arrangements to consider, but there are also new methods of thinking about morality. We shall in particular say a good deal about *contractualism*, which provides a way of making sense of morality in which the consequences of policies for individual welfare are not necessarily decisive. While Part II uses the concepts of standard welfare economics, Part III presents alternatives to the questions that welfare economists ask and to the terms in which they try to answer them.

Part IV finally provides a small sample of technical work in economics that is directly guided by ethical concepts and immediately relevant to moral theorizing. The payoffs from knowing something about both economics and philosophy do not go only to economists. Philosophers have lessons to learn from attempts to formalize moral concepts and to determine their consequences.

At the end of each chapter we provide a brief discussion of relevant literature, and at the end of the book is a glossary of relevant terms. We have tried not to burden the text with too many references. Many more can be found in the survey essay from which this book arose (Hausman and McPherson 1993).

When you are finished with this ramble through the lush forests of moral philosophy and the brushland where it meets economics, we hope you'll see that economics remains partly a moral science. It can't be done without moral presuppositions, and it's hard to do it well without addressing moral issues intelligently. Similarly, moral philosophy can't be done without beliefs about human interactions, and it's hard to do it well without knowledge of the kind that economists seek. Like those who would completely disavow the culture of their parents, economists sometimes try to deny their philosophical lineage. Although they can reform and improve their philosophical inheritance, they can't escape it, and to attempt the escape makes their theories hollow. The philosophical parents of today's social disciplines cannot successfully repudiate their offspring either. Moral philosophy and economics have much to contribute to each other.

2　Two examples

This book will be filled with arguments, but arguments are pale and abstract without examples. One good example may do more to clarify how ethics matters to economics than would a hundred pages of argument. Furthermore, ethics is not just logic. Emotion has its part to play, too, and examples help to engage the emotions. In this chapter our concern is not to argue that ethics matters in economics but to exhibit through examples how important ethics is.

We shall discuss two examples. The first caused an uproar.

2.1　A shocking memorandum

In December of 1991, Lawrence Summers, who was then the chief economist at the World Bank, sent the following memorandum to some colleagues:

Just between you and me, shouldn't the World Bank be encouraging *more* migration of the dirty industries to the LDCs [less developed countries]? I can think of three reasons:

(1) The measurement of the costs of health-impairing pollution depends on the foregone earnings from increased morbidity and mortality. From this point of view a given amount of health-impairing pollution should be done in the country with the lowest cost, which will be the country with the lowest wages. I think the economic logic behind dumping a load of toxic waste in the lowest-wage country is impeccable and we should face up to that.

(2) The costs of pollution are likely to be non-linear as the initial increments of pollution probably have very low cost. I've always thought that under-populated countries in Africa are vastly *under* polluted; their air quality is probably vastly inefficiently low [*sic*] compared to Los Angeles or Mexico City. Only the lamentable facts that so much pollution is generated by non-tradable industries (transport, electrical generation) and that the unit transport costs of solid waste are so high prevent world-welfare-enhancing trade in air pollution and waste.

(3) The demand for a clean environment for aesthetic and health reasons is likely to have very high income-elasticity. The concern over an agent that causes a

one-in-a-million change in the odds of prostate cancer is obviously going to be much higher in a country where people survive to get prostate cancer than in a country where under-5 mortality is 200 per thousand. Also, much of the concern over industrial atmospheric discharge is about visibility-impairing particulates. These discharges may have very little direct health impact. Clearly trade in goods that embody aesthetic pollution concerns could be welfare-enhancing. While production is mobile the consumption of pretty air is a non-tradable.

The problem with the arguments against all of these proposals for more pollution in LDCs (intrinsic rights to certain goods, moral reasons, social concerns, lack of adequate markets, etc.) could be turned around and used more or less effectively against every Bank proposal for liberalisation. (quoted in *The Economist*, February 8, 1992, p. 66)

The memorandum is worth reading carefully, and we would urge you to read it a second time before proceeding further. Summers is not seriously proposing a World Bank program to export pollution to the LDCs. Such a policy faces technical difficulties, and there are moral arguments against it (though Summers points out provocatively that similar moral objections apply to other World Bank policies). One should also not think that Summers has distorted economics in order to serve some personal ideology. On the contrary, his economic logic is exemplary. His only mistake was to put into words uncomfortable implications that most economists would prefer not to draw or at least not to draw in a memo that might be "leaked" to *The Economist*. We've seized on this example, because it is easier to recognize controversial ethical content in economic theory when it is so blatant and apparently repugnant.

2.2 The economic benefits of exporting pollution to LDCs

Air and water pollution lessen the quality of life in many ways, yet most kinds of pollution have no market prices. One cannot go to the hardware store and purchase for $19.95 a 20 percent decrease in the toxic chemicals in the air one breathes. There are few markets in pollution limitation, first because it is not possible to locate all the sources of air and water pollution. (If your neighbors decide to dump left-over weed killer down their drain, who will ever know?) Second, even if it were possible, it would be prohibitively expensive to strike a deal with all the polluters in order to improve your air or water. Third, any deal you strike with polluters will affect your neighbor and vice versa – while walking to the corner, you've got to breathe the same air your neighbor breathes. Any effective deal will require cooperation among your neighbors.

Thus some collective action is often needed in controlling pollution. One way economists can help with the problems of controlling pollution is by *imputing* costs to it. The hope is to figure out what pollution costs would be, if there were markets where pollution could be bought and sold. Economists may attempt to impute pollution costs by examining housing prices in communities that are much the same, apart from their air quality. They can draw inferences from how much people pay for air filters, water filters, or bottled water. They can collaborate with biologists in determining and assessing the costs of damage to health caused by pollutants. In such ways, economists may be able to estimate how much people in developed countries would be willing to pay to lessen pollution in their environment and how much people in LDCs would have to be compensated in order to be willing to accept more pollution.

People might be ignorant of the harms caused by pollution. People in an LDC might be willing to accept toxic wastes for very little compensation, because they are unaware of the contents of the wastes, the harms they might do, or the prospects of the wastes escaping and poisoning groundwater. If their willingness to accept more pollution were based on such mistakes, it would not reflect what was really in their interest.

Summers avoids the problem of LDC negotiators mistaking their interests, because he does not rely on estimates of how eager people in developed countries are to be rid of their pollution or how willing people in LDCs are to accept it. What his three points attempt to show instead is that, insofar as they are *rational*, people in LDCs should be happy to sell pollution rights to people in developed countries for a price that the latter should be happy to pay – for the economic costs of the *consequences* of increased pollution are much lower in LDCs than they are in developed countries. The willingness to accept more pollution in LDCs does not rest on mistakes about the consequences of doing so.

Economists employ complicated techniques to determine economic costs when things are not literally bought or sold, and it will simplify the discussion here if we engage in some make-believe. Suppose pollution could be bought and sold on the market. Since pollution is a bad, what consumers would want to buy would be its *absence*. Let us think of reductions of pollution that consumers could buy as units of a single hypothetical commodity, "environmental quality" (EQ). We can then think about what the price of units of EQ and total expenditures on EQ would be in this make-believe world in which individuals could separately purchase and consume units of EQ, and firms could separately produce and market units of EQ.

Consider whether rational and well-informed individuals, who live in a particular LDC, *Poor*, could strike deals to sell units of EQ to rational and well-informed individuals, who live in a developed country, *Rich*. If *Poor* is one of those "underpolluted" LDCs that Summers refers to, *Poor* currently has a great deal of inexpensive EQ. Environmental quality is inexpensive not only because it is plentiful, but because, as Summers points out, (1) the value added to output by an additional unit of EQ will be very low, (2) the costs in health or aesthetics of a small drop of EQ will be small, and (3) citizens in *Poor* lack other things that they would want to purchase first. In *Rich*, on the other hand, EQ is costly and scarce. So unless the price of a unit of EQ is extremely high or extremely low, individuals in *both Poor* and *Rich* will gain if EQs are sold by individuals in *Poor* to individuals in *Rich*. The possibility for making advantageous trades will disappear only when *Poor* has acquired so much of *Rich*'s pollution that the price of environmental quality in *Poor* is as high as it is in *Rich*. This will happen only when there is much *more* pollution in *Poor* than in *Rich*. For given *Poor*'s poverty, a bad environment will have lower costs for individuals in *Poor*, and they should be willing to pay as much for pollution abatement as are individuals in *Rich* only when *Poor* faces much worse pollution problems.

So if individuals were all rational and well informed, and it were possible for individuals easily to buy, sell, and transport pollution or "environmental quality," there would be active trading between the developed and less developed nations of the world, and pollution would be pouring out of the developed nations and into the less developed nations. But units of EQ cannot ("lamentably"?) be individually appropriated, bought, and sold, and it is hard to transport pollution between nations. Consequently, the World Bank can enhance world welfare by facilitating transfers of pollutants to LDCs in return for some measure of compensation.

Merely shifting pollution to LDCs, without paying any compensation would not, of course, be *mutually* beneficial. But from the perspective of "cost-benefit analysis" (see section 7.4), it would still result in a net benefit, because the developed countries *could* compensate the LDCs and still be better off. One could thus read Summers' memo as also pointing out the advantages of *uncompensated* transfers of pollution to the LDCs.

2.3 Where does ethics come in?

The three points in Summers' essay show that the amount rational individuals in developed countries would be willing to pay to lessen their pollution is more than the amount that rational individuals in LDCs would demand in order to accept more pollution, and that there would be more pollution in LDCs if pollution were easily exchangeable. But why should one conclude that it is "lamentable" that "pollution is generated by nontradable industries"? Why should one conclude, "Clearly trade in goods that embody aesthetic pollution concerns could be *welfare-enhancing*" [our emphasis]? How is one supposed to reach the conclusion that "the World Bank [should] be encouraging *more* migration of the dirty industries to the LDCs"? How does one get from claims about how rational and well-informed individuals *would choose* to claims about *welfare* and from claims about welfare to claims about what the World Bank *ought to do*? We have not yet clarified the logic of Summers' argument.

We would suggest that Summers' argument can be articulated as follows:

1. The economic costs of the consequences of increased pollution in LDCs are much less than the economic benefits of the consequences of lessened pollution in developed countries. (premise)
2. Rational and well-informed people in developed countries would be willing to pay more to lessen pollution than rational and well-informed people in LDCs would demand in return for accepting more pollution. (from 1)
3. For some intermediate compensation C, all rational and well-informed individuals would be willing to transfer pollution from a developed economy to a LDC. (from 2)
4. If all well-informed and rational individuals are willing to make an exchange, then carrying it out makes all of them better off. It increases everyone's welfare. (premise)
5. Shifting pollution to LDCs from developed countries and paying C makes everyone better off. (from 3 and 4)
6. It is a good thing to make people better off. (premise)
7. It is a good thing to shift pollution to LDCs and to pay compensation C. (from 5 and 6)

The conclusion in this reconstruction of Summers' argument is slightly different than "the World Bank [should] be encouraging *more* migration of the dirty industries to the LDCs," but if one assumes that the jobs and revenues provided by dirty industries are "reasonable compensation," then this reconstruction captures Summers' intentions. One might argue that it would be a good thing to shift pollution to LDCs regardless of whether there is any compensation, on the grounds that there is a "net benefit" in such shifts. But it will take more controversial moral premises to establish this stronger conclusion, and we will not comment on such an argument at this point.

The above argument contains two plausible moral premises, statements 4 and 6. In later chapters we shall examine these ethical principles. What is important here is to recognize that they are indispensable. Summers is well aware that dumping pollution in LDCs raises moral questions, and in the last paragraph he briefly refers to some of these. But the tone of the memorandum (which is addressed to fellow economists, not to the public at large) suggests that the three numbered paragraphs make a "scientific" case, while the last paragraph in the memo mentions wishy-washy moral objections. The moral content does not wait for the last paragraph to make its appearance. The three numbered paragraphs are part of a *moral* argument, and Summers' economics is shot through with ethics.

2.4 Should the World Bank encourage migration of dirty industries to LDCs?

The conclusion in the argument above appears to follow from its premises but the logic is not transparent. In particular, one might wonder exactly how 2 is supposed to follow from 1 or how 3 is supposed to follow from 2. If one does not want to accept the conclusion, either one has to challenge one of these links, or one has to question at least one of the premises.

The uproar caused by this memo suggests that most people are not willing to accept its conclusion. But this may be a thoughtless first reaction. Why shouldn't the World Bank encourage migration of dirty industries? Though we can't pretend to speak for all those who find this conclusion objectionable, here are three possibilities. (We will consider others in chapter 14.)

1. Encouraging dirty industries to migrate to LDCs will lead to more total pollution. Developed countries have the incentive and the administrative capacity to enforce pollution controls, while LDCs, for the reasons Summers gives, have less incentive to limit pollution, and they have a harder time enforcing pollution controls. Since many of the consequences of pollution are global, the consequences of encouraging the migration of dirty industries to LDCs will be very bad.

2. Even though people in both developed economies and LDCs would be happy to shift pollution to LDCs for some reasonable compensation, the exchange is *unfair*. Consider an analogous agreement between a billionaire and a beggar whereby the beggar agrees to work sixteen-hour days in exchange for daily gruel and a straw mattress. Both parties may be rational and well-informed, and both may enter the agreement voluntarily. But most people would say that the billionaire is exploiting the beggar. No matter how voluntary, the arrangement is unjust. Indeed the analogy may understate the injustice of dumping pollutants in LDCs, because much of the poverty in LDCs has been caused by the developed countries. A better analogy would involve a billionaire and a beggar, who is now impoverished because of previous plunder, competition, or manipulation by the billionaire. The exploitation seems more egregious if the wealthy party caused the other's poverty.

3. The migration of dirty industries to LDCs will not make them truly
   better off. Something has got to be wrong with Summers' argument or
   his notion of welfare. The economic benefits of these industries will not
   compensate for the harms they will cause.

Although the first objection, that migration of dirty industries will
increase worldwide pollution, is a serious one, it need not challenge
Summers' moral framework. To the extent that the effects of pollution are
not localized, Summers' arguments concerning the net benefits of shifting
pollution do not stand up. If an exchange sought by *Poor* and *Rich* has
consequences for *Q* that create no costs and benefits for *Poor* or *Rich*, then
the exchange will not necessarily be socially beneficial. If the harms of
pollution are not mainly local, then one cannot conclude that the migration of dirty industries will be beneficial, no matter how attractive they
may be to the particular traders.

The second objection, in terms of the injustice of shifting pollution to
LDCs, would not surprise Summers. He alludes to such objections in his
last paragraph, but he offers no response apart from the observation that
such objections "could be turned around and used more or less effectively
against every Bank proposal for liberalisation." The injustice objection
also shows that premise 6, that it is a good thing to make people better off, *or if
it's not
really
make
them better
off.*
needs qualification. It may not be a good thing to make people better off if
doing so involves severe injustice.

Merely pointing out that shifting pollution to LDCs is exploitative
does not show that it is wrong. Most people are prepared to put up
with additional injustice in exchange for a sufficiently large increase
in welfare. Before deciding what is best, one needs to know how
great the welfare benefits will be and how much injustice will result.
It is easy to see why Summers does not broach these questions, but it
is hard to see how one could defend this policy proposal without
addressing them. One misleading feature of this memo is its suggestion
that, apart from some moral belly-aching, the policy implications are
simple.

The third and last objection is not well formulated. It is basically just an
expression of skepticism about the claim that it would really be worthwhile
for LDCs to sell environmental quality to developed economies. If
Summers' memo is right, this skepticism is unfounded. But is Summers'
memo really right?

It is comparatively easy to question whether mutual willingness to
exchange demonstrates mutual benefit on the grounds that the parties may
be ignorant or irrational. But Summers argues that, given the actual consequences of increased pollution in LDCs, rational individuals in LDCs
should be willing to accept pollution for less money than individuals in

developed nations should be willing to pay. Does it not then follow that making the deal would make the parties better off?

The conclusion does not follow, for step 2 doesn't necessarily follow from premise one. Even though the economic costs in LDCs of the consequences of pollution are much lower than the economic benefits in developed countries, rational and well-informed individuals do not have to accept the market's evaluation of the consequences of the pollution. If there were markets on which all varieties of environmental quality could be bought and sold, there would be massive transfers of pollution to LDCs. But those transfers would not necessarily be preferred by the agents involved, and they would not necessarily increase human well-being. Let's see why.

The economic costs of the harms caused by pollution are much lower in LDCs because wages and productivity are lower, because people are more likely to die of other things before they can be harmed by pollution, and because there are other pressing needs upon which individuals will spend their money first. But are economic costs and benefits a reliable guide to what is harmful and beneficial? Given the current unequal distribution of wealth, preventing crippling injuries confers much greater economic benefits in rich countries than in poor ones. But the moral significance of crippling injuries should not depend on whether the victim lives in a wealthy country. One might thus reasonably raise moral objections to regarding economic costs and benefits as a guide to what *ought* to be done. It seems that costs and prices have a contestable moral significance built into them.

Summers' memorandum is an amalgam of economic analysis and moral philosophy. Or perhaps it would be less misleading to say that the economic analysis in Summers' memo already contains an inextricable dose of ethics. We do not pretend to have proven that ethics is mixed up in all of economics and cannot be separated out, and indeed in the appendix we shall consider proposals for isolating a pure "value-free" science of economics. Our point here is illustrative. Economics of the kind exemplified by Summers' memorandum is shot through with controversial ethical commitments.

2.5 A more theoretical example

Perhaps it is not surprising that a memorandum discussing policy issues should have a lot of ethical content. Is the same true when one turns to theoretical economics? Our second example shows that disputes concerning highly abstract theorizing sometimes are at bottom more concerned with morality than with "positive" science.

One striking and fruitful theoretical contribution of the 1950s was Paul Samuelson's model of overlapping generations. In his celebrated paper, "An exact consumption-loan model of interest with or without the social contrivance of money" (1958), Samuelson addresses the following problem: Suppose individuals want to save for their old age, when they cannot produce anything, and supppose nothing lasts from one period to the next. All people can do if they don't want to starve is to strike a bargain during their working years so that those who are younger will support them when they are retired. In a world of endlessly overlapping generations of workers and retirees, what will the pattern of interest rates be?

To isolate the effect of this desire to provide for one's old age from other factors that influence the rate of interest, Samuelson formulates an extremely simplified model in which everyone lives exactly three periods. In each of the first two periods of their lives, people produce one unit of a completely perishable consumption good, while in the third period of life, people produce nothing. To simplify further, Samuelson considers first an absolutely unchanging economy and then one growing eternally with an unchanging rate of growth and an unchanging rate of interest. In these models a rate of interest equal to the rate of growth clears all markets (makes everyone's plans compatible) and is, moreover, Pareto optimal. (A state of affairs is Pareto optimal if it is impossible to satisfy anybody's preferences better without frustrating someone else's preferences – see chapter 7.) In the case of no population growth at all, individuals can save one-third of their output in each of the two periods in which they are productive and then maintain the same level of consumption ($\frac{2}{3}$ unit) during retirement.

Suppose instead that the population increases by 30 percent per period. Then at some time t, there might be 1,000,000 retirees, 1,300,000 mature workers in the second period of their lives, and 1,690,000 young workers in the first period of their lives. In figure 2.1, the thickness of the bar represents the size of the generation. For every retiree, there are 1.3 mature workers and 1.69 young workers. The "biological" rate of interest (the rate of interest that equals the rate of population growth) will equal the 30 percent rate of population growth. So for every bushel of their output that mature workers "save," they get 1.3 bushels back during retirement, while for every bushel of their output that young workers save, they get 1.69 (1.3^2) bushels back during retirement. How much people will save depends on whether they want more total lifetime consumption or whether they care more about equalizing consumption over the periods of their lives. To equalize consumption over the three periods, young and mature workers will need to save about one-quarter of their output, and their lifetime

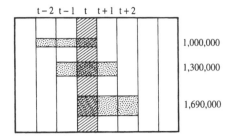

Figure 2.1 Overlapping generations

consumption will be approximately 2.25 units. Their lifetime consumption of 2.25 units can be larger than their lifetime output of only two units, because the number of producers and hence total production keeps increasing. Equalizing consumption across the three periods of life will not, however, maximize the satisfaction of preferences if individuals care only about the total amount of consumption and not about how it is distributed across time periods. Suppose, for example, everyone's utility function U is $\log(10C_1) + \log(10C_2) + \log(10C_3)$, where C_1 is consumption in the first period of life, C_2 consumption in the second period, and C_3 consumption in the third period. ("Utility functions" are mathematical devices to represent preference. See section 3.1.) We multiplied the amount of consumption by ten so that the logarithms would be positive. Then younger workers will prefer to save about 5/8 of their income, mature workers to save about 9/16 of their income, and retired workers to consume about 1.8 units of output. Total lifetime consumption will be about 2.6 units, which is considerably more than total consumption when consumption is equalized across periods.

How can a biological rate of interest be achieved? If young workers transfer resources to retirees, the repayment with interest that they hope for must come from people who are not yet born. If there is no way to bind the unborn, then the only way that people can avoid starving in retirement is for the mature workers to transfer goods to the young workers in return for repayment in the next period when the mature workers will be retired. So it seems that the only bargains people can strike will result in lavish living during the first period of life and penury during the remaining parts. This pattern of consumption is inferior to what would result from a biological rate of interest, because it is unbalanced and because in a growing economy it results in a lower lifetime total consumption. If there were only some way to bind those who are not yet born, then everybody would be better off.

Samuelson discusses two ways in which the biological interest rate might be achieved. The first is via a "social contract" in which individuals collectively agree to an obligation to support retirees. The second is "fiat money" – that is money that has value only because it is common knowledge that individuals are willing to accept it as payment for goods. The biological interest rate can be achieved if the working generations accept the money offered them by the retirees. Samuelson points out that fiat money is very much like a social contract.

All this is highly idealized positive theorizing which has spawned an enormous literature. If one looks carefully at Samuelson's original essay and the immediate responses to it by Abba Lerner (1959a,b) and William Meckling (1960a,b), one is, however, in for some surprises. The first is that halfway through his essay Samuelson drops the question he began with concerning the effects on the rate of interest of the desire to save for one's retirement! Instead his focus shifts to the fact that the "biological" rate of interest (equal to the rate of growth) cannot be achieved without fiat money or a social contract. If the economy never ended, the rate of interest that would obtain in a competitive market in the absence of fiat money or a social contract would be sub-optimal. Everybody would be worse off. If the economy eventually came to an end, then everyone would still be worse off without fiat money or a social contract except the last two generations. Although these are highly theoretical claims concerning what would be the case, their interest is almost entirely normative – for the view that "perfectly competitive" markets lead to Pareto optimal outcomes is central to welfare economics. As we shall see later, perfect competition is generally regarded as an ideal both by economists who support government intervention to remedy market failures and by economists who believe that government ought not to interfere in economic affairs. But in Samuelson's model, perfect competition is not an ideal. Intervention in the market in the form of a social contract or fiat money can improve upon perfect competition.

Meckling's and Lerner's comments are also surprising. They purport to find analytical mistakes in Samuelson's work (erroneously – see Samuelson 1959 and 1960), but in fact they are both driven by normative concerns. From a utilitarian perspective (see chapter 8) and from the "left" of Samuelson, Lerner denies the ethical desirability of a rate of interest equal to the rate of growth. Lerner points out that maximum average utility in any given period is achieved if consumption is equal across the three generations. With a 30 percent rate of population growth and the utility function specified above, average utility per period is about two "utils" if consumption is equalized, while average utility under the Samuelson plan is about 1.75 "utils." Yet, paradoxically, Samuelson's biological rate of interest offers each individual more lifetime consumption (2.6 versus 2.25

units) and hence more utility. The reason why Samuelson's plan can offer every individual more, even though the average utility in every period is less and the output the same is that in each period Samuelson's plan offers more to the retirees, who are less numerous than the young or mature workers. Lerner argues that the apparent superiority of Samuelson's plan is fraudulent in the same way that chain letters are. Consuming less while working and consuming more while retired involves no productive investment and does not increase the available stock of goods. It merely offers everyone a lavish retirement in return for a penurious working life, and it can make good on that promise only if population (or productivity) continues to increase at the same rate. But just as chain letters must come to an end, so must the increasing population. Lerner argues that Samuelson is mistaken in regarding provision for the retired as savings, because in Samuelson's model, nothing can be invested or held over from one period to the next. Social security should instead be regarded as a program in which workers transfer income to retirees. Normative policy disagreements concerning the attractiveness of utilitarianism and whether social security can be sharply distinguished from transfer programs are central to the controversy between Samuelson and Lerner.

Meckling complains from the "right" about the biological interest rate solution, because (we think) he cannot accept the conclusion that the perfectly competitive equilibrium is unattractive. Meckling maintains that since no one can repay loans made by young workers, the only way to save for retirement involves young workers consuming more than they produce. Meckling thereby rules out Samuelson's biological interest rate, and concludes that there is nothing superior to the competitive outcome. But Meckling offers no good argument against the possibility that a biological interest rate could be established by a social contract. Apart from some cavils, his only argument is that it is against the self-interest of young workers to transfer income to the retirees. Consequently, they will not voluntarily agree to the transfer ". . . and the zero-interest-rate equilibrium can prevail only if the sheriff is retained on a permanent basis" (1960, p. 84). But the sheriff is just as necessary if there is no social contract, for whether in repayment or as a gift, it is never in anybody's self-interest to transfer anything to retirees. Contracts to do so require enforcement. Furthermore, if individuals believe that if they respect the social contract or accept the fiat money, then later generations will too, then it is in their interest to honor the social contract and accept the fiat money. So it is doubtful whether a very tough sheriff is needed after all. What's really bothering Meckling is a normative, not an analytic issue. In this hypothetical instance perfect competition does not lead to a good result.

2.6 Conclusions

We do not contend that the Samuelson example is representative of all
work in theoretical economics. Our purposes in discussing both
Samuelson's overlapping-generations model and Summers' memorandum
are, we repeat, only illustrative. Samuelson's essay shows how ethical issues
are sometimes intermingled in highly regarded theoretical economics,
while Summers' memorandum illustrates the role of ethical considerations
in policy-oriented discussions. In both examples economics is linked to
questions concerning the well-being of individuals, economic costs and
benefits are linked to harms and benefits generally, and the smooth functioning of competitive markets is taken to be beneficial. Moral issues form
a background to both cases, and in neither are issues of justice and welfare
easily divorced from one another. There's a great deal to be done to clarify
exactly *how* economics and ethics are interconnected, but we have (we
hope) made plausible the claim that ethics plays an important role in
economics.

Suggestions for further reading

General overviews of the relations between economics and ethics can be
found in Buchanan (1985), Hamlin (1986), and Sen (1987a).

  There has not been any scholarly discussion of Lawrence Summers'
memorandum, although the general issues it raises concerning cost-benefit
analysis have been extensively discussed. See section 7.4 below and the
suggested readings for chapter 7.

  Paul Samuelson's overlapping-generations model (1958) has been much
discussed. For an overview of its influences and of the permutations the
basic model has undergone, see Hausman (1992, ch. 7).

Part I

Rationality and morality

When we say that it is morally right to relieve famine victims, we are expressing our approval of famine relief, and we are at least suggesting that people *ought* to come to the aid of those in danger of starvation. Morality is thus both *expressive* and *normative*.

So is rationality. When we say that it is rational for individuals to have medical insurance, we are expressing approval of doing so and suggesting that people ought to make sure they are insured. Similarly, to characterize a choice as irrational (or immoral) is to condemn it, and not simply to describe it.

Not only are morality and rationality alike in these ways, but "rational" is often used (as in the last example) as a synonym for "prudent," and prudence is a moral virtue. Yet morality and rationality are of course not the same thing.

How are morality and rationality related? Is it always rational to be moral? These general philosophical questions are critical to understanding the relations between ethics and economics, because, as we shall see, economics is built around a theory of rationality. In this part of the book we will explore the relations between economics and rationality in chapter 4 and between rationality, norms, and morality in chapter 5.

Chapter 3 presents the standard theory of rationality and its extensions to circumstances of risk and uncertainty, and it also considers some of the objections to which the theory has been subject. It is the only relatively technical chapter in the first three parts of this book.

Chapter 4 then examines the role of the standard theory of rationality in both positive and normative economics, and it explains how the theory ties positive and normative economics together and makes both appear to be more plausible than they otherwise would be.

Chapter 5, the last chapter in Part I, considers questions such as: What is the relation between a morality and a preference relation? Can one or should one develop a conception of economic rationality that permits a distinction between acting morally and maximizing utility? If the two diverge, is it then sometimes irrational to act morally or immoral to act rationally?

3 Rationality

Economics portrays agents as choosing rationally. Many generalizations concerning how people do in fact choose are also claims about how agents ought rationally to choose. This fact distinguishes economics from the natural sciences, whose quarks and polymers do not choose at all, and whose theories have no similar normative dimension. Economists regard choices not as mental determinations but as *actions*. They arise from *constraints*, *preferences*, and *expectations* (or beliefs). Economists typically take preferences to be pre-determined or "given" facts about individuals and not themselves in need of explanation or subject to rational appraisal. Economic analyses begin with an individual's preferences, whatever they may be. But choices and *sets* of beliefs and preferences may be rational or irrational. Choice is rational when it is determined by a rational set of beliefs and preferences. The rationality of sets of preferences and beliefs is defined within "utility theory." Although this is not a technical book, our discussion cannot proceed without some discussion of the technicalities of utility theory.

3.1 Certainty and ordinal utility theory

Let us suppose we are concerned with the choices, preferences, and beliefs of an agent Q. In circumstances of complete certainty, Q chooses rationally if her preferences are rational and there is nothing available that Q prefers to what she chooses. Except in the case of ties, one can simplify: Q is rational if her preferences are rational and she chooses what she most prefers among those things she can get.

Q's preferences are rational if they are transitive and complete. Q's preferences are *transitive* if and only if, for all objects of choice or "options" x, y, and z, if Q prefers x to y and y to z, then Q prefers x to z. And similarly for the case where Q is indifferent: if Q is indifferent between x and y and between y and z, then she is indifferent between x and z. Though it has been questioned whether transitivity is a requirement of rationality, it is plausible. Suppose (1) Q has intransitive preferences. She prefers x to y and y to z, but prefers z to x, (2) Q already has some of y, and (3) Q is willing to pay a penny to trade what she has for something she prefers. Q will then pay a penny to trade y to get x, another penny to trade x to get z, another penny to trade z to get y, another penny to trade y to get x, and so on until Q realizes that her preferences leave her vulnerable to manipulation. Q will thus not cling to intransitive preferences. This argument showing the irrationality of intransitive preferences is called "the money pump argument." It is persuasive, though some would question it (Schick 1986).

Q's preferences are *complete* if for all options x and y, either Q prefers x to y or Q prefers y to x, or Q is indifferent between x and y. If Q's preferences are complete, then Q is never unable to rank x and y. If asked to choose between two sealed shoe-boxes, one of which contains \$10 and the other \$1, Q may be confident that she is not indifferent, but if she doesn't know which one contains the \$10, she may not be able to form a preference. Such problems will not come up in conditions of certainty, and completeness may be a reasonable simplification for some purposes. But it is questionable whether completeness is a condition of rationality (Levi 1980). Note the difference between being indifferent and being unable to rank. Indifference is ranking equally, not an inability to rank.

We regard Q's preference ranking as a subjective state of Q that, along with Q's beliefs, explains her choices. But many economists would disagree. In accordance with the theory of "revealed preference," they instead attempt to *define* preference in terms of choice. Provided that some consistency requirements are met, choosing x when one might have had y at a lower cost reveals a preference for x over y. Although we agree that choices are important evidence concerning preferences, we think that revealed-preference theory is mistaken to identify preference and choice. Keeping them distinct is useful (1) for clarity about what preference and choice mean, (2) to permit preferences to explain choices, and (3) to leave space for the possibility that agents may choose actions that do not maximally satisfy preferences (see Sen 1973, 1977a; and p. 63 below).

To hold that preferences are rational if they are complete and transitive seems to demand little. It apparently makes it easy to have rational preferences. Yet many theorists would maintain that it is still too demanding, and there are a variety of weaker concepts of rationality, which we cannot discuss here (see Sen 1971 and McClennen 1990, ch. 2).

Completeness and transitivity together establish a *weak ordering* of any finite set of alternatives, and one can assign numbers to options so that preferred options get higher numbers, and indifferent options get the same number. If Q prefers a particular portable computer to \$500 and prefers

$500 to a Big Mac, then one can assign numbers to these three alternatives. For example: computer – 12; $500 – 7; Big Mac – 2. But any other three numbers in the same order – such as (100, 97, 4) or (2 million, 92, 91) – would do just as well. Any such assignment of numbers is an *ordinal utility function*. "Utility" here does not refer to usefulness or pleasure. A utility function is only a way of representing a preference ranking. The *ordinal representation theorem* states that if an individual's preferences are complete, transitive, and satisfy a further "continuity" requirement, then they may be represented by a continuous real-valued ordinal utility function (Debreu 1959, pp. 54–9). Continuity is a technical condition, which we shall not discuss.

The theory of rationality in circumstances of certainty can thus be restated: Agents are rational if and only if their preferences may be represented by ordinal utility functions, and their choices maximize utility. We intentionally avoided saying that they act "in order to maximize utility," for in contemporary economic theory, utility is merely an index or indicator. *Maximizing utility is just doing what one most prefers to do.* Although the utility language was inherited from the utilitarians, some of whom thought of utility as a sensation with a certain intensity, duration, purity or "propinquity" (Bentham 1789, ch. 4), there is no such implication in contemporary theory. To speak of individuals as *aiming to* maximize utility or as *seeking* more utility may misleadingly suggest that utility is an object of choice, some ultimately good thing that people want in addition to healthy children, lower taxes, or kiwi fruit. But the theory of rational choice says nothing about *what* people want. Notice that the theory of rational choice thus does *not* imply self-interest. Someone whose choices are determined by a complete and transitive preference-ordering that ranks the well-being of others very highly is no less a utility maximizer than is the individual who is indifferent to the welfare of others. Thus, when economic theories treat individuals as self-interested – as they often do – they must add *substantive* claims concerning what people want to the standard theory of rationality.

Despite the fact that utility theory makes no substantive claims about what people should prefer, it remains a normative theory concerning how people ought to choose, rather than a positive theory of how people do choose or merely a model or a definition. It lays down conditions that choices and preferences *ought* to satisfy. It is not a positive theory because it says nothing about the extent to which people are rational, and it is not merely a model or definition, because rationality is itself a normative notion. To define what rational preference and choice are, is *ipso facto* to say how one *ought* rationally to prefer and to choose. Since utility theory says nothing about what individuals prefer, it has a much wider scope than

economic theories, which depict agents as seeking more commodities or
larger net returns. Utility theory is employed by psychologists, statisti-
cians, philosophers, and sociologists, as well as by economists.

3.2 Expected utility theory

The standard theory of rationality is silent concerning how agents should
deal with risk or uncertainty, and economists often abstract from the problems that arise when one is not certain. But the theory can be extended to
cover cases of "risk" and "uncertainty." Frank Knight (1921) suggested
that one should speak of circumstances of *risk* when all the alternative
outcomes and their probabilities are known. Someone playing roulette is
in a circumstance involving risk. In circumstances of uncertainty on the
other hand, some of the probabilities are unknown. Building a nuclear
power plant involves uncertainty, because no one knows all the possible
outcomes or their probabilities. In speaking of known or unknown probabilities, we are talking about so-called "objective" probabilities, such as
relative frequencies. For example, the probability with which a coin will
come up heads can be regarded as the limit of the ratio of heads to total
flips as the number of flips grows ever larger. As we shall see shortly, there
is also a subjective notion of probability – as "degree of belief" – which is
important in the theory of decision-making in circumstances of uncertainty.

   In situations of risk and uncertainty – when actions do not lead with
certainty to any particular outcome – actions may be regarded as *lotteries*
with outcomes as prizes. Actions undertaken in circumstances of certainty
can also be regarded as lotteries, though of a particularly boring sort,
since they always pay off the same prize. Standard normative theories of
decision-making under risk and uncertainty begin by asserting that preferences among *lotteries* are complete, transitive, and continuous. As noted
before, completeness is particularly questionable as a condition of rationality in conditions of uncertainty. Second, one needs technical conditions
relating complex lotteries, which have lotteries as prizes, to simple lotteries.
Finally, one needs one further condition of rationality. Suppose, like most
people, Q prefers (other things being equal) more money to less and Q has
a choice between two gambles concerning the flip of a coin. One of them
pays off more if the coin comes up heads, but is otherwise identical to the
other gamble. It seems to be a condition of rationality that Q prefers the
gamble that pays the higher prize if the coin comes up heads, though there
is no violation of completeness, transitivity, or continuity if Q prefers the
gamble with the lower prize. The further condition of rationality that
is violated by a preference for the gamble with the lower prize is called

the "independence" or "sure-thing" principle. It says that if two lotteries differ only in one prize, Q's preferences between the lotteries match her preferences between the prizes. It is called the sure-thing principle because, no matter what the outcome of the lottery, Q is at least no worse off, and with one of the outcomes Q is better off.

These axioms are much more controversial in the case of uncertainty than in the case of risk. Indeed one might argue that talk of probabilities and of lotteries is obscure when probabilities and even the range of possible outcomes are not known. So-called "Bayesians" are more comfortable applying these axioms in circumstances of uncertainty than are non-Bayesians, for Bayesians believe that the probabilities that are relevant to decision-making are *subjective*. They are degrees of belief. And people may have degrees of belief about events for which relative frequencies cannot be defined, such as the outcome of a particular World Cup soccer competition. A particular World Cup is played only once, and the probability that a particular team will win is not the limit of the frequency of its victories in repeated World Series. Bayesians interpret a claim such as "The odds that Brazil will take the series are three-to-one" as expressing instead a subjective degree of belief. An argument resembling the money-pump argument shows that degrees of belief should be probabilities obeying the axioms of the mathematical theory of probability. Whether one should apply expected utility theory in conditions of uncertainty is highly controversial.

If Q's preferences satisfy all the axioms, then they can be represented by a *cardinal utility* function. The (cardinal) representation theorem says that if an agent's preferences are complete, transitive, and continuous and satisfy the independence condition (and other technical conditions concerning compound lotteries), then those preferences may be represented by a utility function that has two special properties (see Harsanyi 1977b, ch. 3; Ramsey 1926; Neumann and Morgenstern 1947; and Savage 1972). First this utility function possesses *the expected utility property*. (The [expected] utility of any lottery is equal to the utilities of its outcomes multiplied by their probabilities.) Suppose Q is offered a gamble over the roll of a die. Q will win $60 if the die comes up 1, and will lose $12 if the die comes up with any other number showing. The *expected monetary value* of the gamble is 1/6 times $60 minus 5/6 times $12 or $0. The *expected utility* of the gamble to Q is 1/6 times the *utility* to Q of winning $60 plus 5/6 times the *utility* to Q of losing $12. Depending on how rapidly Q's utility increases as a function of money, the expected utility of the gamble may be positive, negative, or zero. The cardinal representation theorem says that if Q's preferences satisfy the axioms, then there is a way of representing Q's preferences so that the expected utility of a lottery is the sum of the utilities of the prizes weighted by the probabilities of winning them.

Second, the cardinal representation theorem says that if Q's preferences satisfy the axioms, then an expected utility function (a utility function with the expected utility property) that represents them is "unique up to a positive affine or linear transformation." To say that a function U is "unique up to a positive affine or linear transformation" is to say that any positive affine transformations of U will do just as well as U itself. U' is a positive affine or linear transformation of U if and only if $U' = aU + b$, where a is a positive real number and b is any real number. If a function U, represents an agent's preferences and has the expected utility property then so will all positive affine transformations of U. Furthermore no expected utility function that is not a positive affine transformation of U will represent the agent's preferences, though the will be other merely ordinal utility functions that will also represent Q's preferences.

In the case of ordinal utilities, differences between utilities are entirely arbitrary, since any numbers in the same order represent the preferences just as well. In the case of ordinal utilities, the fact that the difference between U(x) and U(y) is larger than the difference between U(c) and U(d) tells one nothing about the agent's preferences. The relative magnitudes of the numbers are just an accident of the particular utility function chosen. But things are different with cardinal utilities. The cardinal representation theorem establishes that comparisons of utility *differences* are "objective." They do not depend on what scale is chosen. If U(x) – U(y) > U(c) – U(d) and U$'$ is a positive affine transformation of U, then U$'$(x) – U$'$(y) > U$'$(c) – U$'$(d).[1] Although expected utilities are cardinal and comparisons of utility differences are "objective," nothing said so far permits one to make comparisons between the utilities of different individuals. If Q's cardinal utility is 100 and M's is 89, one cannot draw any conclusion about whose preferences are better satisfied. Since any positive linear transformation of these numbers will represent the preferences just as well, their relative magnitude reflects only an arbitrary choice of one particular utility function for each.

As in the case of utility theory concerning choice under certainty, one relates choice to preference by asserting that individuals choose whatever available option is highest in their preference ranking – or, in the case of ties, one of the options tied for first place. Unlike ordinal utility theory, which is a theory of the rationality of preference and choice only, expected utility theory has implications concerning the rationality of *belief*. If one

---

[1] Proof: U$'$(x) – U$'$(y) = aU(x) + b – aU(y) – b = a(U(x) – U(y)). Similarly, U$'$(c) – U$'$(d) = a(U(c) – U(d)). So U$'$(x) – U$'$(y) > U$'$(c) – U$'$(d) if and only if a(U(x) – U(y)) > a(U(c) – U(d)). And since a is positive, this will be true if and only if U(x) – U(y) > U(c) – U(d).

regards the axioms of expected utility theory as conditions of rationality, then people whose degrees of belief concerning uncertain outcomes do not satisfy the axioms of the probability calculus will be irrational. Expected utility theory is thus not only a theory of rational preference and choice, but also a thin theory of rational belief.

3.3 Questions about utility theory

Expected utility theory demands more than does utility theory under certainty, and is much more controversial. Psychologists and economists have found ways to test whether people's preferences satisfy the conditions of expected utility theory, and they have found that they often appear not to. If people don't behave the way that expected utility theory says they ought to, then it may be that people are irrational. People may break the rules, even if they are good rules. But if choice behavior that violates the axioms of expected utility theory is common and seems sensible, then one may question whether expected utility theory is a correct theory of rationality. Some of these results do in fact suggest that expected utility theory is flawed as a theory of rationality. These empirical anomalies, along with general critiques of expected utility (see Allais 1952, Ellsberg 1961, Sen 1985b, Levi 1986, McClennen 1990), have stimulated the formulation of alternative theories of rationality under uncertainty.

Testing a normative theory of rationality is less straightforward than testing a positive theory of actual choice, and controversy can easily arise and persist. We cannot survey the controversies concerning expected utility theory and its competitors here, but we will give one famous instance, which is of some importance to moral philosophy as well as to decision theory. This example will provide some sense of the character of these controversies.

In the early 1950s Maurice Allais formulated the problem shown in figure 3.1 (Allais and Hagen 1979). A ball is drawn from an urn containing one red ball, eighty-nine white balls, and ten blue balls. So the probabilities are known. Depending on the color and the choice of A or B in problem I or of C or D in problem II, one receives one of the payoffs listed in figure 3.1. For example, if someone facing problem I chooses A, then he or she gets 1 million dollars for sure. If they choose B, then they have a 1 percent chance of getting nothing (if a red ball is drawn), an 89 percent chance of winning 1 million dollars and a 10 percent chance of winning 5 million dollars. Many people are inclined in problem I to prefer option A to option B and, in problem II, to prefer option D to option C. Even the prominent Bayesian statistician, Leonard Savage at first expressed these preferences (Savage 1972, p. 103). But these preferences violate the

		Payoffs		
Problems	Choices	Red (1)	White (89)	Blue (10)
I	A	$1 m	$1 m	$1 m
	B	$0	$1 m	$5 m
II	C	$1 m	$0	$1 m
	D	$0	$0	$5 m
III	E	$1 m	$x	$1 m
	F	$0	$x	$5 m

Figure 3.1 Allais' problem

independence principle, for the only difference between the pair (A,B) and the pair (C,D) is in the magnitude of the payoff if a white ball is drawn, which should be irrelevant. In other words, the value of "x" should be irrelevant to one's choice in problem III. Since one gets $x if a white ball is drawn regardless of whether one chooses E or F, the value of $x should give one no reason to favor E or F. Thus, A should be preferred to B if and only if C is preferred to D.[2]

Yet many people still prefer A in problem I and D in problem II. Intuitively the reason is that in choosing B one is giving up a million dollars for sure, while in choosing D one is not. This reason is in conflict with the independence condition, which says that $x (the prize if a white ball is chosen) is irrelevant. It is possible to reconcile a preference for A and D with the independence condition by arguing that the outcomes have not been properly described. The outcome of choosing B if a red ball is chosen is not $0, but $0 plus severe regrets. ("I could kill myself. I gave up a million dollars for sure!") Although some decision theorists have defended the independence condition in this way (such as Broome 1991b, ch. 5), others have felt that such redescription of the outcomes makes expected utility theory empty. They have pointed out that apparent disconfirmations can always be explained away by redescribing the outcomes. Broome's response is to argue for substantive principles of rationality that specify whether it is rationally permissible to distinguish between the outcomes when a red ball is drawn on choosing B (and thus might have had $1 million for sure) and when a red ball is drawn on choosing D. Most decision theorists and economists do not follow Broome here, and they regard preferences for A in problem I and D in problem II as inconsistent with the

---

[2] For those who prefer some algebra, let V be the utility of $5 million, U be the utility of $1 million, and 0 be the utility of $0. Then EU(A) = U, EU(B) = .89U + .1V, EU(C) = .11U and EU(D) = .1V. If A is preferred to B, then EU(A) > EU(B). So U > .89U + .1V, or .11U > .1V. So if A is preferred to B, then C must be preferred to D.

independence condition. It is not clear whether this inconsistency shows that the independence condition is mistaken or that people are irrational.

If one takes the choices of A in problem I and D in problem II to be inconsistent with the independence condition, are these choices evidence against the independence condition or are they evidence of human irrationality? It is hard to see how to make conclusive arguments in favor of one of these alternatives, but we believe that either the payoffs need to be redescribed, or that there is a case to be made against the independence condition. This is because (1) there is no other evidence of irrationality among those preferring A and D, (2) some distinguished decision theorists themselves choose A and D, and (3) plausible alternative theories of rationality have been defended that rationalize choosing A and D. Together these give grounds for questioning whether the independence condition is a requirement of rationality.

Apparent anomalies such as Allais' example are relevant to moral philosophy as well as to economics, because expected utility theory is involved in arguments for moral conclusions, such as remarkable "proofs" of utilitarianism given by Fleming (1952), Harsanyi (1955), and Vickrey (1945, 1960). As we will discuss in detail in chapter 8, utilitarianism is the moral view that actions and policies are morally permissible if and only if they lead to no less total utility than any alternative. D'Aspremont and Gevers (1977) have shown that within one particular axiom system, the choice between utilitarianism and a very different theory of justice resembling the theory defended by John Rawls (see chapter 11) depends on whether one accepts or rejects axioms of expected utility theory and permits or rules out different sorts of interpersonal comparisons. There are also non-utilitarian ethical systems that are built around expected utility theory, such as David Gauthier's (1986) bargaining theory of justice (discussed in chapters 11 and 13).

Although the issues concerning expected utility theory are highly theoretical, they are also of immediate practical importance because alternative theories may yield different recommendations about the "rational" thing to do. For example, in the case of nuclear power mentioned above (which obviously involves uncertainty rather than merely risk), should we rely on our best guess as to the future consequences and maximize expected utility or should we recognize our ignorance of relevant probabilities and use some other principle of choice (Levi 1980)?

In addition to the controversies concerning whether expected utility theory is too narrow or too demanding, some moral philosophers have maintained that there are such things as irrational preferences, quite apart from any questions about consistency. This is a classical view found in Aristotle and Plato. More recent defenders include Thomas Nagel (1970) and John McDowell (1978). Derek Parfit, for example, holds that, "It is irrational to desire something that is in no respect worth desiring . . ." (1984, p. 123). He gives the example of a person who suffers from "future-Tuesday indifference." This individual prefers a greater pain on a future Tuesday over a lesser pain on a Wednesday, merely because he or she does not care what happens on future Tuesdays. Parfit remarks, ". . . the fact that the agony will be on a Tuesday is no reason for preferring it. Preferring the *worse* of two pains for *no* reason, is irrational" (1984, p. 124). Although most economists attempt to avoid any substantive theory of rationality, those economists who hold that rationality implies self-interest are in fact implicitly committed to judging the rationality of preferences (Walsh 1994).

John Broome argues that expected utility theory itself must rely upon judgments that some preferences are intrinsically irrational. Consider for example, some instance of intransitivity: Q prefers x to y, y to z, and z to x. If Q wanted to make trouble for the decision theorist, she could argue that the apparent intransitivity results from misdescribing the objects of her preferences. So "z when compared with y" is a different thing altogether than "z when compared to x." If one calls the first z_1 and the second z_2, then Q may have a fully transitive preference ordering such as z_2, x, y, z_1. Since such a reply to the charge of having intransitive preferences can always be given, transitivity turns out to be an empty condition of rationality, unless one is willing to argue that it is *irrational* to prefer z_2 (z when compared to x) to z_1 (z when compared to y). Expected utility theory has no "bite," unless one is committed to the irrationality of such preferences. David Lewis, Susan Hurley, and John Broome have argued in this way that expected utility theory presupposes substantive principles of rationality.

Although it is good to know something about the ways in which expected utility theory may be too strong or too weak, what's most important for our purposes is to understand clearly what the different varieties of utility theory have to say about rationality. In the simplest terms utility theory sees rational choice as choice that is determined by rational preference and belief, and it sees rational preference as demanding only that individuals be able to rank all options. It is remarkable that such a bare-bones theory of rationality has given rise to so much controversy and (as we shall see) that it apparently has such striking ethical implications.

Suggestions for further reading

The basic model of rationality and its extension in expected utility theory have been widely discussed. Some of the sources that we have found particularly accessible and helpful are Harsanyi (1977b, ch. 3), McClennen

(1990), Gärdenfors and Sahlins (1988), Sen (1971), Machina (1987), and Hargreaves Heap *et al.* (1992).

For philosophical discussions of the plausibility of restricting questions of rationality to questions of consistency and to questions of the rationality of means, see Hume (1738, 1748), Gauthier (1986, ch. 2), Hurley (1989, ch. 5), Broome (1991b, ch. 5), Griffin (1986, chs. 3, 4), Parfit (1984, part 2), Nagel (1970), McDowell (1978), Stewart (1995), and Hampton (1994).

4 Rationality in positive and normative economics

Rationality is a normative notion concerning how people ought to choose, prefer, or reason. So it may seem surprising that it has a large role in positive economics, which is concerned with how people do in fact choose. Since rationality is different from morality, it may also seem surprising that rationality plays a large role in normative economics. But the world is full of surprises, and rationality is ubiquitous in both positive and normative economics.

4.1 Rationality and positive economics

The theory of rationality says that people's preferences are rational if they are complete and transitive and that people choose rationally if their choices are determined by their preferences. If one adds to the theory of rationality the generalization that real people are to some extent rational, then one has the central principles of the positive theory of economic choice. In standard microeconomic theory, individuals are portrayed as having complete, transitive, and continuous preferences for commodity bundles. Their preferences thus can be represented by continuous ordinal utility functions. Consumers are portrayed as choosing the bundle they most prefer from among the commodity bundles they can afford. The standard theory of consumer choice thus limits the objects of preference to bundles of commodities and services, and it makes further assumptions concerning rates of substitution. But these are only further details: in economics the theory of rational choice is simultaneously the theory of actual choice.

Positive economics can be formulated without using the word "rational." Rather than first defining "rational" and then stating that individuals are rational, one can assert that the preferences of individuals are complete and transitive, and that individuals choose whatever they most prefer. But the identification of what is actual with what is rational remains. It does not depend on any particular formulation. It is instead a reflection of the fact that economics simultaneously provides a theory of the *causes* and *consequences* of people's economic choices and of the *reasons* for them.

Everyday explanations of human actions rest upon a psychological theory that is so widely accepted that it seems hardly worth mentioning. According to this "folk psychology," actions result from the beliefs and wants of agents. Sometimes in explaining actions, one only cites the agent's beliefs or only the agent's wants, because the other is obvious in the context. For example, when asked why he robbed banks, Willie Sutton replied, "Because that's where the money is." His explanation takes it as too obvious to require mentioning that he wanted to steal, and it makes us laugh precisely because most of us don't take such a desire for granted. The pattern of explaining action in terms of beliefs and desires is ubiquitous.

Economic explanations of choices in terms of utility maximizing fit this pattern. Economists talk in terms of "preferences" or "utility" rather than "wants," and they often do not mention explicitly the agent's beliefs because they assume that the agent has perfect knowledge and thus believes whatever the facts are. But these are minor complications. In the main, explanations in economics of the choice behavior of individuals conform to the pattern of folk psychology. Economists are more interested in the market *consequences* of individual choices than in the choices themselves, but individual choices are the causal intermediaries that connect "shocks" such as a crop failure or a new tax to their consequences for prices or quantities exchanged.

The relations between microeconomics and folk psychology are worth noticing because folk psychology is both an account of the *causes* of human actions and of the *reasons* for actions. Many philosophers in the 1950s argued that explanations for actions in terms of beliefs and desires were only reason-giving and could not be causal, but in 1963 Donald Davidson argued persuasively that reasons that explain actions must *also* cause the actions they explain.

An example will clarify Davidson's argument. Consider a real-estate agent who attends church regularly. One reason is that the agent believes in God and wants to express devotion to God. Another reason is that the agent meets potential clients at church. Both of these are in some sense "good" reasons to go to church, though most people find the first reason more admirable than the second. Davidson points out, however, that identifying good reasons does not automatically explain actions. One needs to know what reasons actually "led" the agent to go to church. There are many possibilities: (1) It may be that both reasons explain the church-going. (2) It may be that the real-estate agent attends because of piety and only incidentally profits from attending. (3) It may be that the real-estate agent is a hypocrite and attends church only as a way of attracting clients. Or (4) it might be that the "real" reason is that the real-estate agent loves to listen to the church organist. Davidson's point is that to explain an action, one needs to know which reasons were *causally responsible* for it.

One special feature of reasons is that people *evaluate* or *assess* them. Piety is a *good* reason to attend church. "Good" here seems to mean both "(morally) admirable" and "sensible." The desire to make lucrative contacts is a sensible reason to go to church, though not a very admirable one. The desire to reverse the greenhouse effect is an admirable reason to attend church, though according to most people's theology, hardly a sensible one. The desire to resurrect Joseph Stalin is not a good reason to go to church, for it is neither sensible nor admirable. When one cites the reasons why people act, one automatically raises evaluative questions about whether the considerations that led them to act were "sensible" and morally acceptable.

Every theory that takes beliefs and preferences to be reasons that explain choices must incorporate some theory of rationality. Since desires cannot function as explanatory reasons if they do not determine choices or if they do not induce at least a loose ranking of what is better or worse, preferences must not be radically incomplete, and they must have a large measure of consistency. To say, as economists do, that rationality requires that preferences be complete and transitive and that choice maximizes preference satisfaction is one simple way of meeting these constraints on reason-giving explanations. The economist's theory of actual choice must also be a theory of rational choice if explanations in economics are to cite both causes and reasons. To say this, however, is not to offer a defense of the particular theory of rationality that economists endorse, for there are alternatives, such as Herbert Simon's theory of bounded rationality, which also permit one to explain choices in terms of reasons.

Although some philosophers and psychologists have argued against folk psychology, it is hard to imagine humans abandoning this way of understanding their actions. The fact that the theory of actual choice is simultaneously a theory of rational choice thus helps to shore up the theory of actual choice. Suppose one finds evidence that people's preferences are not complete and transitive. Psychologists claim to have found such evidence. For example, with a bit of experimental trickiness, one can get individuals to judge that a bet or investment J is definitely better than another bet or investment K, but to express a willingness to pay *more* for the inferior bet, K. This "preference reversal" phenomenon is well established in experimental settings and it follows that people do not have complete and transitive preference rankings. Such solid evidence dis-confirming central theoretical propositions of positive economics ought to be worrisome.

But most economists are not worried. Why not? One reason is that choice phenomena such as preference reversals are *irrational* and they can be exploited. Consequently, irrational preferences tend to be *unstable*. In recent work, Chu and Chu (1990) sold K bets to experimental subjects for the price they stated they were willing to pay, had them exchange the K bets for the J bets, which the subjects claimed to prefer, and then pur-chased back the J bets for the lower price that subjects claimed the J bets were worth. At the end of the series of transactions the subjects were of course poorer. If the "money-pumping" cycle is this transparent (see Berg *et al* 1985), then it does not take long for subjects to figure out that they are being made fools of and to adjust their stated preferences or the prices they are willing to pay for the bets. Because the theory of actual choice is simultaneously a theory of rational choice, there must be limits on how far wrong it can be.

A defender of the standard theory might then go on to claim that, although not perfectly correct, the standard theory of choice must be a good first approximation because a theory that portrayed choice as irra-tional would typically reveal opportunities for exploiting this irrationality. Since people will learn not to be exploited, acting on such a theory would undermine it.

We do not endorse this argument fully, but it nevertheless matters to the appraisal of economic theory that the positive theory of choice is simultaneously a theory of rational choice and thereby serves to evaluate even as it predicts and explains agents' conduct. The intermixture of posi-tive economics and the theory of rationality makes positive economics more acceptable to many economists and harder to disconfirm.

4.2 Self-interest, preference satisfaction, and welfare economics

Rationality is a normative notion. One *ought* to be rational. One is foolish or mistaken if one is not rational. But it might reasonably be contended that rationality is not a moral notion. One can be a rational villain. What one ought rationally to do need not coincide with what one ought morally to do.

The standard "thin" theory of rationality as utility maximization is not itself a moral theory. Some of those who are wicked, like some of those who are just, might be rational and others irrational. But the stan-dard theory of rationality does not stand by itself. On the contrary, it is embedded in both normative and positive economics, and it thereby smuggles crucial elements of moral theory into positive economics. Before we see how, let us examine what part rationality plays in normative economics.

Positive economics and the theory of rationality jointly determine the character of normative economics. One can in fact virtually derive normative economics from the theory of rationality and components of *positive* economics! Here's how.

Start with the theory of rationality and add a common assumption of positive economics, namely that individuals are exclusively self-interested. A self-interested person S will never prefer x to y if S believes that y is better for himself or herself. If nothing but self-interest affects S's preferences, even when two alternatives affect S's interests in just the same way, then S prefers x to y if and only if S believes that x is strictly better for himself or herself than is y. Rational and exclusively self-interested individuals always prefer what they believe to be better for themselves over what they believe to be worse.

Add then a second common assumption of positive economics, that individuals have perfect knowledge. Self-interested individuals with perfect knowledge prefer x to y if and only if x is *in fact* better for them. How well off an individual is is the same thing as how well satisfied an individual's preferences are. Orthodox normative economics consequently identifies welfare and preference satisfaction. Economists typically make this identification in a flash without noticing that they are defending a controversial philosophical theory. We'll discuss the importance of this identification later in this chapter and in chapter 6.

Once economists have identified well-being with the satisfaction of preferences, the central features of standard normative economics follow naturally. All they need is one innocuous moral principle of *minimal benevolence*: other things being equal, it is a morally good thing if people are better off. Indeed, one might argue that this principle follows from the near tautology: other things being equal, it is a morally good thing if there is more good. Because of the "other things being equal" clause, minimal benevolence is uncontroversial. It does not, for example, say whether it is better or worse to make some people better off at the cost of increasing inequality. It only says that if all other morally relevant considerations, such as equality, are a toss-up, then it is a morally good thing to make people better off. One premise in the reconstruction in chapter 2 of the argument in Lawrence Summers' memorandum came to grief precisely because it did not contain such an "other things being equal clause." Even if shifting dirty industries to LDCs makes everyone better off, it might be morally unacceptable because it is unjust. This observation is fully consistent with minimal benevolence.

If economists accept minimal benevolence and identify an individual's welfare with the satisfaction of his or her preferences, then they will judge that, other things being equal, it is a morally good thing to satisfy an individual's preferences. The main issue in standard normative economics is accordingly to what extent economies enable individuals to satisfy their preferences. Thus the importance of "Pareto optimality."

Although a Pareto optimum is typically defined as a state of affairs in which it is impossible to make anyone better off without making someone worse off, this purported definition is misleading, and it shows how completely economists identify well-being with the satisfaction of preferences. In fact, R is a "Pareto improvement" over S if nobody *prefers* S to R and somebody *prefers* R to S. R is a Pareto optimum if and only if there are no Pareto improvements over R. If one identifies preference satisfaction and well-being, then one can deduce from the definition of Pareto improvements that they make some people better off without making anyone worse off. Notice that there will typically be many Pareto optima, and that many of these will be ethically unattractive. Consider a state of affairs R in which millions of people are starving. If there is no way to make them better off without making someone worse off, no matter how slightly, then R is a Pareto optimum.

If one accepts minimal benevolence, then *other things being equal*, Pareto improvements are moral improvements and Pareto optima are morally desirable. At this point some formal theorems of welfare economics become very important. What is usually called "the first welfare theorem" establishes that the allocation resulting from any perfectly competitive equilibrium among self-interested agents is Pareto optimal. Perfect competition obtains when there are no interdependencies among people's utility functions, there are markets for all goods and services (and thus no externalities), no barriers to entry or exit from any market, and so many traders in every market that no one can influence prices. A perfectly competitive equilibrium obtains when there is perfect competition and there are no excess demands on any market. Given this first welfare theorem, one can conclude that, other things being equal, perfectly competitive equilibria are morally desirable and market imperfections that interfere with the achievement of competitive equilibria are morally undesirable. This is a theoretical defense of *perfect competition*, not a defense of actual markets or of a *laissez-faire* policy, and it is only a defense of perfect competition, *other things being equal*.

A consideration of the "other things" that are morally relevant leads to ethical controversy, which economists would like to avoid. Indeed we conjecture that economists rarely argue for markets on grounds of individual liberties and rights, because they believe that arguments based on premises concerning liberty or rights are more philosophically controversial and ambitious than is the benevolence argument.

Justice is one of the "other things" that must be equal, and a Pareto improvement that leads to distributional injustice may be morally undesirable. But the argument above may be continued, for there is a second welfare theorem. This theorem shows that all Pareto optima can be obtained as competitive equilibria from the right initial distribution of endowments. In other words, one can achieve whatever Pareto optimal outcome one wants by first redistributing the resources individuals bring to their market interactions and then letting individuals trade freely under the highly idealized conditions of perfect competition. One can employ this second welfare theorem to argue plausibly that all other moral concerns, including concerns about justice, can be satisfied by adjusting initial holdings and that perfect competition is thus a moral ideal. The conclusion does not follow, however, because it could be the case that one will have to settle for an outcome that is not Pareto optimal in order to satisfy the other moral constraints.

The welfare theorems do not help with the problem of comparing states of affairs that improve some persons' level of preference satisfaction while harming others. This severely limits the range of social policies on which the Pareto notions can find purchase. Normative economics is not going to be very helpful unless there are other ways of comparing alternative policies. Later in chapter 7, we shall see how standard welfare economics has found ways to say more.

Whether defenders of *laissez-faire* or of extensive government intervention to address market failures, most economists share a moral commitment to the *ideal* of perfect competition. It is this commitment that gives point to the analysis of market failures. (Why should they matter if market successes are not a good thing?) The fact that this commitment appears to presuppose nothing more controversial than minimal benevolence helps resolve a paradox: On the one hand, economists do not see themselves as moral philosophers, and they attempt to steer clear of controversial ethical commitments when doing theoretical welfare economics. Indeed, economists have sometimes supposed that theoretical welfare economics was independent of all value judgments. Yet, on the other hand, when welfare economists address policy questions, they speak with apparent moral authority. They purport to know how to make life better.

What explains how economists can feel themselves possessed of moral authority without the trouble of doing moral philosophy? The answer, we think, is that economists do not regard the identification of well-being with the satisfaction of preferences as a controversial ethical judgment. It seems to be just a part of the standard view of rationality. Once one accepts this identification, one need only add an uncontroversial principle of minimal benevolence to get the argument for perfect competition sketched above.

4.3 Rationality and ethics in positive economics

As one sorts through the complicated story told in the previous sections, one can begin to see how rationality can function as a Trojan horse smuggling ethical commitments into the theoretical citadel of positive economics. At a relatively superficial level, commitment to a theory of well-being as the satisfaction of preferences places constraints on the character of positive economics. It is only plausible to identify well-being and the satisfaction of preferences if (1) individuals are rational, (2) individuals are self-interested, (3) individuals are well-informed, and (4) individual preferences are not formed or deformed in odd ways. If, for example, people come to prefer things because of manipulation by advertisers or because of "sour grapes," then it is harder to believe that satisfying their preferences automatically makes them better off. So one reason, among many others, to avoid incorporating theories of preference formation into positive economics is that doing so would threaten the accepted (moral) theory of individual well-being, and possibly upset the conclusions of welfare economics. The fact that there is little work on preference formation helps to make plausible the identification of well-being and preference satisfaction, and commitment to the preference-satisfaction view of well-being discourages work on preference formation.

But the standard theory of rationality together with standard assumptions about the objectives of consumers and firms introduce evaluative commitments at a deeper level. As we saw above in section 4.1, explanations in terms of reasons raise questions about whether the reasons are good reasons. The answers to these questions are linked to one's attitude toward the explanation. If the reasons why the agent acted are good reasons and there are no special grounds for further inquiry, then once one knows the agent's reasons, nothing puzzling remains and nothing further needs to be explained. But if the reasons why the agent acted are not good reasons, then it is puzzling why they moved the agent to act. One would want some further explanation.

For example, suppose a school-teacher with a salary of $35,000 borrows $10,000, and her reason is that she wants to buy a new car and does not have enough cash to do so without borrowing. This seems a good reason and explains her action. Given her desire for a new car, there is nothing obviously imprudent about taking out the loan, and there seems to be nothing wrong in borrowing the money. There might be other factors that render the action imprudent or immoral, and one might want to ask further questions about why she wants a new car, why she has not saved enough to buy one without borrowing, and so forth. But unless one has particular reasons to ask further questions, the initial explanation is satisfactory. Suppose, on the other hand, the teacher cheats her best friend out of $10,000 for just the same reason. The desire for a new car is not a good reason to cheat one's friends. The desire for a new car may be a good reason to undertake some other course of action, but can it be a reason to do something imprudent or immoral? "How in the world could she do such a thing?" "How could she want a new car badly enough to cheat her friend?" Whether one finds a reason-giving explanation satisfactory depends on one's *evaluation* of the reasons cited – on one's evaluation of the relevance of the reason to the action and on one's evaluation of the prudence and morality of the choice, given the reason. Similarly, one is not satisfied with Willie Sutton's explanation for why he robs banks.

There is nothing wrong with an explanation that cites reasons that do not support the decision taken or that support an immoral and imprudent decision. People often do things for bad reasons, and it may be perfectly true that the teacher cheated her friend of $10,000 because she wanted to purchase a new car. The difference between explanations that cite good reasons and explanations that cite bad reasons involves the attitudes of those giving the explanations: explanations that cite bad reasons pose puzzles. One is satisfied by an explanation that cites good reasons, while one remains puzzled after being given an explanation that cites bad reasons.

Those who are satisfied with economic explanations of choices in terms of preferences for larger bundles of commodities or greater net revenues thus implicitly take such preferences to be good reasons to make the particular choices. Accepting such explanations as fully satisfactory thereby implies judgments of prudence and morality. For example, suppose that a firm knowingly dumps its toxic wastes into a stream and poisons an area of marshland. If the costs of the dumping in terms of possible lawsuits or loss of reputation were less than the costs of disposing of the wastes in some harmless way, then the firm increases its net revenues by dumping the wastes and poisoning the marshland. An economist might cite this fact to explain the dumping even in a case in which the firm would have had good earnings in any case. Suppose one were satisfied with this explanation and did not feel that it was necessary to add something like "and this firm is so concerned about profits that it does not take the environmental consequences of its actions into consideration" or "and this firm did not realize that the dumping would destroy the marshland" or simply "the dirty swine!" Then one believes that seeking larger profits is a good reason for this firm to poison the marshland. If one sees nothing puzzling or requiring comment in the fact that the firm dumped in order to make more profits, then one implies that one does not regard such behavior as immoral or imprudent. For if one thought it were immoral, then one would be puzzled at why the firm did it, when only extra profits were at stake. One would regard the explanation of the dumping in the same say that most people would regard the explanation of the teacher cheating her friend. One would seek some further explanation, such as that the managers did not realize the seriousness of the damage they were doing. Similarly, one would be surprised and alarmed by a biography of Willie Sutton that explained why he robbed banks in terms of the greater amount of money that is to be found in banks than in tobacco shops rather than looking at why he chose a life of crime in the first place.

If one finds the explanation in terms of profit-seeking satisfactory, then one does not find it puzzling that a firm would poison marshland in order to increase its profits. And if one does not find it necessary to explain or to condemn the fact that the pursuit of gain could motivate this action, then one is implying a certain minimum *approval* of the action as prudent and minimally morally acceptable, though not necessarily admirable. This evaluation is *not* part of the explanation itself. It is instead implicit in the *evaluation* of the explanation as not calling for moral judgment and as not raising further puzzles. As a matter of logic, omitting an explanation or condemnation of the motivation does not *entail* any evaluation. But as a matter of pragmatics, it does.

One's implicit approval of the action as prudent and minimally morally acceptable might be based on the judgment that there is nothing morally problematic about poisoning marshland in order to increase profits. But we suspect that most economists have in mind a more complicated explanation based on the judgment that the firm had little choice. Economists would, we believe, maintain that competitive pressures do not permit firms the luxury of moral scruples. Many economists would be inclined to say that if the polluting firm took the high road, it would be driven out of business, and the less scrupulous surviving firms would then cause similar damage.

The argument that competitive pressures exclude moral considerations (or that firms that take morality into account have already been eliminated) is a complicated one, which is seldom carefully presented. Notice first that the conclusion does not follow that taking the high ground never does any good. Even if competitive pressures were to drive the firm out of business (if it refused to pollute the marsh), those pressures might not lead any competitor to open a factory at the same location or to cause the same pollution. All that the competitive pressures argument can show is that the alternative to pollution is not merely lower profits, but bankruptcy and a risk that the pollution will occur just the same.

At this point moral judgment re-enters. To take avoiding bankruptcy as an understandable and unremarkable reason to pollute a marsh is to see nothing needing explanation or condemnation in the choice. This moral and prudential judgment is less objectionable than is the judgment that there is nothing morally impermissible about sacrificing a marsh in order to make larger profits, but it is a moral judgment all the same. If a firm facing bankruptcy hired gangsters to kill the managers of a competitor, economists would not show the same attitude toward the explanation of its conduct.

There are also serious questions concerning the argument that the price of morality is bankruptcy. First, note that the argument does not go through if all firms show the same scruples, for then none is at a competitive disadvantage. So, in giving the argument, one is taking for granted that some firms do things such as poisoning marshes in order to increase profits. Second, the strength of competitive pressures varies enormously. For example, from the time of its formation in 1901 to the present, the market share of the United States Steel Corporation has constantly decreased, yet it has survived (Mueller 1992, pp. 309–10). Third, this selection argument rests on the empirical claim that firms that observe moral constraints will lose out in competition with less scrupulous firms, and it is not obvious that this claim is true.

A reputation for honest dealing with customers, for decent treatment of employees, and for the pursuit of worthy objectives may all increase a firm's profitability. Consider data, such as the following gathered by Robert Frank (unpublished): In 1987, starting salaries in the most prestigious US public interest organizations, such as the American Civil Liberties Union, peaked at $29,000, while prestigious private firms payed up to $83,000. Students in a study at Cornell University claimed that they would have to be paid $10,000 more to work as a lawyer for the National Rifle Association than as a lawyer for the Sierra Club or $15,000 more to write advertising copy for Camel cigarettes rather than for the American Cancer Society. There is thus evidence that "moral" firms can save on wages, and they are likely to have less shirking and lower costs from pilfering or vandalism.

A firm's moral behavior *may* result from a calculation of its good effect on the firm's profitability, but it need not, and we suspect often it does not. A manager or owner may follow certain policies simply because they seem right. The overall effect on the firm's profitability of acting in this unselfinterested moral way may well be more positive than the effect of a more calculated approach, which involved decisions concerning whether doing the right thing would have the desired long-run effects on reputation and profitability (see Frank 1988). These considerations raise doubts about the general argument that competitive pressures compel firms to neglect moral considerations.

Economists should take these issues seriously, since the arguments for resting content with self-interested explanations of immoral behavior have the effect of excusing that behavior. To see nothing remarkable in destructive behavior motivated only by the prospect of additional profits is to endorse a pernicious moral cynicism. To excuse the apparently immoral behavior on the grounds that the firm was forced by competitive pressures to act that way relies on questionable empirical assumptions and risks encouraging much the same moral cynicism. Such approval or excuse should be offered only reluctantly.

We would draw two implications for the explanation of behavior that is *prima facie* immoral. First, any argument that the behavior is mandated by competitive forces should be made explicit and scrutinized. There can be no blanket presumption that such arguments work. Second, if competitive pressures don't offer a satisfactory explanation, then economists should ask whether material acquisitiveness is a good reason in the particular case. One cannot assess explanations in economics without making moral and prudential judgments about how acceptable it is to act for particular reasons. Most of us regard a desire for more commodities as justifying the choice to work longer hours, but not as justifying the choice to rob banks. These moral and prudential judgments are reflected in our satisfaction with the explanation of the longer hours worked and our demand for further explanation of the bank robbing. Judgments of prudence and morality are implicit in attitudes toward explanations of human actions.

4.4 Conclusions

Positive and normative economics are linked via the theory of rationality in complicated ways. Because of these links ethical commitments have an unavoidable role within positive economics. Ethical commitments have some influence in all branches of science, at least on the mores of scientific inquiry and on the questions that are asked. But their influence in economics goes deeper. Unlike the natural sciences, positive economics explains choices in terms of reasons. Consequently, it cannot avoid depicting human beings as to some extent rational. It cannot avoid raising evaluative questions about the reasons it cites to explain choices, and it cannot avoid suggesting answers to them. It's no wonder that students who take economics courses tend to become more selfish and less willing to cooperate, for they are taught in their courses that selfishness is prudent and that selfishness is always acceptable in economic life.

Suggestions for further reading

There has been a good deal of discussion of so-called "folk psychology" by philosophers of psychology. Good contemporary discussions can be found in Churchland (1989), Dennett (1987), Dretske (1988), and Stich (1983).

For discussions of reasons versus causes and of the possible difficulties involved in causal explanation of human behavior, see Davidson (1980), Melden (1961), Rosenberg (1976, ch. 5), Rosenberg (1988, ch. 2), Wright (1971), and Winch (1958).

There is a considerable literature concerning preference reversals. The phenomenon was first discussed in Lichtenstein and Slovic (1971), and the first discussion by economists is Grether and Plott (1979). More recent views can be found in Tversky et al. (1990) and Tversky and Thaler (1990). An overview of economists' reactions can be found in Hausman (1992, ch. 13).

The two main theorems of welfare economics are proven in Arrow and Hahn (1971) and discussed in Graaf (1957), Bator (1957), and Koopman's (1957).

The argument in section 4.3 concerning the evaluative implications of accepting explanations in terms of reasons was suggested by some remarks of Frank Knight (1935).

5   Rationality, norms, and morality

Every society has moral norms, although none can boast of perfect compliance. People approve of behavior that complies with the dictates of their morality and disapprove of behavior that violates moral norms. Those who violate moral norms typically experience negative feelings of guilt or shame. Moral norms enable people to coordinate their actions more efficiently than would be possible without a shared morality. It is in everyone's interest to live in a society governed by moral norms requiring that people tell the truth, keep promises, refrain from actions of violence toward others, and so forth.

Yet it can be costly to do what is morally right. If one is on a sinking ship without a life-jacket, there are obvious advantages in stealing one from another person. One might feel guilty about it later, but people can get over guilt, while they cannot get over death. The central character in Woody Allen's film, *Crimes and misdemeanors*, a distinguished physician who has his mistress murdered to protect his reputation, is surprised at how easily he gets over his guilt. To go to one's death in order to comply with a moral norm against theft might even appear to be *irrational*. Although rationality and morality may often march in step, at a certain point their paths seem to diverge.

How compatible are morality and rationality? This is an old philosophical question, which we cannot hope to settle, but we can explore its ramifications for economics. In this chapter we shall argue that moral considerations deserve a place in economic modeling. To support this conclusion we shall show that moral norms have important economic consequences and that they cannot be explained away in terms that make no reference to morality. We shall also argue that moral commitments should not be regarded by economists merely as individual preferences or sociological facts. But first some clarification is in order, for it is by no means clear whether there is any conflict between morality and the standard theory of rationality presented in chapter 2 above.

5.1 Rationality and self-interest

People often use the word "rational" as a synonym for "prudent." To say that it's not rational to take a midnight stroll through the shrubbery of New York's Central Park is to say that it is not prudent to do so. Because of the risks, it is not in one's *interest* to take such a stroll. There is a close association between rationality and self-interest. In his classic work, *The methods of ethics*, Henry Sidgwick attempts to derive utilitarianism from intuitions concerning the nature of rationality, but in the end he concludes that what he calls "the method of egoism" – that is, self-interested conduct – is just as rational. Robert Frank, in his contemporary classic, *Passions within reason*, writes, "I will use the terms 'rational behavior' and 'self-interested behavior' to mean the same thing" (1988, p. 2n).

The connection between rationality and self-interest is not unequivocal. Though most people would say that it is rational to steal a stranger's life-jacket to save one's own life, most would not say that it is irrational to refuse to do so, and very few people would regard as irrational all actions that apparently conflict with self-interest. Parents who sacrifice their interests for their children are not necessarily irrational. So it seems in ordinary speech as if people are inclined to regard *both* self-interest and moral self-sacrifice as rational.

On the standard account of rationality, preferences are rational if they are complete and transitive, and choices are rational if they are determined by preferences. This theory of rationality places no constraints on *what* a rational individual may prefer, and therefore permits moral preferences and moral choices. According to the standard theory of rationality, someone who prefers honesty to life itself and who accordingly does not steal another's life-jacket may thus be perfectly rational. Rationality and self-interest appear to have nothing to do with one another, and there seems to be no conflict between morality and rationality.

Moral and altruistic preferences are ruled out of many economic models not by axioms of rationality, but by assumptions that the objects of preference are bundles of commodities to be privately consumed and that there are no interdependencies among the preferences of different individuals. In standard economic models a successfully stolen Porsche is the same commodity as one that is purchased or received as a gift, and the agent's preference for the Porsche will be the same. If the objects of preferences are taken to be bundles of commodities and services for personal consumption, then there is no room for moral and altruistic considerations. But this fact does not imply any incompatibility between *rationality* and altruism or morality.

Many people mistakenly interpret the standard theory of rationality as a theory of self-interest. They reason as follows: According to utility theory, it is rational to choose whatever one prefers. Rational choices are determined by one's own interests rather than by anyone else's, and hence rational choices are self-interested. When it is interpreted as a theory of actual choices, utility theory, on this account, reveals that altruistic and moral behavior is actually self-interested. The individual who drowns rather than steal another's life-jacket, like the individual who has no such scruples, does what he or she most prefers and hence acts in his or her own interests. So the person who steals someone else's life-jacket is no more self-interested than is the person who chooses death over immorality.

This conclusion is paradoxical, and the argument is fallacious. To be self-interested is to have preferences directed toward one's own good, not simply to act on one's own preferences. What distinguishes people who are self-interested from those who are altruistic or malevolent is *what they prefer*, and utility theory says nothing about what the content of rational preferences ought to be. Similarly, accepting utility theory as a correct description of people's actual choices and preferences leaves open the question of to what extent individuals are self-interested. So it appears that there is no conflict between morality and the standard view of rationality. We shall argue below, however, that some moral phenomena cannot be accommodated within utility theory.

3.2 The influence of moral norms on economic behavior

Before we can determine whether morality and the standard theory of rationality are compatible and whether and how moral factors can be incorporated into economic models, we need to say a good deal about the nature, causes, and consequences of specifically moral behavior. When philosophers discuss moral norms, they are interested mainly in their validity. But, as Max Weber insisted, one can treat the norms present in a community as objective and causally significant matters of fact quite apart from the question of whether they are worth endorsing. Economists may want to know how the moral norms prevailing in a certain community influence the behavior of the community's members and how moral norms are established, modified, and sustained. One may distinguish *philosophical* inquiries into the validity of moral norms from *sociological* inquiries into their consequences and causes, although we deny that these inquiries are completely separable.

Moral norms are a subclass of social norms, which, following Elster (1989b, p. 113), we take to be prescriptive rules regarding behavior which are shared among a group of people and which are partly sustained by the approval and disapproval of others. Social norms include items such as standards of dress and rules of etiquette. Specifically moral norms are marked out by their subject matter (interpersonal interaction where significant benefits and harms are at stake), their weight (they typically override other considerations), and the sanctions, both internal (guilt) and external (blame), attached to their violation. (See also Elster 1989a, Pettit 1990, and Griffith and Goldfarb 1991.)

Moral norms would be of little interest *unless* they influenced behavior. This point marks an important difference between moral claims and other kinds of assertions. An adequate account of mathematical validity or of truth in physics need not explain why human conduct should be guided by mathematics or physics. But accepted moral claims are *action-guiding*; part of what it means to acknowledge the validity of a moral norm is to have it influence one's actions. A person can coherently, if foolishly, accept the law of gravity and blithely step off the Empire State Building; one cannot, however, accept a moral norm against murder and then cheerfully blow away one's neighbors. Since many economists feel that satisfying explanations require showing that behavior which is apparently influenced by norms is really ultimately self-interested, we need to argue for the obvious claims that moral norms influence actions and that this influence cannot be explained away in terms of self-interest.

As a way of gaining clarity about the role norms can play in economic analysis, we shall consider an example in which moral norms are invoked in explaining so-called "efficiency wages." Usually economists maintain that individuals are paid more because they are more productive. But paying people more may also induce them to work more productively. The idea of an efficiency wage is that simply raising the wages of a group of workers will motivate them, other things being equal, to work more effectively. Efficiency wages refer to the motivational effect of high wages, not to productivity bonuses or piece-work payments.

Efficiency wage theory has attracted a lot of attention largely because it may help to explain two important features of industrial economies. The first feature is the presence of involuntary unemployment. Why don't wages fall to a level consistent with employing the entire labor force? According to efficiency wage theory, paying people more than a market-clearing wage leads them to be more productive. Reducing wages could cost firms more from lost productivity than they gain from the savings in wage payments. The second feature is the so-called "dual labor market." Some observers characterize the US economy as having a "casual" labor market characterized by high turnover and low (market-clearing) wages and a "career" labor market characterized by lower turnover, higher wages and rationed entry through queues of applicants for a limited number of jobs. Here again, the presence of efficiency wages in firms whose jobs are in the career labor market category may be part of the explanation. Firms could hire equally well-qualified workers at lower wages, but they could not motivate them to work as productively.

A variety of attempts have been made to explain efficiency wages in models that assume rational self-interested behavior on the part of both firms and workers. For example, Samuel Bowles and Herbert Gintis (1993) point out that it is costly and difficult for firms to monitor the performance of their workers. If the only sanction firms have is the threat of firing, then firms are not going to be able to motivate their workers unless firing is costly to the workers, and firing will not be very costly to workers unless firms pay more than market-clearing wages. Although Bowles and Gintis are Marxists and argue for the advantages of worker cooperatives, their account of efficiency wages relies only on self-interested maximizing choices by workers and employers, and it does not rely on norms.

George Akerlof, in contrast, has offered a sociological explanation, in terms of what he calls "partial gift exchange" (1982). Akerlof revisits a case study developed originally by the sociologist George Homans. Homans examined "cash posters" at the Eastern Utilities Company, whose job was to record customers' payments on ledger cards at the time of receipt. It was easy to measure the workers' output and to compare it to the company's performance standard. Of the group of ten workers, two barely met the standard of 300 postings per hour, but the average number of postings per hour (353) was 17.7 percent above the standard. Despite considerable variation in performance (the range was from 306 to 438 postings per hour), all workers received the same wage, differential promotion was not an issue, and there were no serious efforts to sanction the slower workers. These facts are hard to reconcile with standard economic theory. If workers prefer gossiping, coffee drinking, or day-dreaming to recording payments on ledger cards, then those who post more than the standard 300 should either slack off or demand more pay. If the company, for its part, wants to increase its returns, then it seems that it should raise its performance standards, at least for the more productive workers. If these workers exceed the standard without any reward, they should be willing to increase their rate of postings further in exchange for additional compensation. Higher compensation for more productive workers should benefit both the firm and the workers.

Akerlof argues that these facts have a straightforward sociological explanation. Both the firm and the workers adhere to a norm of "gift exchange" for effort and wages above the minimum expected. Workers receive a gift of more than the market-clearing wages and in return they give more than the minimum standard of effort. These transactions are governed by the norms of "a fair day's work for a fair day's pay." Further explanation is needed for the absence of pay differentials and for the firm's willingness to maintain low-performing workers in their jobs. Akerlof appeals here to further norms of fair treatment among workers. Introduction of pay differentials or efforts to dismiss the less productive workers might result in withdrawal of some of the extra effort. (Akerlof reports evidence that slowdowns occurred in the past when the company tried to toughen up.) In the presence of a "gift" from the workers of 17.7 percent of output, the firm has need to be cautious about violating workers' norms of fair treatment.

The fact that in this example the norms governing workers' effort decisions are sensitive both to wages and wage differentials introduces a basic difference between the workings of a pure market and a market with gift exchange. Akerlof shows in a formalization of the cash posters' story that the observed phenomena of wage equality and effort above the minimum required are consistent with the firm maximizing profits and the workers maximizing utility in the presence of this relationship between norms and wages.

It is hard to judge whether Akerlof's explanation of the cash posters' case is correct because, as Akerlof notes, it is possible to construct many subtle neoclassical explanations of these facts which avoid any appeal to norms and rely instead on turnover costs, measurement difficulties, and the like. The sociological explanation is plausible, and as Akerlof notes, norms regarding gift-giving are familiar in countries like the United States, and the "ties of sentiment" that develop among workers and even between workers and their employing firm are a plausible ground for the emergence and maintenance of such norms.

The norms that figure in Akerlof's explanation raise further questions. How are they generated? Why does the relation between work norms and perceived fairness take precisely this form? How stable are these norms in response to changes in other factors? Are there other norms whose observance would be more efficient? These are, in our view, serious and interesting questions to pursue. Some might, however, argue that the fact that Akerlof's explanation of the cash posters raises these further questions shows that the explanation is unsatisfactory, because it is not sufficiently "fundamental." Many economists would suggest that a fuller picture would ultimately reduce the norm-guided behavior to sophisticated self-interested choices.

Akerlof's account raises interesting questions about the origin and determinants of social norms to which, at this point, there are no very satisfactory answers. It is, however, a huge leap from recognizing these questions to claiming that good answers to them will reduce everything to self-interest and will produce an explanation of essentially a neoclassical kind. Whether there is an adequate account in terms of economic self-interest is precisely what is at issue here. It begs the question to insist that there must be one.

As this example from Akerlof illustrates, sociological and normative aspects of work relations may influence the macroeconomics as well as the microeconomics of labor markets. The "efficiency wage" story offers a promising route to explaining the existence of involuntary unemployment in equilibrium. (In addition to Akerlof, see Solow 1981, Blinder and Choi 1990, and Bowles 1985). However, an adequate macroeconomic explanation of unemployment grounded in efficiency wage theory requires solving further puzzles. Why don't unemployed workers undercut the prevailing above-market-clearing wage by offering to work for less than those with jobs? Why don't employers actively seek such workers, perhaps differentiating the workforce to pay more to those with established jobs and less to the eager newcomers? Solow (1990, ch. 2) and Weibull (1987) suggest that further social norms come into play – a norm among workers against bidding against their fellows for jobs and a norm among employers against seeking to undercut their existing workforce.

There are many other areas of economic life where it appears that moral norms are influential. The regulation of negative externalities like air pollution and littering, for example, is accomplished partly through legal sanctions, but norms against such "anti-social" behavior also play a significant role. The same may be said about the provision of public goods in general and about voting. Public transport in many European cities operates on an honor system with only sporadic ticket checks.

A particularly central example of a public good whose provision relies on moral norms is the existence of a legal system, including a system of property rights (Arrow 1974). Adam Smith was among those who stressed that no legal system – certainly not one that allowed widespread commercial freedom – could rely purely on criminal sanctions for its enforcement. A widespread conviction that people ought to obey the law is essential to the maintenance of social order. Moral norms *do* apparently matter enormously. Unless these appearances can be shown to be misleading or the persistence of the norms itself explained in terms of rational self-interest, moral norms must be recognized as significant causal factors that are sometimes of major importance.

5.3 How do norms motivate and what sustains them?

Automobile manufacturers sometimes initiate costly recalls of their product even when they are not required to do so. One possible explanation is that there are norms requiring that manufacturers repair flaws in merchandise. So one might explain a particular voluntary recall by General Motors by mentioning the norm and citing the generalization that, other things being equal, agents follow norms. Few economists would be satisfied with this explanation. They would insist that one must explain why the management of General Motors decided to comply with the norm and why the norm persists. As we mentioned before, many economists would go further still and deny that one has an explanation until one has demonstrated that the action is in the "material" or "economic" self-interest of the agents. The qualifiers "material" or "economic" are needed to give some teeth to the constraint. If being in compliance with the norm is itself counted as in the interest of the agent, then it is trivially true that norm-following is self-interested. What economists would like to show is that norm-following increases profits of firms or the consumption or leisure of individuals. Although it is not, in our view, reasonable to insist that only material self-interest motivates, the other challenges are serious. Norms do not descend from the heavens, as the Ten Commandments are alleged to have done. They are somehow created, modified, sustained, and enforced by people, and an explanation of behavior that merely cites a norm, without considering what sustains and enforces it, is shallow.

Let us shift to an example involving individuals where the moral norm explanation is more persuasive than in the case of an automobile recall. A few years ago experimenters left wallets containing identification and a small amount of cash on the streets of New York City (Hornstein *et al.* 1968). Almost half were returned with the cash intact. It is hard to understand how returning the wallets could have been advantageous for those who found them. It is troublesome to pack up a wallet and mail it (particularly in New York City, where there are long lines at the post offices). Presumably the reason why most people returned the wallet was either a direct altruistic concern for the owner of the wallet or a moral norm against appropriating other people's property. Since altruism tends to be weaker when one has no vivid impression of the other person, it seems reasonable to assume that the norm against theft explains why people returned the wallets (Batson 1993). (What would lead you to return a wallet?)

How does a norm motivate individuals to comply with it? One possibility is that the moral *reasons* justifying the norm *themselves* motivate the compliance. People's desire to act on principles that no rational agent could reasonably reject, or their desire not to free-ride, but to do their part in practices of which they approve, can motivate them to follow norms, even when doing so will not benefit them materially. (What motivates you not to steal?) Explanations like this one may not be congenial to economists, but we believe they are often correct. And if such explanations are correct, then the *justification* for a set of norms and not merely the *fact* that the norms are accepted may be important empirically. If people comply with some norms because they accept the moral *reasons* that justify those norms, then a critique of those reasons may have important behavioral consequences. And if reasons have such empirical importance, then economists need to understand how norms are justified.

Economists and sociologists influenced by economists have tended to focus instead on the individual *sanctions* motivating compliance with norms. These sanctions may not be material, and they may consequently be suspect to some economists. But they are very much the stuff out of which everyday life is built. If one returns the wallet, one feels good about oneself, and a thank-you note makes one feel even better. One can tell one's family, friends, and associates what one did, and in response one gains their trust and praise. Indeed in this way it is possible to garner some material advantage, though usually not enough to compensate for the trouble of returning the wallet. If, on the other hand, one does not return the wallet, then, if one has been "well brought up" (and hasn't studied too much economics!), one feels guilty, and if one's failure to return the wallet becomes known to others, one may be censured by them, or one may suffer from knowing that one has lost their self-esteem, even if their censure is never expressed (Pettit 1990, p. 740). More needs to be said about "internal" sanctions such as guilt or self-satisfaction, but this mode of explaining compliance with norms seems clear enough: Individuals comply with norms because of the individual benefits attached to doing so and because of the costs of not doing so. We have no doubt that this is often an important part of the explanation for why individuals comply with norms, although as we have already said, we do not think that it is the whole story.

To say that individuals comply with norms because of sanctions does not get one far. Sanctions have to be applied by people, and it is typically no more advantageous to punish or reward others for complying with norms than it is to comply with norms in the first place. Given that others (including one's "superego") will punish violations and reward compliance, it may be advantageous (though not necessarily materially advantageous) to comply with norms. But this only explains why one person should comply with norms if others do. It does not explain why people generally comply with norms, nor why the norms persist.

One might attempt to explain why norms persist in terms of their social benefits. Groups with strong norms of truth-telling and promise-keeping do better than groups without such norms. But in any sizeable group, no individual can have much effect on the norms obtaining in the group or on average compliance. So although the social benefits of a system of norms may provide a moral reason for complying with them, these benefits do not generally provide a self-interested reason. On the contrary, one typ-ically does better by free-riding on the norm-following of others. Since there are few sanctions attached to sanctioning others, rational individuals who are only concerned about their profits, consumption, or leisure are rarely going to trouble themselves to punish or reward others for violating or complying with norms. So if one knows that one's fellows are rational and self-interested agents of the sort found in economic models, then one should have little to fear in the way of sanctions against violating norms and little to expect in the way of reward for complying with them; and it seems as if norms cannot be effective. But norms are effective, and hence people's commitment to them cannot be explained in terms of economic self-interest.

We do not maintain that this argument is an iron-clad demonstration that norms cannot be generated or sustained by a community of rational and self-interested economic agents. Involuntary attitudes of approval or disapproval may create the needed incentives to conform to norms (Pettit 1990, Brennan and Pettit 1993), or it may be possible to argue that the costs and benefits of sanctioning can make sanctioning rational (Coleman 1990, ch. 10). But the argument should give economists pause. Unless norms are of no economic importance, which is very hard to believe, econ-omists need to broaden their theory of economic behavior to find a place within it for a discussion of when norms will form, of how much influence they may have, and of what their consequences will be. If the existence and influence of moral norms depends on the strength of moral reasons (as we have argued), then economists will not be able to treat moral norms as mere sociological facts that need not be understood or assessed.

5.4 Philosophical implications

The evidence cited above strengthens the case that normative commit-ments matter. In this respect these "sociological" studies bolster the case for taking morality seriously. At the same time, these studies say little about *how* moral norms influence individuals' economic conduct. As Alan Gibbard (1990) has argued, the psychology of norm-guided behavior is not well understood. What exactly does it mean, for example, for a norm to be "internalized"? Gibbard distinguishes the psychological state of "accepting" a norm from the state of "being in the grip" of a norm. The former includes a deliberative judgment and a conscious endorsement of the norm, which typically issue in behavior conforming to the norm. The latter is an involuntary state, in which one finds oneself moved by the demand of a norm without judging the demand as worthwhile and indeed perhaps in the face of a judgment that the demand is pointless or

improper. Did the cash posters, for example, have a reflective understanding of their gift exchange norms? From the point of view of their
overt behavior, it may not matter much, but there may be a big difference
in terms of what kinds of factors lead people to be moved by moral norms
and what factors can change their moral behavior. From the standpoint of
most moral philosophy, which links moral conduct to reasoned decisions,
the cognitive element involved in accepting a norm in Gibbard's sense is an
important feature.

Can philosophers learn from these sociological inquiries about the
content of morality? It would be an obvious mistake to conclude that a
norm is morally acceptable merely because it is widely followed. Yet
understanding the economic role of moral norms may shed light on the
question whether such norms are justified. For example, Kenneth Arrow
(1974) and Melvin Reder (1979) have shown how the virtues of honesty
and trustworthiness may promote economic efficiency in circumstances of
uncertainty. Arrow has also argued more specifically that medical codes of
ethics may be an efficient and socially desirable response to the opportunities physicians possess to exploit their informational advantages over
patients. Arguments of this kind may contribute to the *justification* of
these moral norms. One argument in favor of a norm is that it leads to
good consequences, including consequences for economic well-being.
Anyone who accepts such an argument in the case of a particular norm
has a reason (though not necessarily a self-interested reason) to accept the
norm, and in this way the argument may help explain why people embrace
the norm in their behavior. The good consequences of a moral norm are
not, however, enough to explain its emergence and persistence. As Elster
(1989a,b) has argued, to explain the existence or persistence of the norm
also requires an account of the mechanisms by which the favorable consequences produce or sustain the practice. In biology, natural selection provides such a mechanism. In the social sciences, "functional explanations"
– explanations of phenomena in terms of their beneficial consequences to
society – are more dubious.

Not all moral norms have good economic consequences. The norms
regarding work rules and wages discussed earlier in this chapter seem
ambiguous in this regard. On one hand, these norms promote wage equality, high wages, and stable and productive working groups; and these
would widely be judged to be good consequences. Yet these norms may
also contribute to unemployment. Moreover, more established "in groups"
may benefit disproportionately from these norms, while minority and disadvantaged groups are excluded from these benefits.

What people take to be moral norms may sometimes be subject to moral
criticisms. For example, Amartya Sen has made powerful criticisms of the

norms in many societies that govern the distribution of resources and power within families. These norms discourage women from objecting to intrafamilial inequalities even though the resulting inequalities in the distribution of food between boys and girls apparently lead to millions of premature female deaths in poor countries (Sen 1990). There have been places in which the norms prevalent in the majority culture mandated discrimination against minority group members. What is relevant to whether moral norms are justified is not whether they are socially influential, but whether they are socially beneficial. And even the fact that a norm is socially beneficial is not sufficient to justify it.

5.5 Morality and utility theory

We have argued that economists need to broaden their theory of economic behavior to consider when norms will form and what sort of influence they may have. Doing so requires recognizing that economic agents are not always self-interested and that self-interest is not always material. Economic agents do not only care about the commodities and leisure they may consume. Sometimes they also want to benefit or to harm other people, and even when self-interested, they may care more about the esteem and affection of others than about the size of their houses or the style of their clothing. Since there is nothing in the formal theory of rationality that bars altruistic and moral preferences, these data do not refute the theory. But even if utility maximization and morally motivated conduct are formally consistent, utility theory might not be very helpful in analyzing moral conduct. Amartya Sen (1977a) has argued that, even though utility theory may be too demanding in some regards, such as in its insistence that preferences be complete, it may at the same time impose *too little* structure on problems of choice to allow productive analysis of moral conduct.

Some of the structure that needs to be added creates no formal difficulties. For example, one can distinguish *self-regarding* or *egoistic* preferences from *other-regarding* or *altruistic* preferences by including either the utility or consumption levels of other individuals in a person's utility function. Someone who is altruistic will prefer states of affairs in which others consume more or in which their preferences are better satisfied. Someone who is envious or malevolent will prefer states of affairs in which others do worse. Terminologically, it is useful to refer to the satisfaction of self-regarding preferences by some term such as "personal interests" or "standard of living," which differs from the person's overall level of satisfaction, including the satisfactions of sympathy. But one must be careful not to forget that self-regarding preferences include preferences for the approval of others. There is no canonical usage here, and what is important is not the precise names, but an awareness of distinctions among the concepts (see Sen *et al.* 1987).

Not all non-egoistic concerns are however captured by notions of sympathy or altruism. One may be concerned not only with the level of another person's welfare or consumption, but with how it is attained. In particular, one may wish to be an active contributor to another's well-being. We not only want our children to acquire good moral characters, but we want some of the responsibility for their upbringing. As Arrow has noted, the desire to contribute may have substantially different implications than mere altruism. If many rich people prefer a higher level of consumption for "the poor," then there may be a "free-rider" problem: people want poverty eliminated, but they'd like others to pay for it. If, instead, each wishes to contribute to helping the poor, the "public-goods" or "free-rider" problem goes away (Hochman and Rodgers 1969). More generally, economists should not ignore the desire to *do* certain things rather than simply to enjoy the consequences of their being done. But once again there is no formal difficulty about capturing such desires within utility theory. All one has to do is to include actions involving helping others among the objects of preferences.

A more serious complication arises from the fact that morality is not the same thing as altruism. An altruistic concern for the members of one's family is consistent with blood-thirsty behavior toward the rest of the world. Even a more generalized altruism leaves out important features of morality. Amartya Sen clarifies part of what is left out by distinguishing between "sympathy" and "commitment." Consider a soldier on sentry duty. Her motives in staying alert may include a self-interested fear of punishment and a sympathetic concern for the welfare of those she is guarding. But she may be motivated as well by a desire to do her duty, to live up to a code she has acknowledged as binding on her. Sen proposes to define "commitment" in terms of her willingness to undertake an action (in this case staying alert) *even if* doing so conflicts with self-interested and sympathetic preferences. Returning the wallets in the experiments cited above probably involved commitment rather than sympathy. Notice that this definition of commitment involves a subjunctive. Duty may happen to coincide with personal welfare; but the defining characteristic is that the duty would be carried out *even if* this were not so.

Economists schooled in the theory of revealed preference might insist that if agents chose to stay alert or to return a wallet, then they must have preferred to. Many economists would also be tempted to claim that staying alert or returning the wallet consequently makes the agents better off. But, as we will argue in the next chapter, it is a mistake to equate the satisfaction of preference with what is good for an agent. What about equating what an agent chooses with what an agent prefers? Even though it may be possible formally to model the committed agent as maximizing utility, it may be more *enlightening* not to do so. For then one can begin to consider what role morality might play in *constraining* choices, and one can recognize the special problems of self-control and weakness of will to which moral duties give rise.

By not modeling moral action and deliberation as utility maximization, one can also make sense of the phenomena of reflecting on, assessing, and sometimes revising one's motives or reasons for acting. It may be useful to suppose that individuals have different preference rankings or utilities depending on whether they consider matters from a self-interested or a moral perspective or to suppose that individuals have "metapreferences," that is, preferences concerning what their preferences should be. Multiple-preference systems very naturally model internal conflict concerning such personal choices as whether or not to smoke (Schelling 1984, pp. 57–112) as well as more clearly moral choices such as whether to contribute to charity (Etzioni 1986, pp. 177–80; Frankfurt 1971). Some have argued that the choices of morally influenced persons are better represented in such models (Margolis 1982, Etzioni 1988). However, this approach also raises difficult questions, for it is not clear within the multiple-preference frame-work how to explain which ranking will prevail in which circumstances. If that determination is itself made by a consistent preference ranking at a higher level, then it may make sense to re-invoke standard utility theory.

If one takes seriously the reasons for regarding moral concerns as *competing with* preferences rather than as determining preferences, then there is reason to regard some of morality as irrational in terms of the notion of rationality defined by utility theory. But one might instead question whether utility theory defines rationality in an acceptable way. If one takes acting rationally to be acting on good reasons, then there seems to be no basis for a conflict between rationality and morality. Even though this last statement in defense of the rationality of morality is vague, it is important to recognize that the alleged "irrationality" of moral commitment is very different from what people generally take irrationality to be. Moral commitment is not like hallucinating or falling into a fit, since it depends on reasons and responds to arguments.

5.6 Conclusion: on the rationality of morality

The *homo economicus* of contemporary economics is *homo rationalis*. This fact embodies a commitment to a modeling strategy and to a theory of prudence. The theory of rationality is already a fragment of a theory of morality. But the view of rationality that economists endorse – utility theory – may not provide a rich enough picture of individual choice to permit one to discuss the character, causes, and consequences of moral behavior. Economists need not of course aspire to provide a general theory of human action. Yet they should not shrug their shoulders at the difficulties in meshing moral behavior with economic rationality. For it seems that moral behavior may have important consequences for economic outcomes, and the propagation of utility theory has moral implications.

Suggestions for further reading

For the general contrast between "self-interest" and "present-aim" theories of rationality, see Parfit (1984, part 2). For more on the relations between rationality and self-interest in economics, see Sen (1977a).

Useful discussions of norms can be found in Elster (1989a,b) Pettit (1990), Brennan and Pettit (1993), Goldfarb and Griffith (1992), Coleman (1990), and Frank (1992).

Efficiency wage theory is discussed in Akerlof (1984), Akerlof and Yellen (1986), and Solow (1990).

The possible influence of moral factors in determining the efficiency of alternative ways of organizing the workplace are discussed in Putterman (1984), Bowles (1985), McPherson (1983a), Reich and Devine (1981), and Bowles and Gintis (1993). A related but distinct point is the role of *trust* in governing worker–employer relations, which is discussed in McKean (1975), Arrow (1974), and Gambetta (1988).

General problems concerning the explanation of the provision of public goods and the role that moral norms may play can be found in Taylor (1987), Kelman (1981), Schelling (1978), Mansbridge (1990), and Elster (1989a).

For discussions of the existence of altruism and its possible importance in economics see Arrow (1972), Becker (1981), Boulding (1978), Collard (1978), and Batson (1993).

Multiple-preference rankings are introduced and discussed in Frankfurt (1971), Sen (1977a), Schelling (1984), Etzioni (1986), and Brennan (1988).

Part II

Welfare and consequences

Economic outcomes may be better or worse along several dimensions. Some outcomes may make people better off. Others may show more respect for human dignity. Others may permit greater freedom. To decide which dimensions are more important requires moral judgment.

Economists typically evaluate outcomes in only one way – in terms of individual welfare. Outcome Z is better than outcome Q if and only if outcome Z makes people better off than outcome Q. Since the evaluation of outcomes rests exclusively on their consequences for individual welfare, the theory of individual welfare is crucial to normative economics. Indeed normative economics is often called "welfare economics." As we saw in chapter 4, economists are committed to one particular view of welfare as the satisfaction of preferences.

Economists do not only evaluate outcomes. They also evaluate institutions and policies. Institutions and policies may be better or worse quite apart from their consequences. For example, even if markets led to bad outcomes, they might still be desirable because of the freedoms they involve. But economists in fact evaluate institutions and policies entirely in terms of their welfare consequences. Freedoms are valued only to the extent that they contribute to welfare. The many evaluative questions one might ask about economic institutions, policies, and outcomes are all reduced to the single problem of evaluating outcomes in terms of the extent to which they satisfy preferences.

In Part II we shall address the complexities that arise when one reduces evaluation to evaluation of outcomes by their welfare consequences. Chapter 6 will probe the standard preference-satisfaction view of welfare and discuss some alternatives to it. Chapter 7 is concerned with standard welfare economics and the way in which it depends on the preference-satisfaction view of welfare. Chapter 8 will then discuss utilitarianism, which, like standard welfare economics, evaluates policies in terms of their welfare consequences. Unlike welfare economics, utilitarianism attempts to be a complete moral theory, and it is not necessarily wedded to a preference-satisfaction view of welfare. Utilitarians also suppose that interpersonal comparisons of welfare levels and differences are possible. Despite these differences, there are deep affinities between welfare economics and utilitarianism, and they share many of the same virtues and vices.

6   Welfare

When people in modern Western cultures think about morality, they think first of all about what is morally permissible or impermissible – right or wrong. But there are other matters of moral concern. Of special importance among these are questions about what things are good or bad.

Exactly what is good for a particular agent, Murphy, will depend on Murphy's character, ability, and circumstances, and what is good for Murphy may be very different from what is good for Marlow. But most of the differences between what is good for Murphy and Marlow concern *instrumental* goods – things that are good because they are *means* to something else. If one focuses on *intrinsic* goods – things that are good in themselves – without regard to their consequences, then there may be much less variation from individual to individual. Size 7 shoes are good for Murphy, while size 12 shoes are good for Marlow, but both pairs serve the same end. Notice that there must be intrinsic goods in order for there to be instrumental goods. One central question of moral philosophy has been to determine what things are intrinsically good for human beings. Thus Aristotle, for example, held that happiness was the sole intrinsic good.

All plausible moral views assign an important place to conceptions of individual good, utility, welfare, or well-being. This is obviously true of utilitarianism, which maintains that what is right maximizes some function of the welfare of individual members of society. But even non-utilitarian views that emphasize notions of rights, fairness, and justice need a conception of human well-being. Not only do these views recognize the virtue of benevolence, which requires some notion of human good, but even their core notions often make reference to well-being. For example, justice or fairness is understood in terms of treating the *interests* of different persons properly, and acting rightly will often involve avoiding *harm* to other individuals. And notions of harm and interest are plainly connected to notions of well-being.

6.1 Theories of well-being

In chatting with one's neighbors, as in studying moral philosophy, one finds many different theories of well-being. In some religious views, the ultimate good lies in a relationship with God, while in others such a relationship with God is good because of the eternal happiness it brings. Many people believe that only mental states are intrinsically good, but there is less agreement here than it seems, because there are so many different views of which mental states are intrinsically good. Jeremy Bentham holds that the good is pleasure, while John Stuart Mill holds that it is a diverse set of mental states he calls "happiness." Mystics find the good in contemplative states of mind. Henry Sidgwick argued for the hybrid view that the good is any mental state that is intrinsically desirable.

There are also many defenders of non-mental-state views. Friedrich Nietzsche regards great achievements as the ultimate goods. Others endorse as intrinsic goods a whole pot-pourri ranging from health and intimate personal relationships to achievements such as those Nietzsche admired. The theory of well-being is a messy area of philosophy. It is difficult even to categorize the various theories, and they all face serious difficulties. All of this is enough to send economists running back to their graphs and matrices. But they cannot avoid addressing these philosophical problems if they want to be able to judge when welfare increases or decreases.

Theories of well-being can be classified as either "formal" or "substantive." A substantive theory of well-being says what things are intrinsically good for people. "Hedonism" is an example of a substantive theory of well-being. It says that well-being is happiness or pleasure. Formal theories of well-being specify how one finds out what things are intrinsically good for people, but they do not say what those things are. To maintain that welfare is the satisfaction of preferences is to offer a formal theory of well-being. This theory does not say what things are good for individuals, but it says how to find out – by seeing what they prefer. Formal theories may be compatible with substantive theories. For example, if happiness is the ultimate object of preference, then it could be true both that well-being is the satisfaction of preference and that well-being is happiness.

One reason why economists are attracted to a formal theory of well-being is that formal theories appear to involve fewer philosophical commitments. In particular, economists are reluctant to make substantive claims about what is good or bad for people. By leaving the substantive question of what is good for an individual up to the individual, it seems that economists are showing their philosophical modesty. The preference-satisfaction view of well-being also appeals to the anti-paternalist values of many economists. But as we shall argue in this chapter, it is not clear that formal theories of the good, such as the preference-satisfaction theory, are less philosophically controversial than substantive theories.

Given economists' commitments to utility theory in *explaining* human choices, it is natural that they would look to levels of utility – that is, preference satisfaction – as the fundamental measure of human well-being for evaluative purposes as well. If individuals are exclusively self-interested, then they will prefer x to y if and only if they believe that x is better for them than y is. If they are well-informed, then their beliefs will be true, and x is better for them than y if and only if they prefer x to y. So it's very tempting to take well-being to be the satisfaction of preferences. In applied work, economists often rely on more objective measures of "real income" rather than utility measures, but this is viewed as a compromise with data limitations. Real income is regarded as an imperfect proxy for preference satisfaction.

Yet there are such obvious objections to a preference-satisfaction view of well-being that one wonders how economists could possibly endorse it. Real individuals are not exclusively self-interested. They are sometimes altruistic and all too often malevolent. Real individuals are also ignorant of many things. So people may prefer something that is bad for them because they mistakenly believe it is beneficial or because they want to help a friend or harm an enemy. It is not true that x is better for A than y if and only if A prefers x to y. How then can economists take welfare to be the satisfaction of preferences?

6.2 Is the standard view of welfare plausible?

These objections are not hard to see. It takes no great philosophical talent to recognize that giving a powerful motorcycle to a reckless teenage boy does not necessarily make him better off, no matter how desperately he wants it. Yet economists continue to espouse the preference-satisfaction theory of welfare. Why?

In chapter 4 we explored one reason: If one accepts the standard view of rationality and the standard idealizations of positive economics, then it follows that what one prefers is what is good for one. So, within the theoretical world depicted in many standard economic models, welfare is preference satisfaction. Economists recognize that this world is not the real world, and the fact that welfare is preference satisfaction in standard models does not imply that welfare is preference satisfaction in real life, but they often regard the differences between theory and reality as matters of detail. "If one looks past the complications of actual life to the central realities captured in standard economic models, one can see that welfare is in essence the satisfaction of preferences." This line of thought will not convince anyone who does not see the world the way economists do, but it helps explain why economists are content to identify well-being with the satisfaction of preferences.

Second, even though what satisfies Smith's preferences does not necessarily make Smith better off, Smith's preferences may be the best *guide* to what is beneficial to her. Even though satisfying people's preferences may not necessarily make them better off, there is perhaps no better way to decide how to benefit people. Legislators know less of Smith's circumstances than she knows and they have a less tender concern for her well-being than she does. The judgments of legislators about how to make Smith better off are thus likely to be worse than her own judgments. Furthermore, even if Smith's preferences are not a better guide to what is good for her than the judgments of legislators, it is *safer* to leave the judgment to her. This defense does not attempt to show that welfare *is* the satisfaction of preferences. Instead it denies that economists need any philosophical theory of welfare. Regardless of what human well-being truly is, the best *measure* of well-being is the extent to which preferences are satisfied. But there is no way to defend the claim that preference satisfaction is the best measure of welfare until one has said what welfare is.

We guess that many economists do not take the standard definition of welfare literally. They believe instead that welfare is a desirable mental state, such as happiness. They find it plausible to believe that the best measure of well-being is preference satisfaction, because they believe that the best way to implement a social policy that aims to make people happy is to satisfy preferences. We cannot prove our conjecture that most economists actually take welfare to be a mental state like happiness, but there is a good deal of evidence that supports it. Economists often slide from talking about utility to talking about happiness. Economists often talk about individuals "seeking" utility, which makes no sense if utility is just a measure of the extent to which preferences are satisfied. And it is easy to equivocate on the word "satisfaction." To satisfy a preference is for a preference to come true. It has nothing to do with any *feelings* of satisfaction. Ellen's grandmother's preference that her granddaughter become a doctor is satisfied if Ellen becomes a doctor, even if Ellen's grandmother never lives to see that day and cannot *feel* any satisfaction at the event. But economists often speak of satisfaction as a feeling.

It is questionable whether well-being is in fact a mental state like happiness. Suppose there were an "experience machine" that could give people the highest quality experiences possible (Nozick 1974, p. 41). These high-quality experiences might be intense sensations of pleasure or they might be experiences of climbing Everest or composing a symphony. Let them be whatever experiences mental-state theorists of well-being claim are ulti-mately and intrinsically good. The mental-state theorist would then have to say that all people would be better off permanently hooked up to a reli-able experience machine rather than living their own lives and experienc-ing the decidedly mixed mental states that come with them. If one believes that those who are hooked up to the experience machine are missing out on some of the intrinsically good things in life, even though they are not by assumption missing out on any good mental states, then one cannot accept a mental-state view of well-being.

6.3 Implications of taking well-being to be the satisfaction of preferences

Even if the theoretical and practical defenses of measuring welfare by the satisfaction of preferences do not succeed, they permit one to see why sen-sible economists so readily link welfare and the satisfaction of preferences. Let us now look more carefully at the consequences of a preference-satis-faction view of welfare for economic evaluation.

Measurements of well-being have many purposes – to establish bench-marks for equality, to assess progress over time, to compare living stan-dards across communities, to weigh the comparative claims that different persons may justifiably make on social resources, and so on. Different conceptions may suit different purposes. We shall argue in this section that the view of welfare as the satisfaction of preferences is unsuitable for most of these purposes.

6.3.1 Changing and conflicting preferences and preferences based on false beliefs

To regard welfare as the satisfaction of preferences leads to complications when preferences change. As Richard Brandt (1979, ch. 13) and Derek Parfit (1984, ch. 8) point out, if an individual's preference ranking changes, then it is unclear whether the individual is made better off by sat-isfying or frustrating the original preferences. It seems that one faces within an agent's life something akin to the problem of interpersonal utility comparisons, which we will discuss in the next chapter (Gibbard 1986).

Should one care about satisfying preferences that a person no longer has? Should anyone be concerned to satisfy Hausman's childhood desire to be a garbage collector? Surely not (according at least to Hausman now!).

But why not? Is it just that his current desire not to be a garbage collector is stronger? But what if his current desire isn't stronger? Most people, including most economists, would give *no* weight to satisfying past preferences in cases such as this one. But can one repudiate past desires without repudiating a preference-satisfaction view of the good? If one says that satisfying past desires does not count, because giving people what they no longer want brings them no "satisfaction," then one has shifted from a preference-satisfaction to a mental-state theory of welfare. It seems that an acceptable account of welfare and rationality needs to look beyond preferences to reasons.

This theoretical problem of preference change is linked to a practical problem. Suppose, as seems plausible, that policies and institutions have systematic effects on preference rankings. (Surely the billions spent on propaganda and advertising must have *some* effect on preferences.) Assessments of policy must then depend in part on one's views concerning *which* preferences to promote or concerning which institutions provide a suitable framework within which desirable preferences will develop (McPherson 1982, 1983b). Should one be concerned about the extent to which one satisfies current preferences, when one judges that they are in any event likely to change? Should one aim to modify preferences to make them easier to satisfy? A preference-satisfaction theory of well-being makes some of these questions very difficult to answer, and it suggests implausible answers to others. In particular, a preference-satisfaction view of well-being apparently has the alarming implication that (other things being equal) we should educate people to have easily satisfied preferences.

Problems also arise when an agent has false beliefs. If citizens of New York State prefer to locate a nuclear power plant in the middle of New York City because they falsely believe that long-distance power transmission poses greater risks than do nuclear power plant accidents, then frustrating their preferences would be more likely to make them better off than satisfying them. Even if policy-makers should in general honor people's preferences, they should not necessarily agree with their beliefs. But this leaves the policy-maker in a bind, because preferences virtually always depend upon beliefs. The only consistent ways out of this impasse are either to follow people's preferences, even if they depend upon beliefs that are false and unreasonable, or to employ some substantive theory of welfare (Hausman and McPherson 1994).

Conflicts within an agent's preferences create problems too. The standard model of rationality rules out conflicts among preferences, but one cannot rule realities out of the real world, and such conflicts obviously exist. There are many conflicts between "first-order" preferences, such as a preference for smoking, and "second-order" or "metapreferences," such as a preference that one does not prefer to smoke. Such conflicts can give rise to internal struggle, feelings of regret and deprivation, and apparently inconsistent behavior, such as purchasing cigarettes but then locking them away or flushing them down a toilet. In addition to such conflicts between first-order preferences and metapreferences, there are also conflicts among first-order preferences themselves. A preference-satisfaction view of well-being provides few resources to deal with such conflicts. If Jones does not have a consistent preference ranking, then there is no way one can say whether anything is better for Jones than anything else. If Jones has two or more preference rankings which conflict with one another, then there is no way one can say whether x is better for Jones than y unless x happens to be above y in all of Jones' rankings. Without privileging one of the rankings, one cannot say which ranking would be best for Jones to keep and which would be best to drop. Indeed one cannot even make *sense* of the notion of how good it is for Jones to have one preference ranking rather than another without invoking some preference ranking.

Although preference changes and conflicts among preferences may be unimportant in some applications, the dependence of preferences on beliefs looms large in many policy problems. All three of these difficulties are both theoretical and practical, and a preference-satisfaction view of well-being cannot cope with them very well.

6.3.2 Assessing preferences

On the preference-satisfaction view, one makes Smith better off by satisfying her preferences regardless of how idiosyncratic or obnoxious they are and regardless of how they were formed. But some of the uses of the theory of welfare apparently demand that one discriminate among preferences.

Consider preferences that are idiosyncratic or based on highly contestable beliefs. One may not believe that satisfying the preferences of a starving man who begs for money to make a sacrifice to his god will make him better off. If the notion of individual well-being is to be employed in weighing the strength of claims for social provision, it must permit reasoned social agreement on the relative "urgency" of claims to different goods (Scanlon 1975). One might thus acknowledge a moral obligation to feed the person, but not to finance his worship (Scanlon 1975, Sagoff 1986). One can see here one reason for preferring "in-kind" provision to transfer payments, for if we give this man money he will not use it to alleviate the needs that give rise to our obligation to assist him. Those who identify welfare and preference satisfaction might claim that this resistance to honoring idiosyncratic preferences is purely practical: we would open ourselves to all kinds of manipulation and misrepresentation if we let people's subjective reports of their needs govern public distribution of benefits. One might also object that it is paternalistic not to respect the worshipper's preferences. But paternalism and anti-paternalism are views about what it is permissible to *do*; they are not views about what individual welfare is.

Should public benevolence or justice be sensitive to what people prefer? What moral pull should satisfying Hausman's preferences have on McPherson? Thomas Nagel has argued that if something is valuable to people *only* because they want it, then providing it has *no* direct moral importance for others (1986, ch. 9). According to Nagel, others have no reason to satisfy Hausman's preferences unless they can make sense of why what he wants is worth wanting, or why his life will be better in some substantive way if he gets what he wants. Suppose, for example, that Hausman wants the Chicago Bulls to win the NBA basketball championship for a fourth time. The effect of the Bulls' performance on Hausman's mental state may give others some reason to want his preferences to be satisfied. McPherson may not want to see him distraught. But Nagel maintains that apart from the consequences on Hausman's mental state, others have no moral reason whatsoever to root for the Bulls. This line of thought implies that social policy should not be concerned with satisfying preferences.

Consider those who have expensive tastes. An even-handed concern to satisfy their preferences appears to be *unfair*. A person who has cultivated a taste for "prephylloxera claret and plover's eggs" (Arrow 1973, p. 254) may be miserable without them and, in one sense, worse off than someone in similar circumstances who delights in beans and franks (see also Dworkin 1981a). But should social policy be responsive to such preferences? Defenders of a preference-satisfaction view may argue that what is at issue is fairness rather than well-being: the person *is* worse off without the plover's eggs, but policy-makers don't have to care. Although this answer may explain how it can be just to ignore the preference for plover's eggs, it does not show how the benevolent can also discount expensive tastes. Defenders of more objective views of well-being on the other hand, can simply deny that the well-being of fancy eaters is lower at all; there is no need to explain away the policy-maker's indifference to their "plight." If one refuses to get all choked up about failures to satisfy expensive preferences, then either one's benevolence is limited or one does not accept a preference-satisfaction view of welfare.

Racist, sadistic, and other anti-social preferences raise similar problems. Presumably it is bad to satisfy them, if for no other reason than that doing so frustrates other (and characteristically stronger) preferences. But should such preferences count at all (Harsanyi 1977a, p. 56)? Given a hedonistic or a preference-satisfaction view of well-being, it seems that anti-social preferences ought to count and that a benevolent person should, other things being equal, strive to satisfy them. More objective views of well-being, on the other hand, could permit one to deny that individuals are made better off when their anti-social preferences are satisfied.

Defenders of a preference-satisfaction view of welfare have some ways of deflecting the claims of those with anti-social and expensive preferences without questioning the identification of well-being and the satisfaction of preferences. First, they can claim that some moral issue such as justice, which is distinct from benevolence, is involved. Second, they can note that preferences are malleable and that expressions of preferences respond to incentives. The frustration of expensive and anti-social preferences would discourage their expression and might contribute to changing them. In these ways, frustrating such preferences would in the long run enable more preferences to be satisfied. These points are well-taken, and they provide additional reasons not to satisfy expensive and anti-social preferences, regardless of whether one identifies welfare with the satisfaction of preferences. But they do little to defend preference satisfaction as a *measure* of well-being, and economists are more concerned with the practical question, "How should one measure well-being?" than with the philosophical question, "What is well-being?"

A final difficulty concerns preference formation. People may have particular preferences because of previous coercion or manipulation, or they may come to prefer things as the result of problematic psychological mechanisms. Some people, for example, want things precisely because they cannot have them ("the grass is always greener on the other side of the fence"), while other people spurn what is beyond their reach, like the fox who judged the unobtainable grapes to be sour (Elster 1983; Sen 1987b, 1990). For example, women who are systematically denied roles in public life or equal shares of consumption goods may learn not to want these things. Their level of preference satisfaction may then be much higher than their level of well-being. It seems that those who are benevolent need to consider not just preferences, but the *origins* of preferences or the *justifiability* of preferences. Women who have been systematically oppressed may not have strong preferences for individual liberties, the same wages that men earn, or even for protection from domestic violence. But liberties, high wages, and protection from domestic violence may make them better off than giving them what they prefer. Satisfying preferences that result from coercion, manipulation, or "perverse" preference formation mechanisms may not make people better off. The defender of a preference-satisfaction view of welfare can point out that if people's preferences adjust to policies, then one may in the long run satisfy their preferences better by ignoring their present preferences and giving them instead what they will come to want. However plausible this may be as a defense of a preference-satisfaction theory of welfare, it is no defense of measuring welfare by the satisfaction of actual preferences.

6.4 Modifying the preference-satisfaction view

The preference-satisfaction view has a number of awkward implications. It suggests that expensive and anti-social preferences count. It suggests that one should not look behind the preferences that result from manipulation or perverse psychological mechanisms. It flies in the face of shared views of the urgency of objective needs. And the preference-satisfaction view leads to serious puzzles in cases of preferences based on false beliefs, changes in preferences, and conflicts between preferences.

One reaction to these difficulties is to reject the preference-satisfaction view and endorse some other theory of welfare. In the next section, we will consider two plausible candidates. But there is another alternative. Rather than maintaining that well-being is the satisfaction of *actual* preferences, one can maintain that well-being is the satisfaction of self-interested preferences that are "rational" or "well-informed." This modified theory of well-being is still a formal theory. It does not say *what* a rational or well-informed person prefers. It says that what is good is whatever people rationally prefer for themselves.

It is more plausible to maintain that well-being is the satisfaction of suitably "laundered" self-interested preferences than to maintain that it is the satisfaction of actual preferences. This view grants that people may prefer something that is bad for them, because of ignorance or because of a concern to benefit or harm others. Such preferences would not be rational and self-interested, and so satisfying them would not make the person better off. Furthermore, satisfying preferences that result from coercion and manipulation no longer count as benefitting a person, if but for ignorance or irrationality the person would not have had such preferences. When actual preferences change, there need be no puzzle about how to make the person better off, because the person's rational preferences may not have changed. One might also maintain (although this is more controversial) that racist, sadistic, or other anti-social preferences cannot be rational, and so those who are concerned to benefit people can discount such preferences.

A rational self-interested preference-satisfaction view of well-being thus resolves most of the difficulties facing the actual preference-satisfaction view. Yet, as we shall see in the next chapter, it does not resolve all of them. It also makes an individual's state of well-being even less measurable than does the actual preference-satisfaction view. Not only does the economist face the problem of determining what people prefer, the economist now needs to determine which of these preferences are "rational," "self-interested," and "well-informed." Filling in what is meant by these terms so as to make this a well-defined theory of well-being is difficult, and the result is unlikely to be the sort of theory of well-being that economists would find easy to use. If it could be shown that everyone shared rational self-interested preferences for a certain list of substantive goods, then the rational preference-satisfaction view would specify the same constituents of welfare as some substantive theory, and it might actually be easier to measure welfare on a rational preference-satisfaction view than on an actual preference-satisfaction view. But few people think that a rational preference-satisfaction theory dovetails so nicely with any substantive theory of well-being.

6.5 Alternative theories of welfare

Substantive theories of welfare purport to say which things are intrinsically good. Traditional hedonistic mental-state views, to which, as we suggested, economists still pay secret allegiance, are substantive theories, as are "perfectionist" views (Griffin 1986, ch. 4; Raz 1986, ch. 12) and what Parfit calls "objective-list" views. Substantive views are "objective" in the sense that what is good for people is not determined by whether people believe it is good for them. Their objectivity in this sense does not imply that subjective states do not matter, and most substantive theories of the good count pleasures as goods and pains as bads. Objective views are nevertheless problematic because it seems that what is intrinsically valuable varies to some extent from person to person. Objective views should nevertheless be tempting to economists when they make well-being more readily measurable.

One objective view that may be relevant to economists is John Rawls' notion of "primary goods." In *A theory of justice* (1971), Rawls sees well-being as the satisfaction of rational preference or desire, but he does not regard this conception as appropriate for the purposes of a theory of justice. How well off people are depends on their own efforts, on their luck, and on the materials or opportunities for a good life that society provides. What social policy should attend to is not welfare, but that aspect of welfare to which society contributes. Rawls proposes that the relevant aspect of well-being be measured by an index of "primary social goods." Goods such as education or income are all-purpose *means* or, as Rawls put it, things that you want, whatever else you want (1971, p. 92; see also chapter 11 below). Primary social goods are not proxies for utility levels.

In Rawls' view, on the contrary, utility levels are not at issue in discussions of justice. Primary social goods offer an alternative basis for a more settled social agreement on what is both important to well-being and also a social responsibility (1982). Rawls' approach avoids the expensive tastes and anti-social preferences problems and, as he argues, provides a more impartial perspective for comparing what society contributes to the well-being of different individuals than a preference standard does.

Amartya Sen defends a theory of well-being in terms of the "functionings" an individual attains. A person's functionings are those things that the person does and experiences. Walking, playing the piano, being well-nourished, loving one's friends, understanding Chinese, and appreciating cubism are all functionings. But, like Rawls, Sen does not think that social policy should concern itself directly with the functionings people achieve. Social policy, insofar as it is motivated by a concern for welfare, should instead focus on "capabilities" (1987c, 1992a). A capability is the ability to achieve a certain sort of "functioning." For example, literacy is a capability, while reading is a functioning. People may value capabilities for their own sake as well as for the functionings they permit – you're glad to know you can walk around even if you are inclined to stay put. The emphasis in social policy should not be on what people make of their capabilities (that is on functionings), nor, in contrast to Rawls, on the *means* to achieve certain functionings, but on capabilities and hence on *freedom*, broadly understood. Sen criticizes the primary-goods approach because it focuses exclusively on the external *means* that permit people to attain various functionings. A concern for well-being must also attend to internal features of persons' circumstances, such as physical handicaps, which may profoundly affect well-being. For example, being well-nourished is a functioning whose achievement may be impaired either by internal obstacles (such as a digestive disorder) or external ones (a lack of money to buy food).

Specifying a measure of well-being requires somehow weighting the many different capabilities and functionings each person possesses. This issue of weighting might seem to bring preferences in through the back door. Ultimately, it might be objected, the importance of different functionings depends on the weight they are given in people's subjective preferences. However, while people's preferences for functionings and the capabilities they presuppose are relevant to their weight, a reasoned public discussion over these weights need not wind up concluding that individuals' subjective preferences about them are their only or most important determinant.

Even if the problems of weighting and measuring the components of well-being are greater for more "objective" approaches than are the problems of measurement in standard utility theory (which is not clear), it can still be argued, following Sen, that "it is better to be vaguely right than precisely wrong." In particular, these objective approaches to well-being focus research on well-being in directions that link up more naturally to the normative terms in which policy is debated.

6.6 Conclusions

The identification of well-being with the satisfaction of preferences is questionable in itself. It mistakenly suggests that social policy should attend to all preferences, even if they are expensive, anti-social, or the results of false beliefs, manipulation, or problematic psychological processes. The focus on preference satisfaction fails to link up with the normative terms of policy debate, and it leads to difficulties and implausibilities when preferences change and conflict. Moreover, the standard notion of utility is not easily measurable, and even if it were, economists cannot defend a measure of individual well-being as a good operational proxy without having some defensible conception of what it is supposed to be a proxy for. The only real advantage of identifying well-being with the satisfaction of preferences is that it apparently links welfare problems immediately to fundamental economic theory. But the link is of little value unless the theoretical "welfare" problems are truly problems of human welfare or well-being.

Suggestions for further reading

For an extended defense of an informed preference-satisfaction view of individual well-being, see James Griffin's book *Well-being* (1986). The introduction to Amartya Sen's and Bernard Williams' *Utilitarianism and beyond* (1982) contains a critical summary of arguments against preference-based approaches to measuring well-being. Richard Arneson has provided the most powerful general response in defense of preference-satisfaction views of welfare (1990). See also Mill (1863), Rawls (1982), Scanlon (1991), and Sen et al. (1987).

The problems that arise in respecting preferences when there are uncertainties are discussed in Machina (1990), Hammond (1983), Broome (1991b, ch. 10), Harris and Olewiler (1979), and Hausman and McPherson (1994).

Sen's views on capabilities and functionings are developed mainly in two of his essays (1985a and 1987c) and are discussed at length in Nussbaum and Sen (1993).

7   Efficiency

When economists attempt to evaluate economic institutions, policies, and outcomes, they ask whether they make people better off. Given their theory of welfare, they are asking how well institutions, policies, and outcomes satisfy preferences. Most economists also deny that evaluations should be based on comparisons of how well satisfied are the preferences of different individuals. So they cannot assess policies by adding up their consequences for the welfare (that is, preference satisfaction) of different individuals. Indeed it seems that alternative policies and institutions can only be compared when one of them satisfies at least one person's preferences better without satisfying anyone else's preferences less well. It is for this reason that efficiency has such a special importance in standard welfare economics. For "efficiency" in theoretical economics is not fundamentally a matter of saving time or materials in production or distribution. An efficient state of affairs is one in which it is impossible to make someone better off (in terms of preference satisfaction) without making someone else worse off. The character of welfare economics is determined by its focus on welfare, its identification of welfare with the satisfaction of preferences, and its rejection of interpersonal welfare comparisons.

7.1 Interpersonal comparisons of well-being

If policy 1 benefits Ira and harms Jill, while policy 2 benefits Jill and harms Ira, then there is no way to say which has the greater welfare benefits, unless one can compare how much Ira and Jill are benefitted and harmed. Since the costs and burdens of alternative policies usually fall on different individuals, this case is typical. Interpersonal comparisons of some sort are necessary unless normative economists confine themselves to recommending only policies that harm no one. Furthermore, virtually all ethical systems require one to make interpersonal comparisons of well-being. To be rationally benevolent one must be able to judge where one's efforts will do the most good. To treat the interests of different people equally, one must be able to compare the net effects of one's actions on the interests of each.

Economists writing near the beginning of this century, such as A. C. Pigou, argued that overall welfare is maximized by equalizing incomes as much as is consistent with retaining incentives to produce. Citing diminishing marginal utility of income, they maintained (not implausibly), that an extra one hundred dollars contributes less to the well-being of someone with an income of $50,000 than to the well-being of someone with an income of $5,000. Other things being equal, a more equal distribution of income increases total welfare. This argument assumes that one can make interpersonal comparisons of the amount that one hundred dollars contributes to the well-being of different people with different incomes. If interpersonal comparisons cannot be made, then this argument cannot be made either.

If well-being is the satisfaction of preferences, then interpersonal comparisons of well-being are comparisons of the extent to which preferences are satisfied. So-called "unit" comparisons of utility *differences* are needed to compare the benefits and harms policies might cause to different people. One need only compare how individual utilities change, not their levels. Comparisons of utility levels are also needed if, for example, policymakers want to know who is worst off. Unlike comparisons of well-being made on the basis of some substantive view of well-being, one is not comparing amounts or intensities of the *things* or *states* individuals possess. An interpersonal comparison of preference satisfaction is not a comparison of Jill's and Ira's *feelings* of satisfaction or happiness. A comparison of how much pleasure Jill and Ira feel might be difficult to make because it is hard to measure mental states; but there is no conceptual problem in making the comparison. Interpersonal comparisons of preference satisfaction, on the other hand, are not comparisons of mental or physical states but of the extent to which the world is as Jill and Ira prefer. Indeed Ira and Jill may not even know whether some of their preferences are satisfied. An interpersonal utility comparison must compare how well satisfied Ira's and Jill's preferences arc, not how much satisfaction Ira and Jill feel.

What sort of a comparison is that? The main way economists and philosophers have attempted to understand these comparisons is via what Kenneth Arrow calls "judgments of extended sympathy" (see also Kolm 1972). Suppose one asks people to express preferences not only among ordinary alternatives, but also among "extended" alternatives, such as the alternative of being Ira with some option x and being Jill with y. One might then say that Jill-with-y is better off than Ira-with-x if Jill-with-y is preferred to Ira-with-x.

This way of understanding interpersonal comparisons faces serious difficulties. For example, McPherson might think that Jill is better off with y, because y involves Jill accomplishing something that McPherson greatly admires, while Hausman might think that Ira is better off with x because, given x, Ira is more contented than Jill is with y. *Whose* extended preferences decide whether Ira or Jill is better off? John Harsanyi argues that these difficulties can be avoided if, rather than employing one's own preferences to compare Jill-with-y and Ira-with-x, one compares how well off one would be with x if one had Ira's preferences to how well off one would be with y if one had Jill's preferences. In Harsanyi's view, there is a single impersonal extended preference ranking to which our empathic abilities are a fallible guide. Judgments resulting from putting yourself in someone else's shoes in this way can be used to construct interpersonal comparisons. Alfred MacKay calls this the "mental shoehorn" tactic (see MacKay 1986 and Griffin 1986, ch. 7).

What could this "universal" extended preference ranking be, to which empathy supposedly provides access? It cannot be a ranking in terms of some *theory* of what makes human life good, because economists disavow any substantive theory in favor of the view that well-being is the satisfaction of preferences. The ranking cannot be based on comparisons of Jill's and Ira's well-being, for there is nothing to measure except where they are in their preference ranking. Furthermore, the interpersonal welfare comparison is supposed to be determined by the impartial extended preference and thus cannot be the basis for the preference. The ranking cannot be based on a "bare" preference for Jill's state over Ira's, for the actual mental shoehorn technique people employ in thinking about what life is like for others depends on their *not* jettisoning all of their preferences and values. Once one has set aside all one's own preferences, what could a preference for (y, Jill) over (x, Ira) be based on? "If this proposal for comparability uses (basic) preference purged of any particular point of view, it looks like using preference purged of what is needed to make sense of preference" (Griffin 1991, p. 54). What then can the ranking be based on?

In our view extended preferences cannot provide the basis for interpersonal comparisons. Even if they were unanimous, which is often not the case, they answer the wrong question. A unanimous extended preference for (y, Jill) over (x, Ira) demonstrates that everyone would prefer to be Jill with y rather than Ira with x. But what is at issue is whether Jill's preferences are better satisfied with y than Ira's preferences are with x. The two issues are distinct. Everyone might prefer to be Jill with y even though Ira's preferences are better satisfied with x, simply because they admire Jill. One might, for example, prefer to be Keats, even with his early death, rather than Queen Victoria, yet nevertheless believe that Victoria's preferences were better satisfied than Keats' preferences. If well-being is the satisfaction of preferences, then interpersonal comparisons of well-being must be interpersonal comparisons of the extent to which preferences are satisfied. But can one make sense of such comparisons (Hausman 1995)? How could they be made? Economists are thus on strong ground in denying that interpersonal comparisons of welfare (interpreted as preference satisfaction) are possible, although the arguments most often made against the possibility of interpersonal comparisons, such as Lionel Robbins' (1935, ch. 6), focus on the subjectivity of preference and on the difficulties of testing, rather than on the conceptual problems emphasized above. Economists are, however, on such strong ground that they undermine their own commitment to a preference-satisfaction view of welfare. For people do make interpersonal welfare comparisons, which would be impossible if welfare were the satisfaction of preferences, and economists need to be able to compare policies with different winners and losers in a non-arbitrary way, which is also impossible unless some other view of welfare is adopted.

Notice that these problems also apply to a view of welfare as the satisfaction of rational, informed, and self-interested preferences. Regardless of what constraints one places on which preferences count, one must confront the conceptual difficulties involved in comparing the extent to which the preferences of different individuals are satisfied. If on the other hand one adopts a substantive theory of welfare rather than a preference-satisfaction view, then one can make ready sense of what is involved in interpersonal comparisons, although there may still be serious practical difficulties in actually making them. For example, if one defines welfare as an index of primary goods (see section 6.5), then an interpersonal comparison depends on how much education, wealth, liberties, and so on individuals have.

7.2 "Efficiency" as Pareto optimality

If welfare is taken to be preference satisfaction, and the extent to which the preferences of different individuals are satisfied cannot be compared, how can one say anything substantial about economic welfare? The welfare economist's answer lies in the notions of a "Pareto improvement" and of "Pareto efficiency" or "Pareto optimality." If one is minimally benevolent and in favor of making people better off, then, other things being equal, one should accept the principle (which John Broome calls "the principle of the personal good") that "If two prospects are equally good for everyone, they are equally good, and if one of two prospects is better for someone than the other and at least as good for everyone, then it is better" (1989, p. 11). If in addition one identifies being better off with having a higher utility, then (other things being equal) one will endorse Pareto improvements and efficient (or Pareto optimal) allocations.

There are, however, problems with endorsing Pareto improvements. First, doing so may be unappealing when it involves honoring people's "nosy" preferences regarding others' conduct (see the discussion of Sen's liberty paradox below in chapter 12). Second, it has been proven that one cannot consistently endorse Pareto improvements in circumstances of uncertainty if one also holds that individual and social preferences satisfy the axioms of expected utility theory (Hammond 1983, Seidenfeld *et al.* 1989). Unanimity in individual rankings may rest on offsetting disagreements in both subjective probability judgments and in preferences among options involving no uncertainty, and there may be no coherent set of social rankings and probability judgments. For example, the bourgeoisie and proletariat may both prefer an armed workers' revolt but only because they each have opposing aims and form different estimates of the likely consequences. The fact of their agreement does not establish that an armed revolt would be socially *better* (see also Levi 1990).

The most serious problem that would result if economists only endorsed Pareto improvements is that true Pareto improvements are rare: Economic changes usually involve winners and losers. For example, suppose that there is a single consumption good (bread) in some fixed quantity, and everybody prefers more rather than less of it. Then *every* distribution of bread that exhausts the bread supply is a Pareto optimum. Moreover, R may be Pareto optimal and S may be suboptimal without R being a Pareto improvement over S. Suppose there are 10 loaves of bread to distribute between A and B. A Pareto efficient allocation that gives 7 loaves to A and 3 to B is not a Pareto improvement over the allocation that wastes 2 loaves and gives 4 to both A and B. Very few economic states can be ranked in terms of the relationship of a Pareto improvement. If R is a Pareto improvement over S, then *nobody* can prefer S. If everybody in R except for Donald had triple the income in R as they would have in S, but Donald had one penny less, then (assuming that Donald for reason of that penny prefers S), R is not a Pareto improvement over S. Notice that with just a tiny bit of redistribution, R could be transformed into another state R' that would be a clear Pareto improvement over S. This point, which is crucial to cost-benefit, will be discussed later in the chapter.

The Pareto notions have some real ethical appeal, for, other things being equal, it is better to make people better off, and the satisfaction of preferences surely has something to do with well-being. But they have little bearing on questions of fairness. Economists often suggest that questions of economic welfare be factored into questions of efficiency (to which the Pareto concepts are by definition pertinent) and questions of equity, upon which theoretical welfare economics has little to say (Okun 1975). This factoring is questionable for several reasons. One reason is that perceptions of fairness affect welfare and thus have implications for efficiency (Hirsch 1976, pp. 131f). For example, it seems obvious that sizeable welfare costs result from the moral resentment of those who live in depressed inner-city areas in the United States.

Although one may question the normative appeal of preference satisfaction, and one may suggest that questions of equity are as important as questions of efficiency and not necessarily separable from them, the Pareto notions are at least coherent and clear. And they have some force, too. For example, consider the following potential exchange situation between A and B. A has a Toyota and B has a Ford. Each values what he/she has, but would prefer to exchange. Exchanging is the "cooperative" solution. It is a Pareto improvement over the initial allocation. Yet unless both parties can count on being protected from non-Pareto-improving outcomes, they may hesitate to interact at all. For, if A could have both the Toyota and the Ford, that would be best for A and worst for B, and it would be worst for A if B could have both. Property rights prevent either from forcibly appropriating what belongs to the other and thus enable the cooperative solution to arise voluntarily (Hardin 1988, ch. 3). The Pareto notions help one to understand the roles that property rights and exchange play, and they permit one to see why some systems of property rights are better than others.

Perfectly competitive markets are in this regard "good" institutions, for the outcomes of interactions on them are Pareto efficient. But real market outcomes may be suboptimal, particularly (though not only) in the case of *externalities*. As we saw in the introductory discussion of the Lawrence Summers memorandum, sometimes the costs and benefits of an agent's actions do not fully register as costs or benefits for that agent. Those who pollute the air or deplete the fish in a lake need not take the costs imposed on others into account in their private calculations of economic benefit. Nor can someone who builds a lighthouse collect from all those who benefit from it. One solution to the problems posed by externalities is a more refined assignment of property rights so that either polluters will have to compensate those with a right to clean air or those who want clean air will have to pay those who would like to pollute not to do so. As Ronald Coase proved (under some fairly restrictive assumptions), the same "optimal" amount of pollution will result with either assignment of rights (1960). Since the "transactions costs" – the costs of finding the parties one needs to bargain with and striking and enforcing these bargains – , are often prohibitive, clear rights assignments do not solve all the problems. Government provision of collective goods (such as light-houses), government restrictions (such as hunting and fishing limits or limits on pollution), or government taxes or subsidies can mitigate sub-optimal outcomes. Most economists regard taxes and subsidies as prefer-able to restrictions or mandates, since they are more efficient and permit a greater range of individual choice. But recall the discussion in chapter 4. To tax rather than fine polluters may imply that firms have an acceptable reason to pollute whenever polluting increases their net revenue and implicitly denies that they have good reason not to pollute even when it is profitable to do so (Kelman 1981).

7.3 How welfare economics narrows normative questions

An example may clarify how the Pareto notions may be put to work, while also showing how a standard economic treatment of policy questions narrows the morally relevant issues. Consider the question of whether government should provide food or health care in kind, or whether it should instead provide a cash supplement to those in need. Many econo-mists would offer a simple argument why the government should supply cash: Construct the graph in figure 7.1. The vertical axis represents quan-tity of health care (h), while the horizontal axis represents the quantity of some composite consumption commodity – that is, of everything else con-sumed (ee). Points in the plane represent possible individual consumption bundles, which contain non-negative quantities of health care q_h and the "everything-else" commodity, q_{ee}. As one moves northeast, the amount consumed increases, and if one assumes that people prefer more of both health care and "everything else" to less, then northeast is also the direc-tion of preference. The curving lines, I_1, I_2, and I_3 are "indifference curves" for some individual – call her Alice. They are called indifference curves because they are drawn through points (consumption bundles) between which Alice is indifferent. For example, Alice does not care whether she consumes bundle F that contains lots of health care and comparatively little of "everything else" or bundle G that contains little health care and lots of "everything else." The fundamental principles of the standard theory of consumer choice imply that indifference curves have the shape that they do and that they do not cross. Since some points on I_2 are north-east of points on I_1, every bundle on I_2 is preferred to every bundle on I_1. If Alice is able to "move" from I_1 to I_2, her preferences are better satisfied, and she is better off.

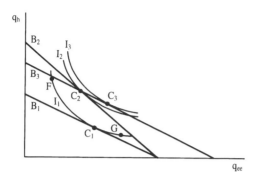

Figure 7.1 Cash vs. in-kind benefits

The straight lines sloping downward to the right represent three different budget constraints on Alice. Given an amount of money to spend
equal to B_1, Alice can only afford consumption bundles on or below the
line B_1. Since points above and to the right are preferred to those below
and to the left, Alice will consume a bundle on her budget line – moreover,
apart from some technical complications, a bundle on an indifference
curve that is tangent to her budget line.

Suppose that Alice begins with the budget constraint B_1, and that her
consumption is C_1, which is on the indifference curve I_1. Suppose then that
the government decides to subsidize health care. This does not change the
amount of money Alice has to spend, but it does make health care
cheaper. Her budget constraint will now look something like B_2 and her
consumption will be C_2 on indifference curve I_2. Alice is better off, she
consumes more health care, and she may consume more or less of everything else.

But suppose that instead of subsidizing health care, the government
gave Alice enough cash to allow her, if she wished, to purchase C_2. Since a
cash allowance to Alice does not change the relative prices of health care
and everything else, it will shift her budget constraint to B_3, which is paral-
lel to her original budget line, B_1, and passes through C_2. But given her
preferences, Alice will not consume C_2. She will instead consume C_3 on
indifference curve I_3. The cash payment must satisfy Alice's preferences at
least as well as the in-kind health-care benefit, and it will typically satisfy
her preferences better. The cash payment is apparently Pareto superior to
the in-kind benefit, because no one will prefer the in-kind provision, and
many people will prefer the cash payment.

But the advantages of the cash payment do not stop there. It is also
apparently cheaper to give people cash than to give them health-care
benefits, because one needs no bureaucracy to process claim forms or to

investigate medical frauds. Since cash benefits are cheaper to administer, one can satisfy all recipients' preferences at least as well with cash benefits as with in-kind provision at a lower cost to taxpayers, or one can provide even more benefits.

Some objections to this argument for cash payments can be formulated in terms that are consistent with taking welfare as the satisfaction of preferences. Thus, one could argue that taxpayers may themselves have preferences for certain kinds of consumption patterns among the recipients of assistance, and hence the welfare of taxpayers may be increased by resorting to in-kind provision. Notice that an obvious response to this line of argument is to object on grounds of liberty to constraining the consumption decisions of persons needing assistance in order to please taxpayers. This objection, however, departs from the welfare economics framework by appealing to the value of freedom. A second argument against cash provision that can be cast within the standard welfare economics framework appeals to the difficulty of monitoring claims for assistance. Cash benefits create incentives to feign illness, while the luxuries of waiting in line at a free medical clinic are not very enticing to the healthy.

The central arguments in favor of in-kind provision cannot, however, even be expressed explicitly in a framework that focuses exclusively on welfare as the satisfaction of preferences. These arguments are openly *paternalistic*. Regardless of how strongly the poor want more health care, "we" know that more health care would be good for them. Paternalism is the view that it is sometimes right to coerce individuals for their own good. The paternalist case for in-kind benefits is not a frivolous one to be dismissed without argument, by supposing that what people most prefer is automatically what is best for them. Whether or not one is inclined to support some paternalistic policies (such as mandatory seat-belt laws or prohibitions on recreational drugs), it is important to recognize the morally significant differences between *judging* that someone is acting against her interest, *persuading* her to act differently, and *coercing* her. To deny that individuals always prefer what is good for them is merely good sense. It is *not* paternalism. Indeed in his classic critique of paternalism in *On liberty*, John Stuart Mill notes explicitly that people may well be wrong about what is good for them (see also Gerald Dworkin 1971, 1988, and Joel Feinberg 1986). If you think that a friend would be better off not smoking, even though your friend thinks otherwise, you are not being paternalistic. (You're probably right!) Nor are you being paternalistic if you attempt to *persuade* your friend to give up smoking. But, if you throw away your friend's cigarettes or get the government to make smoking illegal, then you're behaving paternalistically.

It may be good social policy to give people cash with no strings attached. But whether there should be any paternalistic strings attached to benefits needs to be considered rather than assumed away by supposing that whatever a person prefers is automatically best for the person. Furthermore, the most forceful objections to paternalism are not that it is welfare-reducing but that it improperly interferes with freedom. These aspects of the discussion are very poorly handled when the analysis is confined to Paretian welfare concerns.

Although the value of freedom lurks within the standard argument for cash benefits, the argument remains within the terms set by orthodox economic theory. There is no mention of needs, of the presuppositions of individual dignity, of opportunity, of rights, or of fairness. There is no concern with the moral *reasons* that make individuals willing to pay taxes to provide such benefits. Are people motivated by a general concern to satisfy the preferences of others, or do they instead see themselves as obligated to help others in *need*? Might they regard people as having *rights* to food or medical care which justify taxing others? These are hard questions even to ask within the framework economists employ.

7.4 Cost-benefit analysis

We have criticized the focus on the Pareto concepts on the grounds that welfare is not the satisfaction of preference and that focusing only on welfare unreasonably narrows the terms in which one might want to evaluate institutions and policies. What has bothered normative economists, in contrast, is the fact that the scope of the Pareto concepts is so limited. *Somebody* almost always prefers that the government *not* intervene to build a dam, or to save an endangered species, or to clean up a river. So even though externalities often lead to suboptimal outcomes, the feasible remedies are rarely true Pareto improvements. As sharp and clear as the Pareto concepts are, their scope is too limited.

Economists have struggled to increase the range and apparent force of welfare economics in three ways. We have already commented on one of these in chapter 4: economists have proven striking welfare theorems that apparently establish the ethical attractiveness of perfect competition. A second way to stretch Paretian welfare economics via the development of formal theories of social choice will be discussed later in chapter 12. The third direction in which welfare economics has moved in extending the Pareto notions is the most important in practice. Recall the case mentioned before in which everybody's income in R is three times what it was in S, except Donald's, who is a penny poorer. It is tempting to say that R is an improvement, for Donald *could be* compensated, and then one would have a Pareto improvement. In an example such as this one, R is a *potential Pareto improvement* over S, for the "winners" in R (compared to S) could compensate the losers and have some left over for themselves (Hicks 1939, Kaldor 1939). If one transported pollution to the LDCs without paying any compensation, then one would make people there worse off. Transporting the pollution to the LDCs would, however, still be a potential Pareto improvement because, as Summers argues, the benefits to the developed countries would be larger than the costs to the LDCs. The developed countries could afford to pay enough compensation to make everyone better off. Public works, licensing, enforcement, taxation, and subsidies can be good things, even if they are not unanimously wanted. One sense in which they can be good things is if they are potential Pareto improvements.

The notion of a potential Pareto improvement provides one possible justification for cost-benefit analysis (Mishan 1971, 1981). In theory (but *not* in practice), one asks the "winners" in each policy how much they would pay to institute the policy, and one asks the "losers" how much compensation they would require not to oppose implementing the policy. The policy with the largest net benefit is best, other things being equal. If everybody were to get an equal share of the net benefits, the policy with the largest net benefit would be a genuine Pareto improvement over the other alternatives (with the net benefits or costs of those similarly distributed). But in reality some people win and others lose and the policy with the largest net benefit is only a potential improvement.

One can also defend cost-benefit analysis as a way to implement a utilitarian policy of maximizing total welfare. Here is how the basic ideas of cost-benefit analysis are introduced in one recent text:

The basic notion is very simple. If we have to decide whether to do A or not, the rule is: Do A if the benefits exceed those of the next best alternative course of action, and not otherwise . . .

Going on a step, it seems quite natural to refer to the 'benefits of the next best alternative to A' as the 'costs of A'. For if A is done those alternative benefits are lost. So the rule becomes: do A if its benefits exceed its costs, and not otherwise.

. . . The only basic principle is that we should be willing to assign numerical values to costs and benefits, and arrive at decisions by adding them up and accepting those projects whose benefits exceed their costs.

But how are such values to be arrived at? If we assume that only people matter, the analysis naturally involves two steps. First, we must find out how the decision would affect the welfare of each individual concerned. To judge this effect we must ultimately rely on the individual's own evaluation of his mental state. So the broad principle is that 'we measure a person's change in welfare as he or she would value it'. That is, we ask what he or she would be willing to pay to acquire the benefits or to avoid the costs . . .

The second step is to deduce the change in social welfare implied by all the changes in individual welfare. Unless there are no losers, this means somehow valuing each person's £1. If income were optimally distributed, £1 would be equally valuable regardless of whose it was; that is what 'optimally distributed' means . . . And if income is not optimally distributed most economists would argue that it should be redistributed by cash transfers rather than through the choice of projects. But what if we think that cash will not be distributed, even if it should be? Then we may need to value the poor person's extra £1 more highly than the rich person's. (Layard and Glaister 1994, pp. 1–2)

We quoted so much because this quotation reveals so much about how economists tend to approach problems of policy evaluation. Layard and Glaister claim that the "only basic principle" is that the considerations bearing on policy evaluation must always be comparable and indeed roughly quantifiable. This is a basic principle – and indeed a controversial one – but it is hardly the only one, and Layard and Glaister immediately assume another: that only people matter. This second principle is controversial too and has been explicitly challenged by those concerned with the consequences of human actions for animals (for example, Singer 1975) and the non-sentient environment (for example, Stone 1988). Layard and Glaister then jump from the premise that only individual people matter to the conclusion that only the *welfare* of individual people matters. They do not say why one should believe that the only thing that matters is welfare. What about, for example, people's rights and liberty? The next sentence asserts that we should accept the individual's own evaluation of his welfare (which Layard and Glaister equate with a mental state, despite the official identification of welfare with preference satisfaction). From comments they make later, it seems that they would argue for this assertion on the basis of principles of anti-paternalism and democracy. (The reliance on such principles suggests that Layard and Glaister do not believe that only welfare matters.) The final paragraph then equates the net benefits of projects with their aggregate welfare consequences. These cannot of course be determined without making interpersonal welfare comparisons. If one assumes that willingness to pay can serve as an interpersonal comparable measure of individual welfare, then projects whose benefits exceed their costs will increase total welfare. This assumption is implausible, however, as we shall argue below.

Regardless of the justification for basing social policy on willingness to pay, it is in practice costly to ask people how much they would pay or how much compensation they require, and their answers may be neither truthful nor accurate. Economists have accordingly devised cunning methods of gleaning such information from data on prices and quantities traded and sometimes from responses to surveys. Much of cost-benefit analysis is devoted to devising, criticizing, and improving methods of imputing costs and benefits.

The progenitors of cost-benefit analysis equated potential Pareto improvements with improvements in productivity, efficiency, or real income, and they hoped to separate the study of these uncontroversial economic benefits from controversial questions concerning distribution. John Hicks makes the point as follows,

> whether or not compensation should be given in any particular case is a question of distribution, upon which there cannot be any generally acceptable principle . . . If measures making for efficiency are to have a fair chance, it is extremely desirable that they should be freed from distributive complications as much as possible. (1939, pp. 711–12; see also Kaldor 1939, p. 550)

However, this hope of separating questions of efficiency from questions concerning distribution was dashed, and when the dust settled, it turned out that even the preference for policies that yield *actual* Pareto improvements is not in general free of distributional commitments. Consider figure 7.2, which we borrowed with some modifications from an influential essay by Paul Samuelson (1950). The utilities of two representative individuals R and P are measured along the two axes, and the two curves represent the possible utility combinations depending on whether technology T_1 or technology T_2 is employed. Technology I, which is the status quo (perhaps in 1920), involves a rail transport system with few goods or people carried on highways. Technology II involves an extensive road system like the one currently in use in the United States. The utility status quo in 1920 is, let us suppose, point S, and the result of changing to an automobile technology will, other things being equal, result in the utilities for R and P represented by point Z. Z is of course not a Pareto improvement over S, because P is worse off, but Z is a potential Pareto improvement over S, because R can pay compensation to P and the economy can move along the T_2 curve to Z'. However, one cannot conclude, as Kaldor and Hicks hoped, that T_2 is more efficient than T_1, or that it involves greater physical productivity or a larger real income, because S here is also a potential Pareto improvement over Z – one can move from S along the T_1 curve to S', which is an actual Pareto improvement over Z. Furthermore, even if the choice were between S and Z' rather than between S and Z, so that what was at stake was an actual Pareto improvement rather than merely a potential Pareto improvement, one would still not be justified in concluding that T_2 is more efficient than T_1. Only in the case in which one utility possibility curve is inside of the other can one make a "pure" efficiency comparison that does not take a particular distribution for granted.

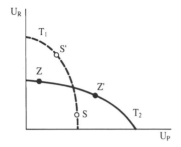

Figure 7.2: The interdependence of equity and efficiency

Furthermore, cost-benefit analysis compares "willingness-to-pay" rather than comparing the welfare gains or losses of different people. Obviously willingness-to-pay has something to do with welfare and preference. If a person greatly prefers x to y, then the person will typically be willing to pay much more for x than for y. But willingness-to-pay also depends on how much money one has and on expectations concerning what it is appropriate to purchase and for what price. One might get very misleading information concerning the relative value of a car and a spouse by investigating how much someone would be willing to pay for each! Since willingness-to-pay depends on wealth as well as preference, it is possible for a policy that has strong claims to be welfare-increasing not to have any "net benefit." If the benefits accrue to the poor and the costs to the rich, what the poor would be willing to pay for the new policy might not be enough to compensate the rich. Nevertheless the policy might have large net benefits if there were a more even distribution of wealth, and someone willing to make interpersonal comparisons might be convinced that the welfare of the poor would increase more than the welfare of the rich would decrease.

It is easy to see why many are uneasy about using cost-benefit analysis to make social choices. Like the other Pareto criteria, it ignores questions of justice, but unlike the other Pareto criteria it sanctions policies that make some people worse off. The compensation considered is only hypothetical, and some people win and some lose. Questions of fairness are obviously pressing in such circumstances. If each policy had different winners and losers so that in the long run everyone was a winner as often as he or she was a loser, the unfairness might wash out. But there is a bias in cost-benefit analysis against the preferences of the poor, because preferences in cost-benefit analysis are weighted with dollars, and the poor have fewer of these (Baker 1975). Exactly those people whom it seems policy-makers should be most concerned to protect are those who are most likely to be harmed. Proponents have consequently explored ways of modifying cost-benefit analysis to compensate for possible injustices (Harberger 1978, Little 1957).

It is also questionable whether social policy should be based on the unreflective and unargued preferences that economists infer from people's economic choices. Some preferences, such as preferences for a certain sort of community, are hard to signal when one buys groceries, cars or even homes. Furthermore, people's preferences for public goods of all sorts respond to *arguments* and may be quite different after public debate than they were before. Substituting cost-benefit analysis for public deliberation means that people's preferences are never subjected to such challenges. Finally, it is questionable whether decisions about roads or schools or tanks should be equally responsive to all preferences, whether or not they are weighted by wealth. For example, Americans may prefer a larger military budget for many reasons. They may believe that the break-up of the Soviet Empire is only a giant ruse designed to trick the United States into lowering its guard. They may believe that the instabilities following the break-up of the Soviet Empire will require major military interventions by the United States. They may believe that lower military budgets will cause massive unemployment. Are not the reasons relevant? Should a decision about the size of the military budget respond only to the strength of people's preferences (or to their willingness-to-pay), or should it look to the *reasons* for the preferences?

Cost-benefit analysis is the most promising device economists have found that avoids invoking interpersonal utility comparisons while still permitting judgments in cases involving both winners and losers. The hope of those developing cost-benefit analysis was that one could make such judgments by endorsing potential Pareto improvements. The conclusion has been that no such blanket endorsement is possible because there is no way to judge changes that affect distributions while remaining neutral on distributive questions (Little 1957, Streeten 1953, Samuelson 1950) and because it is questionable whether policy should be determined by the preferences implicit in private economic choices.

To stop here would leave welfare economists with little to say, and practical applications of welfare economics are needed. The difficulties seem to have been dealt with in two ways. One is by increasing modesty: one cannot always endorse potential Pareto improvements, but at least economists can identify them and leave the endorsing to politicians. Second, welfare economists have perhaps moved implicitly toward reuniting considerations of efficiency and equity. Blanket endorsements of potential Pareto improvements are unjustifiable, but there are ways to adjust such measures for equity concerns, and perhaps equity-adjusted potential

Pareto improvements can be endorsed with more confidence. But economists are queasy about the final step of actually endorsing any one way of adjusting for equity concerns.

7.5 Conclusion: welfare economics in limbo

If one evaluates policies exclusively in terms of their consequences for individual welfare, and one takes welfare to be the satisfaction of preferences, and one denies that it is possible to compare how well-off different people are, then there seems to be little that one can say about which policies and institutions are better. Economists are in precisely this position. Straining against these self-imposed shackles, economists have managed to salvage a practical method of evaluation – cost-benefit analysis – but it rests on shaky foundations, precisely because the fundamental evaluative apparatus of contemporary normative economics is so narrow. One cannot reasonably evaluate policies, institutions, or states of affairs exclusively in terms of their success at satisfying the interpersonally non-comparable preferences of individuals. For welfare is not preference satisfaction, and it seems that things such as freedom, equality, and justice also matter.

Suggestions for further reading

There is an extensive literature concerning interpersonal comparisons. Elster and Roemer (1991) is an excellent recent collection. Other contributions include Robbins (1935, ch. 6), (Harsanyi 1977b, ch. 4), MacKay (1986), Davidson (1986), Gibbard (1986), and Hausman (1995).

The inconsistency between rationality and the Pareto principle in circumstances of uncertainty is proven and discussed in Hammond (1983), Seidenfeld *et al.* (1989), Broome (1989), and Levi (1990). The most extensive discussion of the ethical appeal of Pareto optimality has been concerned with Sen's paradox, which is discussed below in section 12.4. See the suggested readings for chapter 12.

For critical discussion of the argument in favor of cash over in-kind provision of benefits see Hochman and Rodgers (1969), Okun (1975), Thurow (1977), Kelman (1986), and Blackorby and Donaldson (1988).

For general discussions of cost-benefit analysis see Mishan (1971, 1981), Sugden and Williams (1978), Ng (1983), and Layard and Glaister (1994). Especially via the work of Richard Posner, the compensation criterion has had a major impact on legal theory. See Posner (1972), Baker (1975), Coase (1960), and Coleman (1984). Coase's work has also spawned a line of thinking which proposes to contribute to economic welfare not by government provision, but by clearer rights assignments in order to make feasible a wider range of private enterprise. See Coase (1960), Demsetz (1964, 1967), and Cowen (1988).

8   Utilitarianism and consequentialism

Consequentialism is the doctrine that one should judge things morally by their consequences. It specifies a particular *structure* for ethics. First one needs to decide what is intrinsically valuable. Questions of intrinsic value are not necessarily the most *important* moral questions, but they must be answered first because everything else depends on their answers. Then one assesses actions, policies, and institutions in terms of their "contribution" – that is, their own value and the value of their consequences. Welfare economics presupposes a consequentialist moral theory.

In particular, a consequentialist takes an action, policy, or institution to be morally *right* or *permissible* if its contribution is no worse on the whole than the contribution of any alternative. If the contribution of a particular policy is better than that of any alternative, then the policy is morally *obligatory*. Whether a policy or action is right or wrong depends *both* on how things will be if it is implemented and how things will be if any alternative is implemented. The right thing to do may have very bad consequences when the consequences of the alternatives are even worse.

So a consequentialist says that one should do whatever maximizes the good. A utilitarian is a consequentialist who says that what is good is welfare. There are different varieties of utilitarianism depending on whether one takes welfare to be some mental state like happiness, whether one takes welfare to be the satisfaction of actual preferences, whether one takes welfare to be the satisfaction of "rational" or "informed" preferences, or whether still another conception of welfare is adopted. The fundamental thesis of utilitarianism is that one should do whatever maximizes total or average welfare. Utilitarianism is not a selfish doctrine. On the contrary, it may require great sacrifice. Indeed, one objection that has been pressed against utilitarianism is that it may require too much sacrifice. For example, it is sometimes argued that utilitarianism may be unreasonable in requiring that people refrain from favoring their friends or family over strangers in cases where more total utility is produced by helping strangers.

In order to get clear on what utilitarianism is and to assess its plausibility, it helps to consider examples. Think, for example, about how a utilitarian would approach the question of whether capital punishment is justified. Since the entire focus of utilitarianism is on the *consequences* of a policy such as executing certain classes of criminals, questions such as whether murderers *deserve* to die will be irrelevant. The relevant question is instead whether capital punishment results in more total welfare than the alternatives. So a utilitarian argument for or against capital punishment will depend on factual issues such as whether capital punishment deters people from committing crimes, whether criminals who are not executed might commit other crimes, and whether convicted criminals might come to contribute to total welfare. *Everybody's* welfare, including that of the criminal, counts.

8.1 Clarifying utilitarianism

The above description of utilitarianism leaves many questions unanswered. First, "welfare" can mean many different things. Clearly happiness and the satisfaction of preferences are not the same thing, and a utilitarianism that aims to maximize happiness is not the same as one that aims to maximize the satisfaction of preferences. The major nineteenth-century utilitarians (especially Bentham, Mill, and Sidgwick) took utility to be a mental state like happiness or pleasure (or, more precisely to be that property of objects that *causes* such mental states – see Broome 1991a), but few contemporary moral philosophers agree. Most contemporary utilitarians take welfare to be the satisfaction of rational (and perhaps also self-interested) preference. Preference utilitarianism might be described as a kind of grandiose welfare economics. It shares the welfare economist's approach to evaluation, but it attempts to be a general moral theory rather than merely a theory of economic evaluation, and it is undismayed by the difficulties involved in making interpersonal utility comparisons. As we have already seen in chapter 6, it is hard to come up with a plausible concept of welfare, let alone one that is also sufficiently measurable that one can calculate the effects of actions on the total amount of this good.

A second difficulty is that the consequences of actions, policies, and institutions are typically uncertain. Legislators may institute a policy believing mistakenly that its consequences will be better than any of the alternatives. Did they do the right thing, because the expected consequences were better than the alternatives, or did they do the wrong thing because it turns out that the consequences of some alternative would have been better? Since it is awkward and paradoxical to take the first alternative and say that the policy was "right-from-their-perspective" but "wrong-from-a-later-perspective," it seems better to say that the legislators made the wrong choice, no matter how rational, blameless, or even noble they were in making their mistake. To say this is not to deny the undeniable truth that utilitarian appraisals of actions, policies, and institutions always depend on beliefs about what their consequences will be. It is instead to insist merely that appraisals should change as beliefs change. On this view, one should not judge the goodness of people by the rightness of their actions. Instead one should judge people by examining whether they did what appeared to be right on the basis of the knowledge they had. For example, Milton and Rose Friedman argue that the Federal Reserve's failure to rescue failing banks in 1930 and 1931 and to prevent the money supply from contracting had the disastrous consequence of bringing on the Great Depression (1980, ch. 3). If they are right, then there seems to be no question that the Federal Reserve did the wrong thing. But our judgment of the wisdom and character of the decision-makers must depend not on such hindsight but on our understanding of their motivation and of what they should have known. Utilitarianism should be construed as an *objective* account of what actions or policies are morally right. What is right is whatever *in fact* maximizes happiness.

Third, to apply utilitarianism to guide moral deliberation and conduct, one needs some way of measuring welfare and of comparing the changes in the welfare of one individual with the changes in the welfare of another. As we noted in chapter 7, the difficulties involved in making interpersonal comparisons of well-being may be enough by themselves to sink any form of preference utilitarianism.

Fourth, one needs to be clear on *whose* welfare counts. Should one consider only the welfare of currently living human beings? What about the welfare of those who are not yet born (and who might, as the result of our action, never even be conceived) (Parfit 1984, ch. 17)? Most policy decisions have implications for those who are not yet born. Are their interests adequately represented via the concerns of those who are now living for those who will come after them? What does "adequately" mean here? It seems that issues of fairness, which cannot themselves be justified in utilitarian terms, intrude here. (These issues concerning the interests of future generations are, by the way, as worrying for standard welfare economics as they are for utilitarianism.)

In addition to deciding which human interests count, there is also the question of whether one should consider the welfare (or at least the pains and pleasures) of other sentient beings. Most people believe that there is something morally wrong about inflicting suffering on animals "needlessly." Commercial farming of animals for their meat and hides raises moral questions. If utilitarians count the pleasures and pains of all sentient beings, then they can explain quite naturally why the treatment of animals matters morally, but they will face difficult problems in comparing human and non-human welfare (Singer 1975). (Cost-benefit analysis may be in even more trouble determining what a chicken would be willing to pay to roam freely!) Utilitarianism does not, however, apply so easily to other issues in "environmental ethics" concerning the preservation of species or natural beauty.

Fifth, should utilitarians be concerned with total or average happiness? Since the average is just the total divided by the size of the population, total and average utilitarianism will always agree when the population is fixed. But if alternative policies have consequences for how many people there will be, then what is permissible for the total utilitarian can be very different from what is permissible for the average utilitarian. Average utilitarianism seems initially more appealing. A very large population of only middling average happiness might have a larger sum than a smaller population that has a high average amount of happiness, yet the latter seems more desirable. On the other hand, average utilitarianism conflicts with a version of the Pareto principle: imagine a state of affairs in which everybody is extremely well-off and the question arises of whether a couple should conceive a child who will have an excellent life, but who will pull the average down slightly. The average utilitarian would have to recommend against bringing this additional child into existence, while the Pareto principle would speak in favor. Average utilitarianism also encourages the repugnant thought that it would be a good thing if two-thirds of the world's population could somehow simply disappear. And it seems absurd to believe that moral questions about population growth should depend on historical research concerning past happiness – as they would if one believed that population should be limited so that future people have lives that are at least as happy as the average so far. These theoretical issues bear directly on currently pressing problems concerning population control (Parfit 1984, part IV).

Sixth, the utilitarian needs to make clear how utilitarianism is supposed to guide individual action and social policy. Actions and policies are morally obligatory if they maximize utility, but it does *not* follow that individual decision-making or social policy-making should consist in efforts to calculate the welfare consequences of the actions and policies. This conclusion is most obvious in the case of individual decision-making. Not only is calculating the consequences of one's actions on the happiness of the whole present (and future?) human (and animal?) population of the world fraught with uncertainties (and not much fun), it is also likely to introduce lots of bias, since people tend to take a more favorable view of the overall consequences of actions that benefit them. Calculation is itself an action, and not one that is likely to maximize utility. Furthermore, uncoordinated actions by numerous individuals may lead to bad aggregate consequences that could be avoided by having people follow simple rules. People are more likely to perform actions that in fact maximize welfare if they do not calculate the welfare consequences of their actions and, instead, act on general rules, such as "Tell the truth," "Keep your promises," and so forth.

In policy-making there is more scope for investigating the welfare consequences of alternatives, but in many circumstances policy-makers are also better advised to adhere to rules, for it is difficult to tell what the consequences of policies will be and what impact they will have on individual welfare. For example, even if there were some welfare-maximizing policies that violated basic liberties, the legislature might do better overall to accept constitutional limitations that rule such policies out of consideration.

At this point it might appear that utilitarianism is pulling some sort of disappearing trick. Now you see it, now you don't; and traditional moral principles are back in full force. Utilitarianism has a rather nebulous existence in a society where neither individuals nor governments regulate their actions by direct calculation of utility consequences (Williams 1973). But even though it is probably true that the best way for individuals to maximize utility is to stick to many of the traditional moral rules, utilitarianism does not automatically endorse all of traditional morality. It seems plausible that rules against lying maximize utility; but it is not obvious, for example, that moral taboos against paid adoptions ("baby-selling") or euthanasia maximize welfare. Furthermore, even when traditional moral commandments, such as "Tell the truth" have a compelling utilitarian justification, a utilitarian can hardly insist that one comply with them even in circumstances in which one is convinced that violating them would result in more welfare.

As we have seen, there are many versions of utilitarianism and many open problems. Yet utilitarianism remains an extremely powerful ethical view, particularly when one is concerned with issues of public policy, because it makes ethical questions in principle matters of straightforward calculation. Such calculations may be difficult to carry out and in some cases utilitarianism will not give any definite advice because of problems in learning the effects of actions or policies and in measuring their welfare consequences. But there will be clear cases, and the reasons for indecision and disagreement will be precisely known.

8.2 Justifying utilitarianism

Utilitarianism is a tempting ethical theory. In many cases it matches common intuitions well; it neatly shows what morality is all about and why it matters; and given its many historical connections with economics, it should be particularly tempting to economists. In principle, it shows how moral questions may be decided: all it takes is a calculation of the consequences of actions or policies. Evaluations depend on the facts concerning the consequences of alternative policies. Utilitarians can cite the imperfections of human knowledge of consequences to explain why ethical questions are so hard to answer. If actual ethical systems are to a considerable extent implicitly utilitarian, then the utilitarian can offer a plausible explanation as to why moral codes differ in different societies. Leaving one's grandparents out to die in the cold may have been morally permissible among those living in the harsh conditions of the Arctic, because it may have maximized welfare in those conditions. The same policy is morally impermissible in contemporary New Zealand, because it does not maximize welfare there. According to utilitarianism, what is morally right or wrong depends heavily and sensibly on what the facts of the case are. Utilitarianism is "absolutist" in one sense – whatever action maximizes welfare is *the* morally right action to perform – but it is not absolutist in the sense of supporting inflexible formulae for conduct. Whether an action is right or wrong depends on the consequences. Even killing an innocent person might in some circumstances produce more welfare than any alternative action and thus turn out to be morally obligatory.

Yet, as we pointed out in the previous section, utilitarianism gives rise to many complications, ambiguities, and doubts. In the face of such difficulties, can any truly compelling reasons be given to take seriously the idea that the morally right thing to do is to act to maximize the sum of persons' utilities? Such ultimate questions are difficult for any moral view to answer. But utilitarians do have more to say. In fact, deeper justifications of two kinds can be given, and the different justifications point to different ways of resolving some of the ambiguities noted in the previous section.

The first kind of justification rests on the claim that utility is the only intrinsically good thing. If the basic ethical obligation is to promote good states of affairs, utilitarianism will follow naturally. This is the justification for utilitarianism offered by J. S. Mill and Henry Sidgwick. A second approach relies on the notion of equal respect (Griffin 1986, ch. 9). Interpreting equal respect as giving equal weight to everyone's *interests* leads naturally to utilitarianism. The defense of utilitarianism in terms of equal respect can also take the form of a contractual argument (see chapter 11). In one version of a contractual approach, ethical principles arise from a willingness on the part of reasoning actors to consider their interests from an impartial point of view. Assume that people have an interest in promoting their own welfare. If they take up an impartial point of view, they will endorse moral principles that serve individual interests impartially, and they will thus endorse utilitarianism. Such contractualist arguments for utilitarianism have been formalized and cast into axiomatic form. From axioms about morality that characterize these premises, one can "prove" utilitarianism – although, of course, only relative to the axioms assumed. (For references and further discussion, see chapter 11.)

Although these two justifications share a disposition to view one's own interests from an impersonal point of view, they point toward differing interpretations of utilitarianism. The former kind of argument – in which utilitarianism derives from the attraction of maximizing the good – leads naturally to maximizing the total utility of all sentient beings (whether human or not), whereas the equal respect or contractualist arguments point toward maximizing average utility. Consequently, as noted in the preceding section, these two outlooks have sharply different implications with regard to population policy.

The two approaches to justifying utilitarianism also point toward different notions of what utility is. An "intrinsic good" justification of utilitarianism points away from preference-satisfaction notions of utility. It is hard to see why it should be considered objectively good ("from the viewpoint of the universe," as Sidgwick put it) that a state of affairs a person happens to desire should come about. It seems more comprehensible that one should regard mental states and other *substantive* goods as possessing intrinsic value. "Contractualist" views and views that emphasize equal respect turn the spotlight in contrast on the satisfaction of interests. This emphasis makes it more natural to think of something like the satisfaction of rational preference as the notion of utility which makes utility worth maximizing.

8.3 Contemporary consequentialism

During the decades that preceded the 1980s, utilitarianism appeared to be almost dead. Although it continued to influence policy-makers, most philosophers did not take it seriously as a moral philosophy. Even economists abandoned utilitarianism in the face of the difficulties posed by interpersonal utility comparisons. And to pound the final nails in the coffin, John Rawls, in *A theory of justice* (1971), offered not only systematic criticism but an alternative theory that was suitable for guiding policy. The resurgence in practical moral philosophizing that was so prominent in the 1970s usually took for granted some sort of rights perspective rather than any sort of consequentialism.

Yet by the end of the 1980s utilitarianism and consequentialism were alive again and highly influential in both theoretical and applied moral philosophy. In many recent works (listed at the end of the chapter) consequentialism has been resurrected and transformed. Contemporary consequentialists defend very different ethical theories, with Richard Brandt, for example, developing a sophisticated mental-state variant of utilitarianism and Amartya Sen developing a view of consequential evaluation in which rights, capabilities, and functionings play a more central part than happiness. Despite its diversity, this work shares many of the features of modern economic theory and should thus be attractive to economists.

First, most contemporary consequentialists draw a specific connection between ethics and the theory of rationality. John Harsanyi (1977a, p. 43), for example, writes: "Ethics . . . is a theory of rational behaviour in the service of the common interests of society as a whole." Most theorists do not go quite this far, but, as Samuel Scheffler especially has stressed, refusing to make trade-offs among different objectives and to maximize some objective opens one to charges of irrationality.

This discussion of the rationality of non-consequentialist ethical theories (see section 8.5 below) has the non-consequentialist on the defensive, and the charms of maximizing theories, to which economists have long since succumbed, have been seducing philosophers as well. Much of this new ethical theorizing is thus more congenial to economists and more easily integrated into normative economics than are, for example, rights-based ethical views (see chapter 9). The consequentialist theories defended by contemporary philosophers are, to be sure, not easily operationalized, but the difficulties of putting them to work are not insuperable either. Some of this work, such as Harsanyi's, would in many cases justify returning to old-fashioned utilitarian policy analysis.

Second, no prominent theorist except Richard Brandt now defends a hedonistic conception of utility. All of the other specifically utilitarian theorists on the list join economists in taking utility not as an object of preference, but as an index of preference satisfaction. Yet none of them joins economists in regarding utility as an index of satisfaction of *actual* preferences. Although the refusal to identify welfare with the satisfaction of actual preferences sets moral theorists apart from welfare economists, the distance is smaller than in the case of rights theorists or hedonists, and there are greater opportunities for building bridges. It might, for example, be possible to operationalize some of the conditions moral theorists have placed on "rational" and "well-informed" preferences and thereby to strengthen the moral basis for the conclusions of welfare economics.

Third, some of this new work on utilitarianism and consequentialism is influenced by developments in economics and game theory, and more of it could be. In Russell Hardin's utilitarianism, for example, human ignorance of consequences and the difficulties of measuring and comparing utilities hold center stage, and concepts from game theory are put to work generating the outlines of a utilitarian theory of property rights and of their limits. Hardin's game theory is elementary and his derivations are informal; and there are further important opportunities for collaboration between economists and philosophers in developing institutional implications of utilitarianism in circumstances of scarcity, uncertainty, opportunism, and so forth. We shall have a little more to say about these opportunities in chapter 13 below.

Of particular interest in this resurgence of consequentialism has been the development of consequentialist moral theories that are not utilitarian – of theories that take the good consequences to be maximized to be other things than happiness or the satisfaction of preferences (see especially Parfit 1984). Although it is difficult to find empirical proxies for some of these good consequences, the more objective the goods to be maximized, the more opportunity (other things being equal) for empirical application. If philosophers can specify a well-defined and clearly measurable good to be achieved, then the welfare economist can step in and discuss how best to achieve it.

One important objective good in many of these theories is the satisfaction of needs, and even utilitarians emphasize it, though not as a fundamental and intrinsic good. For example, although James Griffin is an informed-preference utilitarian, he argues that policy should focus on needs, because governments can more easily tell what people need than what will satisfy their informed preferences (1986, ch. 3). This emphasis on the empirical tractability of needs is ironic, given the aversion economists have felt towards distinguishing needs from mere wants. But this aversion seems not to have stemmed from empirical difficulties in studying needs. It has arisen instead from *theoretical* objections to drawing the distinction and giving needs any special weight. It seems to us that here is a case where moral philosophers are more practical than economists! In political discussions of economic policy, concern about human needs is already ubiquitous, and if philosophers can provide both a rationale for taking needs seriously in practical social decision-making and a principled way of drawing the distinction between needs and wants in such contexts (Braybrooke 1987, Thomson 1987), then economists can put their modeling tools to work in helping to devise policies that will satisfy needs.

The deep problems of utilitarianism, particularly concerning interpersonal comparisons of well-being, do not preclude operationalizing utilitarianism. One could, for example, stipulate a single utility function that very roughly represents everyone's preferences. Preferences represented by such a common utility function would most plausibly be defined not over marketed goods and services, but over more fundamental "commodities." Thus, one might want to argue that while some people prefer eating in restaurants and others prefer eating at home, what is really at work is a common preference for tasty, nourishing food, with different choices resulting from differences among people in the opportunity costs of producing meals at home. There might then be little problem determining the total utility of alternative policies, apart from the general difficulties of predicting their consequences. The hard part would not be making the operationalization of utilitarianism workable, but justifying it. What basis could one have for regarding the single utility function as representing, however crudely, nearly everybody's preferences and as capturing their relative strength? Can the idea of a shared "deep" utility function underlying apparent differences in preferences be rendered both plausible and practically workable? Would such an operationalization of utilitarianism be any less arbitrary than cost-benefit analysis, which, as we saw above, has also been regarded as operationalizing utilitarianism?

8.4 Is utilitarianism plausible?

The most powerful objection to utilitarianism is that in some cases it clashes sharply with our intuitions. Suppose, for example, that false testimony by one of the witnesses to the Rodney King beating in Los Angeles could have ensured a conviction at the first trial of the officers accused of police brutality. Given the very bad consequences of the officers' acquittal – the massive Los Angeles riots – it seems that a utilitarian would judge that the witness ought to have committed perjury. Yet most people believe that perjury is morally impermissible.

There are three possible responses to this apparent conflict between utilitarianism and what most people believe is right and wrong. First, utilitarians can argue that the conflict is only apparent. In his celebrated essay, "Two concepts of rules" (1955), Rawls distinguished questions about the design of institutions from questions concerning the enforcement of their norms. Even if perjury would maximize utility, perjury is forbidden by law and custom, and new laws and customs permitting perjury whenever one conscientiously believed that perjuring oneself would maximize utility would not be favored by a utilitarian or anybody else. So perjury should be forbidden by law and custom even in a case such as this one where committing perjury would maximize utility. Rawls demonstrates, however, only that perjury should be illegal and socially proscribed. He does not show that it is morally wrong for the witness to commit perjury. Rawls has not ruled out the possibility that it might still be morally obligatory to break the law and to do what is socially proscribed.

The utilitarian can still question whether the conflict between utilitarianism and moral intuition is serious. Russell Hardin (1988) stresses that hypothetical examples such as this one usually presuppose knowledge that is unattainable. The witness cannot be sure that the perjured testimony will lead to a conviction or that the perjury will not be detected. So the best thing to do is to adhere to the rule against perjury. When one takes into account the unavoidable uncertainties, it turns out that utilitarianism does not in fact recommend perjury. In response, many people would say that whether perjury is morally right or wrong in this case does not depend on whether it would be detected or on whether it would insure a conviction. The intuitive objection has not been completely answered.

A second response to the apparent conflict between utilitarianism and moral intuition is to challenge the authority of "intuition." A utilitarian would want people to be educated to have strong moral feelings that promote desirable conduct in typical situations. It will be good on the whole if people are strongly moved by such feelings, but they have no independent evidential force that can help in resolving hard cases (see Hare 1981). Even if the morality most people were taught were devised by a utilitarian, well-brought-up people should feel a strong repugnance toward perjury and should have the moral "intuition" that perjury is wrong.

In reply, the critic of utilitarianism can question what basis there could be for morality apart from intuition. If people can't take their intuitions seriously (though not uncritically), they have no way of arguing for or against any moral principles. So one arrives at a third response to the apparent conflict between intuition and utilitarianism, which is to reject utilitarianism. Utilitarianism remains unpalatable to most people (though perhaps not to most economists), but its difficulties in our view are not obviously greater than those of alternative ethical theories.

8.5 Consequentialism and deontology

It might be thought that consequentialism is not subject to similar intuitive objections. Since consequentialism *per se* does not specify what counts as "good," one might think that all ethical theories could be regarded as consequentialist. For example, those that stress freedom rather than welfare might be regarded as seeking to maximize freedom, while those that stress duties might mandate maximizing conformity with duty.

Consequentialism cannot however encompass all moral theories, because it assumes that there is some "agent-neutral" way to rank states of affairs with respect to goodness. For example, every consequentialist view that counts intentional killings as bad will imply that other things being equal it is obligatory to kill one person if one can thereby prevent two intentional killings. But such a conclusion is drastically at variance with most people's moral views. Everyday morality incorporates "agent-relative" reasons or values. The fifth commandment does not say, "Minimize killings." It says, "Thou shalt not kill."

Moral systems like the Ten Commandments are called "deontological." In Samuel Scheffler's terminology, deontological (non-consequentialist) ethical theories employ both "agent-centered prerogatives" (they sometimes *permit* agents to act in a way that does not maximize the good) and "agent-centered constraints" (they sometimes *prohibit* agents from acting so as to maximize the good). Both prerogatives and constraints are problematic. How can it be morally permissible, let alone morally obligatory, intentionally to choose what results in less good? Deontological theories not only conflict with consequentialism; they appear to conflict with rationality itself.

One reaction is to conclude that deontological moral systems are indeed irrational. If one is serious about regarding killing as wrong and if one is convinced that murdering one innocent person will prevent the murder of two others, then only irrational squeamishness should prevent a rational individual from committing the single murder. Of course, refusing to murder an innocent person does not appear to be mere squeamishness. It seems to be the right thing to do. The consequentialist might argue that appearances are misleading because our intuitions are geared to common, real-world circumstances, not to philosophers' hypothetical examples, and cases in which one can be sure of preventing two murders by committing one almost never occur.

This claim on behalf of the consequentialist is questionable. Conflicts between deontological constraints and rationally minimizing harms do in fact arise frequently in everyday life. Consider, for example, the case of Baby Jessica, a toddler who fell into a well in Texas a few years ago. After a massive human effort costing hundreds of thousands of dollars, she was rescued, although unfortunately she was permanently injured. The resources that were used to rescue her could have prevented the death and injury of hundreds of other children if they had been devoted instead to better prenatal care. The distribution of health-care resources is shot through with similar examples. Consequentialism and rational benevolence imply that resources should go where they do the most good. The consequentialist would maintain that acting otherwise is irrational.

It is possible to bring about a formal reconciliation between the theory of rationality and deontological views forbidding murder or insisting that we do whatever possible to rescue those in danger. If one distinguishes between x being murdered and *my* murdering x, then there is no inconsistency in preferring x being murdered to two others being murdered and preferring two others being murdered to *my* murdering x. Similarly, there is no inconsistency in preferring that Baby Jessica die rather than hundreds of other children, yet preferring the death of hundreds of other children to *my* standing by and letting Baby Jessica die. In order to make such reconciliations more than *ad hoc* gimmicks, one needs to say something about why it is "reasonable" not to be indifferent between x being murdered by somebody or other and my murdering x or between Baby Jessica dying and my not saving her. Here again we can see that utility theory presupposes a substantive background theory of "rational requirements of indifference." But there is a new wrinkle. The background theory here, which determines when it is rational to distinguish among actions and outcomes, depends on substantive moral principles.

The above proposal allows the evaluation of the goodness or badness of a state of affairs (or set of consequences) to vary with the perspective of the person doing the evaluating (Sen 1982b). An onlooker might readily conclude that it is morally better for one person to be murdered rather than for two to be murdered or for one child to perish rather than hundreds. But *from the standpoint of the persons involved,* what is at stake is whether *I* commit a murder or whether *I* stand by and let a child die. One may act on one's own moral commitments and judge that despite the good consequences of performing the murder or letting the child die, the act is wrong. Everyone might agree both that two murders are worse than one and that from the point of view of one facing the prospect of committing a murder, carrying out the murder is morally worse than failing to prevent two murders from happening. Although what is right or wrong on such an account depends on the consequences, the account is not "consequentialist" and is indeed ruled out by consequentialism, which presupposes an agent-neutral evaluation of states of affairs.

It might seem at first glance that evaluator-relativity is less likely to be a consideration in public policy than in personal morality, because policy should be made from an impersonal point of view. But as the Baby Jessica case and other examples from health-care policy show, it is not obvious that policy should attempt simply to override moral concerns to help or not to harm. If Americans were consequentialists and did not rescue Baby Jessica, but also did not look the other way when hundreds of thousands of other children needlessly died, then the United States would in important ways be a better society. But if Americans could ignore Baby Jessica's plight with no more than a self-congratulatory recognition of how rational they were, who knows how inhumane they might become?

8.6 Conclusion: Should economists embrace utilitarianism?

Economists ought to be strongly attracted to utilitarianism because it is so similar to standard welfare economics. Just define the rough and ready utility functions that will represent the preferences of the individuals affected and stipulate a way of making the interpersonal comparisons, and the way to utilitarian policy analysis is open. Economists would not have to give up their focus on outcomes or their view of welfare. Of course it is a bold and controversial step to stipulate what the utility functions should be and how the utilities of different people should be compared, but this step is not any bolder than the identification of welfare with the satisfaction of preferences. Taking this further step and moving from Paretian welfare economics to utilitarian welfare economics would enrich normative economics. Unlike purely Paretian welfare economics it would then be possible to appraise policy alternatives in which none is Pareto superior to the others, and an alternative with more total utility has a stronger claim to be regarded as just than does an alternative with merely a larger net benefit.

Yet many of those concerned with policy would take issue with the suggestion that economists become more explicitly utilitarian, precisely because they would like to see economists make a more radical break with current practice. They would argue that normative economics needs to treat notions such as freedom, rights, and justice as intrinsically valuable rather than continuing to focus exclusively on welfare. We turn to these other dimensions of evaluation in the next part of the book.

Suggestions for further reading

Classic writings on utilitarianism include Bentham (1789), Mill (1863), and Sidgwick (1901). The collection of essays by John Plamenatz (1967) provides a number of helpful philosophical treatments of problems of utilitarianism. An illuminating exchange on utilitarianism by two contemporary philosophers can be found in Smart and Williams (1973). A helpful volume with emphasis on economic aspects is Sen and Williams (1982).

The most important consequentialist works are those of Richard Brandt (1979), John Broome (1991b), James Griffin (1986), Russell Hardin (1988), Richard Hare (1981), John Harsanyi (1977a), Shelly Kagan (1989), Derek Parfit (1984), Peter Railton (1984), Amartya Sen (1982b), Singer (1979), and Smart (1973). Brandt, Hare, Harsanyi, Singer, and Smart are clearly utilitarian, while the others reject theories of human well-being that are characteristic of utilitarianism.

Applications of consequentialist moral philosophy to practical issues abound. See particularly Glover (1990) and Singer (1986).

For discussion of the rationality of deontological moral principles that permit options not to do what maximizes the good or forbid maximizing the good, see Nagel (1986, ch. 9), Scheffler (1982, 1988), Kagan (1989), and Kamm (1992).

Part III

Liberty, rights, equality, and justice

The concept of human well-being is crucial in moral theory, but people also care deeply about freedom, rights, equality, and justice. These notions may be hard to grasp but they are still important, and indeed people risk their lives pursuing them. Economists would be wrong to take welfare to be all that matters. Even if economists themselves had no interest in anything except welfare, they would still need to understand these other values in order to understand the goals of policy-makers and to help devise policies to achieve them.

But it is patently not the case that economists are indifferent to these other moral concerns. They do not think of them in the way that anthropologists think about the myths of unfamiliar cultures. On the contrary, economists care just as deeply about freedom and justice as do other people. Concepts such as rights or fairness may be hard to understand, but they are important enough that it is worth making the effort. Furthermore, one should remember that welfare is just as elusive and puzzling.

In Part III we shall be discussing many important moral notions, under the headings of liberty and rights (in chapter 9), equality (in chapter 10), and justice (in chapter 11). Our way of classifying the issues is an expository convenience, and readers should not take it too seriously. What is important to keep in mind is that there are *many* important moral notions that are distinct from the notion of well-being.

At the same time, we shall also discuss three kinds of moral *theories*: libertarianism (in chapter 9), egalitarianism (in chapter 10), and contractualism (in chapter 11). It is natural to link libertarianism with liberty and rights because these are the central concepts in libertarian theories. But liberty and rights are also important to non-libertarians. It makes sense to discuss egalitarianism while discussing concepts of equality, but concepts of equality are important in theories of justice that are not egalitarian. It is natural to place the discussions of justice and contractualism in the same chapter, because contractualist theories focus on justice. But justice is important in all moral theories. We want particularly to emphasize that the importance of the concepts introduced in this part goes beyond the importance of the particular theories that characteristically invoke them.

9 Liberty, rights, and libertarianism

Many people have a passionate commitment to individual liberty. They may object to paternalistic laws, such as laws requiring the use of seat belts, as infringements on freedom regardless of whether these laws increase welfare. Many would favor protecting the freedom of those with unusual lifestyles or unpopular religious convictions even if it means *diminishing* welfare. Social deliberation, unlike welfare economics, often treats protecting freedom and enhancing welfare as independent goals.

It is ironic that normative economics focuses on the Pareto efficiency concepts because economists value individual freedom very highly. Indeed we would guess that economists value freedom *more* than most non-economists. When economists have criticized socialism, for example, they have not only questioned whether it can "deliver the goods," but they have also argued that economic and political power must be kept separate in order to protect individual liberty (Friedman 1962, ch. 1). Economists also value the prosaic liberties that are part of market life such as the freedom to change jobs, to start a business, or to move from place to place. Thus, for example, many economists favor effluent taxes over direct state regulation of pollution not only because the taxes are purportedly Pareto superior to the regulation, but also because the regulation is a greater threat to freedom. Similarly, economists often favor cash over in-kind transfers because cash transfers leave the recipients freer.

The efficiency case has been a part of "scientific" welfare economics because it has appeared to rely only on uncontroversial moral premises; the argument in terms of freedom has been reserved for "unscientific" essays because its moral premises have appeared more "philosophical." No doubt contentment with the efficiency standard has also been fostered by a belief that the Pareto standard itself promotes liberty, because it values outcomes that best accommodate the voluntary choices of individuals. But Pareto optima do not always respect rights or maximize liberty. Consider a problem such as homelessness. If one thinks only of welfare and not of liberty or rights, one will not begin to appreciate what is at stake.

The concerns about liberty that underpin economists' normative judgments should be incorporated systematically into their methods of evaluation. Doing so raises problems of *definition*, of *moral justification* and of *weighting*. In other words, (1) What is freedom? (2) How can claims about the moral importance of freedom be defended? and (3) How can liberties be incorporated along with other values into a coherent scheme of ethical evaluation?

9.1 Freedom

We find it useful to follow Gerald MacCallum's (1967) suggestion and to regard "freedom" as a relation among three things: (1) an agent, (2) obstacles or costs of some kind and (3) some of the agent's objectives. The last aspect is controversial, since it seems that whether an agent is free to do X does not depend on whether the agent wants to do X (Carter 1995). But without reference to an agent's objectives, there would be no way to identify obstacles. An agent is free in some regard when there are no obstacles of a particular kind preventing or discouraging the agent from doing something. X may not be legally free to purchase beer, because there is a law prohibiting the sale of beer to minors, and X is a minor. X may be legally free to purchase beer, but physically unable to do so because there is no beer available. X may be legally and physically free to purchase beer, but unable to do so because of a lack of money. This lack of economic liberty follows in part from laws, which prevent X from simply taking the beer, but also from social conventions and choices of others. X may be legally, physically, and economically free to purchase beer, yet not at liberty to do so for religious reasons. Rather than thinking of different meanings of the term "freedom," it is helpful to think about different kinds of obstacles to different sorts of objectives.

People are free and unfree in various ways. Some freedoms are of great moral importance, but others are not, and there are substantive disagreements about which sorts of freedom are important. In his influential essay "Two concepts of liberty," Isaiah Berlin argued that social policy should aim to protect "negative" liberties rather than to promote "positive" liberty. One protects negative liberties by respecting a protected sphere around individuals and placing few obstacles in the way of their efforts to satisfy their preferences. Negative liberty has nothing to do with natural or internal impediments to action. Promoting positive liberty, in constrast, involves attempting to realize some idealized conception of the self.

Libertarians often hold that the only morally significant limitations on freedom are those that result from deliberate attempts of others to prevent people from pursuing their goals. People who are starving obviously face crushing material obstacles to the pursuit of their objectives, but libertarians typically deny that such limitations are infringements on liberty unless they are the result of deliberate attempts by others to prevent these people from living as they please. Those who see competitive markets as always promoting freedom do not deny that market outcomes sometimes place barriers in people's way. They deny instead that these obstacles, as the unintended consequences of voluntary interactions, are morally objectionable.

Most people do not have such a narrow view of what freedoms matter. Berlin himself argued that the barriers that others unintentionally place in one's way may be morally significant limitations on freedom. Many people would regard *all* obstacles to agents' pursuits of their objectives as morally significant if they result from the actions of others or if they could be removed by others.

The extent of an individual's freedom depends on how many possibilities are open to her, how easy they are to attain, how important in her plan of life these possibilities are, how far they are influenced by the actions of others, and how the society at large values these possibilities. Any assessment of the extent of liberty in a society requires in addition that one aggregate the liberties of different persons (Berlin 1969, p. 130). This is a mind-boggling amalgam of disparate elements. Some philosophers have suggested ways of cutting down the complexity. Rawls, for example, distinguishes a relatively short list of "basic liberties," including for example freedom of conscience and freedom of expression. Then, within this short list, he further distinguishes between "liberty" as a formal notion and "the worth of liberty," which depends on having the means to exercise the freedom. Others have similarly distinguished "formal" from "effective" liberty. Sen's capabilities (p. 82 above) may also count as morally significant freedoms. For example, if one is literate, then one is free from intellectual obstacles to reading. This usage of the term "free" highlights the important point that a political regime that countenances illiteracy has much in common from the standpoint of liberty with one that bans books.

The concept of "autonomy" or "self-determination" is important in thinking about freedom. Autonomy can be used to refer to a *capacity* to govern oneself, a *condition* of self-governing, an *ideal*, or a matter of moral *authority* (Feinberg 1986, p. 28). The most important of these notions are the capacity to be autonomous and the condition of autonomy (Raz 1986, pp. 204f). It is easier to identify factors that may impair the capacity to be autonomous than to list the factors that enhance the capacity. External factors such as poor or deliberately misleading information, inadequate opportunity for reflection, and a limited range of alternatives among which to choose threaten the capacity to be autonomous. Internal threats to autonomy include limited abilities, such as illiteracy, and psychological defects, such as an inability to cope with uncertainty.

The condition of autonomy is just as complex. It involves satisfying one's own preferences rather than having them satisfied by others. It involves actively accomplishing rather than merely enjoying well-being. And autonomy also involves aspects such as self-possession, individuality, authenticity, integrity, self-control, initiative, and responsibility (Feinberg 1986, pp. 32, 40–4). This condition of autonomy may be valued simply as a matter of fact: most people care rather a lot about being the sort of person characterized here. Alternatively, autonomy can be defended as constituting a partial ideal of the person – something people *should* care about, even if they don't. This latter view has the potential to pose a threat to negative liberty and political freedom.

Autonomy as an ideal of the person is often connected to some notion of the "real interests" or "true needs" of the person, which governments should promote. In two famous passages from *The social contract* (1762), Rousseau wrote

that anyone who refuses to obey the general will shall be forced to do so by the whole body; which means nothing more or less than that he will be forced to be free . . .

. . . along with the civil state, man acquires moral liberty, which alone makes him truly master of himself; for the impulse of mere appetite is slavery, and obedience to self-imposed law is liberty. (1968, p. 64)

The defender of autonomy in this sense thus sees the agent's significant objectives not as whatever the agent wants ("the impulse of mere appetite") but what is truly in the agent's interests. Erecting barriers to doing what one wants may remove subtler obstacles that stand in the way of doing what is truly in one's interests, just as a law against jay-walking may help pedestrians to get to their destinations (MacCallum 1967, p. 330). Promoting autonomy may thus, as Berlin warned, conflict with promoting negative liberties and a wide range of choice.

An analysis of morally significant individual freedoms must take a stand concerning how important various objectives are to individuals. It might allow the individual's preferences to determine the importance of actions and states of affairs, but this is as controversial and substantive a moral decision as is any specification of the "true interests" of individuals. In addition to determining what matters and how much, an analysis of morally significant individual freedoms must specify what kinds of obstacles are of moral concern. The freedom that matters is the absence of obstacles of the specified kind to pursuit of significant objectives.

9.2 What are rights?

The precise definition of a "right," both in law and in morality, has commanded much attention from scholars in this century. Broadly, one might characterize a right as protecting or promoting a way of acting or a way of being treated. A right specifies that a range of actions or conditions open to an individual, such as driving, voting, or being sheltered, should be protected or promoted (see Martin 1993). Such normative direction may be embodied in law or convention, or it may have the status of a moral demand or recommendation.

Rights are often linked to liberties – and for good reason, since one kind of liberty (such as the freedom to emigrate) simply *is* a right, and notions of freedom are important in analyzing rights and in making sense of their rationale. Although the details need not concern us, legal analysts following Hohfeld (1919) have recognized that rights involve complex clusters of permissions and constraints regarding the actions of individuals. Rights typically involve both "privileges" for the right-holder and correlative duties for others. Rights conceived of as the flip-side of the duties of others are called "claims." For example, the right of workers to strike after their contract expires implies both a *privilege* to strike and a *duty* on the part of others not to interfere in certain ways. Rights also involve "powers" and "immunities." For example, occupational safety and health laws provide workers with *immunities* from efforts by firms to assign them certain duties, and thereby limit the *powers* of firms to determine aspects of working conditions. Rights are clusters of claims, privileges, powers, and immunities, though different elements may be central in different rights. Claims are central in what are called "rights," and privileges are central in what are called "liberties." But rights are not just claims, and liberties are not just privileges.

Legal rights are probably the most familiar kind of right. For example, the legal right to strike consists roughly in there being laws permitting workers to strike and prohibiting others from preventing them. Other sorts of *conventional rights* may be less familiar, but they are equally straightforward. For example, company policy may give workers the *right* to seventeen days of paid vacation. *Moral rights* are more puzzling. It is appealing to think of them as analogous to legal rights. Just as legal rights are determined by legislation, so moral rights are determined by the "moral law." But unlike legal rights, some moral rights might not be widely acknowledged or respected. In what sense can they then be said to exist? The point of talking of moral rights is to assess legal and conventional rights, for example to criticize the former rights of the white minority in South Africa or to urge that in the US rights to health care ought to be recognized in law or convention. To say that an agent has a moral right is to say that it is morally justifiable to grant the agent a legal or conventional right (Mill 1863, ch. 5; Sumner 1987).

9.3 The importance of rights

Rights serve the dual roles of safeguarding people's *interests* and of providing them with control over their *choices*. Very often these two purposes will coincide, since people usually try to choose what is in their interest and regard themselves as having an interest in controlling their own choices. So, for example, giving an artist a property right in a painting she has created both serves her interest in being able to profit from the painting and gives her control over its disposition.

Sometimes these two goals – of safeguarding interests and of providing control – will differ. For example, infants and non-human animals have interests but cannot make choices, and the point of assigning rights to such beings is apparently to protect their interests. One may, however, want rights to recognize the value people attach to controlling their own choices, rather than simply safeguarding their interests. Suppose for example that someone makes use of a vacant private condominium owned by Madonna without her permission. When should such a trespasser be said to have violated Madonna's property rights? So-called "liability rules" would say that paying Madonna her standard rental fee fully respects her property rights. Liability rules protect Madonna's interests, but they do not protect her right to control. One may therefore prefer "property rules," which hold that her rights have been violated unless one gets her consent. Most theorists argue that either an interest-based ("benefit") or a control-based ("choice") conception of rights is the valid one. However, we are attracted to the view of Coleman and Kraus (1986) that, depending on facts and circumstances, a particular right may protect interests, or choices, or both.

Rights are important in economics for at least three reasons. First, clear definitions of rights, especially of property rights, promote economic efficiency. A familiar result in transactions-cost economics, well illustrated by current problems in the former Soviet Union, is that the absence of clear property rights results in socially wasteful efforts to defend ambiguous claims and discourages investment because investors cannot be sure that they will reap the rewards.

Second, rights, and again especially property rights, are often taken as starting points in economic analysis. For example, analyses of the distributional properties of economic arrangements often begin from a given allocation of property rights. In adopting such a starting point, economists may find themselves assuming uncritically that this starting point is morally justified – that the rights recognized in the existing property regime really are the "true" rights in some normative sense. A crucial controversy among rights theorists that is of great importance to economists concerns whether there are "welfare rights" – that is, rights *to* things such as food, housing, and health care. We return to this point below.

Finally, rights may be invoked to limit the pursuit of economic goals. Most people today would recognize that the institution of slavery violates human rights and should therefore be forbidden, regardless of whether it might contribute to economic growth. More controversially, one can criticize socialism on the grounds that it violates people's rights in outlawing "capitalist acts between consenting adults" (Nozick 1974, p. 163) or one can criticize *laissez-faire* capitalism on the grounds that it violates people's rights to work or their rights to minimum subsistence. The legitimacy of welfare rights is a primary issue regarding this third role of rights. Should the public provision of health care to those unable to pay for it be viewed as a matter of *right* legitimately claimed by the needy, or is it instead best viewed as a matter of *charity* based on and limited by the good will of the affluent? Answers to this question will depend on the kind of justification offered for rights. Even if there are no welfare rights, governmental provision of charity might still be justified on the ground that people prefer welfare benefits to be provided, but need state action to eliminate the temptation to "free ride" on the charitable efforts of others (Friedman 1962, Hochman and Rodgers 1969).

9.4 The justification of rights

Why should there be moral rights, and what rights should there be? How can moral rules, which are independent of actual law or custom, have prescriptive force? One traditional answer is that human beings can "perceive" what the correct moral rules are and recognize that they must be followed. Locke put it this way,

The State of Nature has a Law of Nature to govern it, which obliges every one: And Reason, which is that Law, teaches all Mankind, who will but consult it, that being all equal and independent, no one ought to harm another in his Life, Health, Liberty, or Possessions. (1690, section 6)

Similarly, the authors of the American Declaration regarded their claims concerning rights to be self-evident. The problem with such a view is that it leaves one with nothing to say to those who fail to acknowledge this "plain and intelligible" law of nature except that they must be "biassed by their Interest, as well as ignorant for want of study . . ." (Locke 1690, section 124). Kant gives a second answer: equal respect for rational agents generates moral rules and rights. This view is notoriously difficult to interpret and is tied up with Kant's metaphysics, which we cannot pursue here. A third answer, which is related to Kant's, is that rational individuals who are concerned to promote their interests would choose to adhere to some set of moral rules. We will explore this contractualist answer in chapter 11. A fourth answer is that of the utilitarian: correct moral rules maximize total welfare, and it is the moral attractions of maximizing total welfare that gives the rules their force. There are other possibilities too, but these are the main alternatives in modern Western moral philosophy.

Each of these ways of justifying rights provides guidance concerning what set of conventional rights agents ought to be granted. The four are unanimous in defending some rights, such as a right not to be killed or a right to enter into contracts. But these moral theories do not always agree. A full theory of moral rights cannot be developed without taking sides on fundamental questions in moral philosophy. Even more challenging from the perspective of those who would hope to employ the moral vocabulary of rights and liberties to evaluate economic institutions and outcomes are the indeterminacies within each of these theories concerning exactly what rights agents have.

9.5 Weighing rights, liberties, and welfare

The remaining problem concerning rights and liberty is incorporating them systematically in schemes of moral evaluation. This problem takes different forms given different accounts of why liberty or rights are valuable. On instrumental or consequentialist views such as utilitarianism, the problem of rights articulation can be formulated as one of selecting rules that maximize good consequences. This is straightforward in principle, although difficult problems of strategic coordination may arise in devising effective rules. The choice of rules may also be influenced by limitations on persons' ability to calculate.

What about cases where rights protections are viewed as intrinsically valuable? One option here is simply to include rights protections or violations effects on liberty among the consequences, weighting them according to some scheme that reflects their moral importance. For example, other things being equal, a murder would be worse than a natural death, because the murder would involve a rights violation in addition to the welfare losses attached to a death. When a job applicant loses out because of employer discrimination, the bad consequences include not only the welfare loss entailed by the worker's unemployment but also the violation of the applicant's right to equal treatment. This approach seems, however, to capture only part of the value of rights protection.

When we discussed the rationality of duty or rights-based moral systems in chapter 8, we touched on some of the difficulties about incorporating such factors into an overall moral evaluation. Recall the example of a witness considering committing perjury in order to insure a conviction in the Rodney King beating case. In this situation, committing one serious wrong will most likely not only increase total welfare, but it will prevent others from perpetrating more serious wrongs. If the police officers accused of beating Rodney King at his first trial had been convicted, Reginald Denny would not have been dragged from his truck and severely beaten, and hundreds of store-owners would not have suffered theft and arson. But many would say that perjury violates people's right to a fair trial, and that it is simply *wrong*, regardless of how many rights violations it might prevent. Even those who would not go so far as to rule out perjury regardless of the consequences would maintain that the moral pressure on an individual not to "do evil" goes beyond an impersonal weighing of the consequences. The consequentialist view does not capture the sense that the moral imperative on me is that *I* should not commit perjury.

One way to preserve a more thoroughly non-consequentialist version of rights protection is to adopt Robert Nozick's view of moral rights as absolute "side-constraints" on action (1974, pp. 28–35). In this view, an individual's obligation is not to strive for a minimum of rights violations, or a maximum of any social welfare function. Rather, agents may do as they wish, within the constraints imposed by rights. If everyone acts morally, then there will be no rights violations. It is not, however, permissible for anyone to violate rights in order to prevent other rights violations. Rights are simply not to be violated. This absolute lack of trade-offs not only of rights against other good things, but of lesser violations of rights against greater ones, is an implication of Nozick's view which has been found disturbing by many philosophers (for example, Nagel 1983), and we suspect most economists would agree. Indeed Nozick himself seems to blanch before the full implications of his own view and suggests that, in the unlikely event that the consequences of respecting rights were catastrophic (as they might be in case of a famine), it might be permissible to violate them after all (1974, p. 30).

As we discussed before, it is possible to permit rights to have an important role without accepting the extreme "side-constraint" view Nozick defends. One can allow the evaluation to vary with the perspective of the person doing the evaluating. So individuals can justifiably demur when offered the prospect of violating the rights of others, even if doing so will minimize overall rights violations. Furthermore, quite rigid constraints may be justifiable even from an explicitly consequentialist perspective. Although utilitarians and Kantians offer quite different stories about *why* rights are necessary and *why* they should have teeth, they join in defending a set of rights that sharply constrain individual action and social policy.

9.6 Libertarianism

Libertarians are defenders of political liberty, property rights, and economic freedoms. In appraising economic institutions, libertarians focus on rights and liberties. Some libertarians emphasize political and economic liberties and property rights because they believe that defending rights and liberties most enhances welfare. We shall, however, mainly discuss the work of philosophical libertarians, who maintain "that the only relevant consideration in political matters is individual liberty" (Narveson 1988, p. 7; see also Machan 1982, p. vii). In libertarian writings, liberty – the fundamental value – is linked to a rights-based view of justice, and the liberties with which libertarians are concerned should be regarded as rights. For philosophical libertarians, acts and policies are just if and only if they do not violate anyone's rights.

What distinguishes philosophical libertarianism is both this identification of justice with respecting rights and a distinctive view of the content of rights and of the duties rights entail. For example, most libertarians hold that redistributive inheritance taxes violate individual property rights and are morally impermissible. But this is only true if property rights include the right to bequeath one's property without any encumbrances. If property rights did not include the right to bequeath one's property, then there would be no rights violation, just as the "entailments" on landed estates that required that they be willed entirely to the eldest son did not violate the legally recognized property rights of the English gentry. Libertarians defend strong and encompassing property rights. Furthermore, it might appear that property rights could conflict with welfare rights to subsistence, health care, and so forth. It would seem that one could not conclude that redistributive taxation is morally impermissible without adjudicating among these conflicting rights. But libertarians deny that such conflicts arise because they maintain that the duties that rights imply are almost exclusively "negative" duties not to interfere.

Libertarians typically deny that there are any welfare rights. For example, libertarians hold that right to life is a right not to be killed, not a right to be given subsistence. In propounding such a view, libertarians are not necessarily endorsing selfishness, although some, such as Ayn Rand's (1964) "objectivist" followers, do espouse egoism. Most libertarians value beneficence and charity as virtues. They only insist that individuals must not be forced to be beneficent or charitable. The libertarian need not admire Mr. Bumble and the other officers of the Parish who (in Dickens' *Oliver Twist*) allow paupers to starve to death. A libertarian may find Mr. Bumble a hard-hearted hypocrite. But libertarians who accepted the legitimacy of existing property rights would see no *injustice* in the wretched treatment of the indigent. The indigent have no welfare rights to food or shelter. On the contrary, insofar as the workhouse relies on taxation to provide its inadequate relief, it is violating the rights of tax-payers and unjustly taking their property. Justice requires that one not interfere with the pursuits of individuals, unless those pursuits themselves violate rights.

Even supposing that the existing property rights were legitimate, how is protecting them supposed to serve freedom better than preventing starvation? If one adopts a "moralized" definition of coercion, which says that A is coerced only when *unjustified* force is used against A, then it would be proper to say that the enforcement of justified property rights through legal authority does not involve coercion. If one thinks of negative liberty as the absence of coercion of this kind, then a system that enforces existing property rights maximizes negative liberty. This argument is questionable because it is doubtful whether existing property rights are justified and because the moralized definition of coercion is controversial. To claim that coercion only exists in the context of unjustified force would imply, uncomfortably, that putting a convicted murderer in prison does not involve coercing him. More generally, linking coercion and liberty conceptually to the definition of rights makes it impossible to conceive of rights as maximizing liberty or minimizing coercion, for to do that one needs conceptions of liberty and coercion that are independent of rights conceptions (see Martin 1993).

Some libertarians, such as Loren Lomasky and Hillel Steiner, defend some rights to positive assistance, such as a right to be given a fair trial or an infant's right to nurture (Lomasky 1987, pp. 164, 260). But even libertarians who grant the existence of such rights want to limit them narrowly. The duties to provide these particular benefits are, like the duties not to interfere, supposed to be easy to comply with without compromising the character of an individual's projects, and the benefits are crucial to the possibility of pursuing any projects at all. But some rights to positive assistance, such as children's right to nurture, impose serious burdens on others. These burdens are problematic because libertarians maintain that value lies in the separate endeavors of individuals, and justice lies in not interfering in those endeavors unless they threaten the rights of others.

It is not obvious that taking freedom to be the fundamental value automatically commits one to a rights-based view of morality, to a particular view of the content of rights, to the view that rights rarely obligate others to give positive assistance, or to the view that enforcing existing property rights necessarily maximizes liberty. Indeed, Joseph Raz, for example, argues at length that valuing autonomy commits one to an extensive role for government in providing the public goods that facilitate the achievement of autonomy (1986, ch. 8). Raz's argument depends upon an interpretation of liberty that most libertarians would reject.

In Robert Nozick's well-known version of libertarianism, natural rights – rights that do not depend on consequences – secure individual autonomy. Justice is respecting rights. According to Nozick's entitlement theory of justice, an outcome is just if it arises from just acquisition of what was unowned or by voluntary transfer of what was justly owned. Just acquisition is acquisition that violates no rights and makes no one worse off, and transfers are, in the relevant sense, voluntary just in case none of the limitations on individual choices arise from rights violations. Only remedying or preventing injustices justifies redistribution or other interferences with voluntary action. A view such as Nozick's clearly places heavy demands on a theory of rights, which Nozick unfortunately leaves undeveloped (see Nagel 1983). Justice is entitlement and depends on the actual history, not on the resultant pattern. Since the past is, as a matter of fact, full of injustices, Nozick's libertarianism might in practice require extensive redistribution. Notice that Nozick's entitlement theory rules out redistributive taxation as unjust only if one accepts a particular view of the content of rights. If just acquisition gave one the right to transfer only 80 percent of one's property, then a 20 percent transfer tax would violate no rights. Even if Nozick is right that justice is determined by entitlement, not by "pattern," patterns might re-enter the story at a higher level when one is deciding what the content of rights should be (Pogge 1989, ch. 1).

Some of Nozick's most striking arguments in favor of this "entitlement view" show that even minimal efforts to regulate the pattern of distributive outcomes involve extensive interference in people's lives. In a much-discussed example, Nozick argues that taxing the income of a star basketball player like Wilt Chamberlain interferes with the choices of Wilt's fans, who would happily pay a premium to see him perform (1974, pp. 161–3). Although Nozick never defends his libertarian system of rights, he does present it as having an appealing coherence. Since the point of rights is to secure liberty and to permit individuals to pursue their own projects, considerations of welfare never justify interferences with individual rights.

Since, in addition, Nozick takes rights to be absolute side-constraints, even efforts to protect rights cannot justify infringements of rights. Thus Nozick argues that only an extremely minimal state can be justified. Notice that accepting the priority of liberty and rights over welfare does not by itself force one to accept the libertarian political program, since a more-than-minimal state might serve liberty better than a minimal state.

The philosophical libertarian's commitment to liberty is in principle independent of any welfare consequences, but libertarians would like it to be the case that protecting freedom also makes people better off, and libertarians need to show that some of their more extreme proposals, such as privatizing all streets and highways (Block 1982) would not lead to disastrous consequences. Jan Narveson (1988, p. 183) puts the point vividly: ". . . those who toil in the libertarian fields devote the lion's share of their efforts to persuading us that the alleged benefits of the State are illusory . . ." Moreover, many who support libertarian policies are motivated by welfare concerns. Friedrich von Hayek, for example, argues that economic prosperity, social innovation, and political democracy are best advanced by keeping governmental action to a minimum (Hayck 1967, 1976). Most libertarian economists are less influenced by distinctive philosophical commitments than by specific reasons for doubting the efficacy of government intervention to improve efficiency or redistribute income. The literature on property rights and transaction costs that derives from Ronald Coase's arguments in "The problem of social cost" (1960) usually reaches libertarian policy conclusions, but philosophical libertarians would reject Coase's consequentialist view of rights as welfare-enhancing devices to reduce transactions costs and to alleviate the suboptimalities caused by externalities.

Rights and liberties are central elements in the European and American moral and political heritage. They are complex and controversial, but so are conceptions of welfare. Normative economics should undertake more explicitly the responsibility of investigating how well economic arrangements serve liberty and to what extent they secure rights. Welfare economics should be only one part of normative economics, not the whole of it.

Suggestions for further reading

Isaiah Berlin's celebrated essay, "Two concepts of liberty," has provoked much discussion. A valuable collection of essays inspired by Berlin's work is Ryan (1979). MacCallum (1967) is a valuable commentary on Berlin.

For discussions of autonomy, see especially Feinberg (1986, pp. 31f), Dworkin (1988, ch. 1), Raz (1986), and Christman (1989).

On the definition of rights, Hohfeld (1919, p. 38) regards claims as "the limited and proper meaning" of "right." Wellman (1985), Sumner (1987), and Thomson (1990) follow Hohfeld terminologically, though none of them is committed to construing pure claims as the paradigm cases of rights. See also Feinberg (1973, chs. 4–6) and Waldron (1984). For a defense of a "choice" construal of rights, see Hart (1955), while Raz (1984) defends a benefit construal. For general discussions of rights see Dworkin (1977), Sumner (1987), Thomson (1990), and Martin (1993), and for a sustained discussion of the difficulties of defending libertarian property rights see Waldron (1990).

Amartya Sen (1982b) discusses the option of including rights violations among the consequences that a consequentialist should take into account. Thomas Nagel, on the other hand, has argued powerfully for preserving a non-consequentialist component in rights evaluation (1986, ch. 9).

Lomasky, Narveson, Steiner, and Machan as well as Nozick (1974) provide systematic accounts of a libertarian viewpoint. Friedrich von Hayek's systematic treatise (1960) argues that a variety of consequentialist considerations support the case for limited government and wide protections for negative liberty. Mises (1949) is the classic libertarian discussion of economics.

10   Equality and egalitarianism

The notion of equality is of tremendous practical importance in discussions of economic policy and also of fundamental theoretical importance in ethics. As Ronald Dworkin, James Griffin, and Amartya Sen have all argued, the concept of equality lies at the heart of moral theories. Sen argues that all moral theories prescribe that people be treated equally in some regard (1992a, p. 3). For example, although libertarian theories appear to be strongly anti-egalitarian, they require equality of rights. Utilitarianism requires that everyone's welfare counts equally. What makes moral theories so different is that the things different moral theorists seek to equalize are not perfectly correlated with one another. Equalizing one thing conflicts with equalizing another. Dworkin and Griffin go further and maintain that a more substantive notion of "equal respect" defines what morality is all about. In Dworkin's view, conflicts between different political philosophies can best be understood as conflicts over the interpretation of equal respect (Dworkin 1977, Kymlicka 1990).

Appeals to equality play an equally crucial role in discussions of economic policy. Welfare-state programs have attempted to diminish inequalities in incomes and status, and concerns about inequalities constitute the main grounds upon which interferences with market outcomes have been defended. To judge whether such programs are advisable, one needs to understand what (if any) sort of equality can be a moral ideal.

An example may help to clarify why one needs to think carefully about the notion of equality. One consequence of inequalities in the United States is that there are many thousands of homeless people. The homeless population can be roughly classified in three groups. The first group consists of those who have lost their foothold in the economy through disruptions such as firms relocating to other states. In the second group are people with mental, physical, or behavioral disabilities. A lack of funds for residential treatment, outpatient care, and occupational rehabilitation has left these people homeless. The third group consists of people without any identifiable disability who have had only a casual connection to the labor force.

Does the value of equality urge that members of these groups be treated similarly or differently? Do the similarities between those who have lost their jobs "through no fault of their own" and those who cannot get jobs because of handicaps require that the two groups be treated equally or do the differences demand that they be treated unequally? Should an egalitarian support treating those with congenital disabilities differently from those who may have suffered damage from drug addiction? Should one view the third group, the casual workers, as cursed with an inability to muster the effort to sustain regular employment, as showing a personal preference for leisure, or as just plain lazy, and how should one's view affect what equality demands? In the public debate about homelessness in the United States, it is typically taken for granted that policy concerning the homeless should depend on what causes the inequalities that give rise to homelessness. Why and how the causes of inequalities matter to their ethical evaluation are controversial questions. One needs to understand what sort of equality one supports.

As this example suggests, it is hard to judge which economic differences between people are morally justified. Should equal wages be a goal when workers may have to provide for families of different sizes? Is the value of equality served by transferring income from those who work hard to those who prefer to surf? Notions of equality of opportunity, of circumstance, or of treatment are just as problematic. Do laws that prevent convicted felons from voting involve equal or unequal treatment? Does providing a more expensive education to those from deprived backgrounds enhance or diminish equal opportunity? Are affirmative action programs an implementation or a violation of equal opportunity?

To determine what to equalize, one needs to understand what one wants equality *for*. Determining what to equalize and determining why the pursuit of equality is morally justified are inseparable inquiries. There are also serious problems when the pursuit of equality comes into conflict with the constraints imposed by rights or with other objectives such as welfare or liberty. So as with our discussion of liberty and rights in the last chapter here too we face problems of *definition*, of *justification*, and of *weighting*. What should be equalized? Why should it be equalized? How important is equality? We shall begin with the second question.

10.1 Why equalize?

To decide *what* to equalize, it helps to know *why* one wants to equalize anything at all. Furthermore, judgments about how *much* to equalize and about how much weight equality should have plainly depend on the role of equality in overall schemes of moral evaluation. A commitment to moral and political equality is deeply embedded in American political traditions and in Kantian moral philosophy, but the basis for this commitment and its implications for economic equality are controversial. Economic equality may have instrumental value, because economic inequalities may give rise to evils, such as widespread poverty, political subjugation, and social instability. But if equality is only desirable as a means to unrelated ends, such as aggregate welfare or social stability, then it seems to be of no more moral significance than are good health care or nutrition, which also have great instrumental value.

David Miller poses this puzzle concerning equality as follows:

Why should *equality* be thought desirable? Equality after all means a leveling of differences; it means a smoothing down of irregularities or idiosyncrasies. Although I may from an aesthetic motive decide to trim my rose bushes to an equal height or polish my wine glasses to an equal shine, to treat people in such a way would be at best perverse and at worst immoral. The pursuit of equality seems to be impaled on a fork: either the ultimate end of the pursuit is not equality at all but some other value or values which have become confused in the popular mind with equality, or our societies are aiming at a goal that cursory inspection reveals to be quite monstrous. (1982, p. 73)

In response Miller points out that even if economic equality, like negative liberty, has mainly an instrumental value, it may also have an intrinsic connection to some of the ends it serves, just as negative liberty has an intrinsic connection to autonomy. Miller lists four different ends which equality, including economic equality, may serve and to which equality has an intrinsic connection.

First, *equality is sometimes required in order to be fair*. If there are benefits or burdens to distribute, then, other things being equal, it is unfair to distribute them unequally. But fairness and justice involve more than equality, and an equal distribution is often unfair. It seems unfair, for example, for all students in a course to get the same grade regardless of their performance. But in the absence of good moral reasons for an unequal distribution, fairness requires equality. Kai Nielsen makes the point this way:

I have in mind the sense of unfairness which goes with the acceptance, where something non-catastrophic could be done about it, of the existence of very different life prospects of equally talented, equally energetic children from very different social backgrounds: say the children of a successful businessman and a dishwasher. Their whole life prospects are very unequal indeed and, given the manifest quality of that difference, that this should be so seems to me very unfair. (1985, pp. 7–8)

Second, equality is a good thing, because *some measure of equality is necessary for self-respect*. Except when they have behaved stupidly or immorally, individuals should be able to say, "I am as good as anybody else; I may not be as clever or hard working as you are, but I am as good as you are" (Davies 1963, p. 45; quoted in Benn 1967, p. 69). The great inequalities that characterize the United States today make it very difficult for individuals at the bottom to maintain their self-respect. The homeless are not only impoverished and uprooted, but they are also often regarded with suspicion, fear, and contempt by the more fortunate. Especially when they compare their lives with those they see on television, they have great difficulty preserving their self-respect.

Third, equality is a good thing, because *equal treatment implements the duty to show equal respect.* "While [people] differ profoundly as individuals in capacity and character, they are equally entitled as human beings to consideration and respect" (Tawney 1931, p. 34). "[Man] knows himself as a man only in society with other men. He needs, as other animals do not, self-respect and the respect of others; he needs to be treated by others as if his needs and purposes mattered to them" (Plamenatz 1967, p. 93). The issue is not how well those who are at the bottom are able to maintain their self-respect, but how they are *treated.* Showing equal respect implies recognizing that, apart from those with severe mental deficiencies or ill-nesses, all people have capacities to deliberate for themselves, to engage in relationships and activities that are intrinsically valuable, and to develop skills and traits that are admirable (Miller 1982, p. 81; Lukes 1977). Large economic inequalities are inconsistent with the social acknowledgment that everyone has such capacities, and they violate the duty to show equal respect.

Equality is also necessary for "fraternity." There should be some measure of solidarity among the inhabitants of a nation and there should be no systematic barriers to social intercourse. Inequalities are objection-able in part because they place barriers to friendship, community, and love. "What is repulsive . . . is that some classes should be excluded from the heritage of civilization which others enjoy, and that the fact of human fellowship, which is ultimate and profound, should be obscured by eco-nomic contrasts, which are trivial and superficial" (Tawney 1931, p. 139).

Equality is thus not only a means to unrelated goals. It is of intrinsic moral importance because it is linked to fairness, self-respect, equal respect, and fraternity.

10.2 Equality of what?

Understanding why equality is morally important helps one to see why certain kinds of inequalities are deeply disturbing, while others may be permissible. Yet close attention to specific egalitarian proposals brings out troubling ambiguities. For example, should people whose ability to feel discomfort has been numbed be allocated few resources on the ground that deprivation has less effect on them? Should society compensate those who are born with poor eyesight or poor coordination or poor ability to discipline themselves to work? Reflection on such hard cases and on the theoretical problems of defining equality has stimulated a searching recent discussion of the ideals of (1) equality of welfare, (2) equality of resources or primary goods, (3) equality of opportunity for welfare, (4) equality of "capabilities" or "access to advantage," and (5) "complex" equality.

10.2.1 Equality of welfare

Economists might naturally interpret egalitarians as aiming to equalize welfare, because welfare is the central moral notion in normative economics. But to interpret the ideal of equality as involving equality of welfare also discredits the ideal in the eyes of most economists. For to claim that two people are equally well off is to make an interpersonal utility comparison, and economists typically doubt whether interpersonal utility comparisons are possible and do not want policy conclusions to depend on them. Most economists would also object that equalizing welfare destroys incentives.

Furthermore, equality of welfare is not a very attractive ideal. Why should one want to make good the losses of those who like to gamble? Don't those who work hard and choose prudently *deserve* to be better off than those who are lazy and thoughtless? Why should those who are unhappy without expensive wine have more of a claim on social resources than those who are content with cheap beer? Why should Tiny Tim's sunny disposition and modest wants cancel out his claims to an expensive wheelchair (Cohen 1989, p. 918)? In terms of the underlying moral values which equality may serve, one might make a case that equality of welfare would promote fraternity or equal respect. But it is hard to see equality of welfare as promoting fairness or self-respect. For reasons such as these, philosophers rarely defend equality of welfare.

10.2.2 Equality of resources

Ronald Dworkin argues that egalitarians should be concerned to equalize *resources* rather than welfare. "Resourcist" views maintain that the levels of welfare people wind up achieving depend on personal choices and characteristics that are no concern of social policy. The proper concern of an egalitarian should not be welfare, but the resources people have available to pursue their ends. Rawls' primary goods, as all-purpose *means*, are resources, and, as we shall see in the next chapter, his two principles of justice constitute one variant of resource egalitarianism.

Resource egalitarianism involves some complexities, since it would be inefficient for everyone to have exactly the same bundle of resources. Down parkas and snow-mobiles are not needed in Tahiti. What resource egalitarians want is for everyone to have bundles of resources that are "equivalent," though not identical. One might say that resource bundles are equivalent if nobody would want to trade her bundle of resources for anyone else's. Dworkin urges us to imagine that the actual resource bundles were determined as a competitive equilibrium in a hypothetical market in which all n people began with claims to $1/n$ of every resource. People's actual resource holdings would vary, but no one would want to trade for anyone else's. It is possible to show, for certain simplified cases, that any resource distribution satisfying this no-envy condition could be reached through a sequence of Pareto-improving trades starting from a condition in which everyone has the identical resources. To state the result more precisely: When all resources are external and alienable, a competitive equilibrium arising from initially identical resource bundles can be shown to be both Pareto optimal and "envy free" in the sense that no one will prefer another's bundle of commodities to his own. Hal Varian (1974, 1975) has proposed the label "fair" for envy-free Pareto optima, and has defended this conception of fairness as ethically appealing (see also Foley 1967 and Baumol 1986). An important stimulus to the study of envy-free allocations of resources has been their apparent ability to provide a standard of equity that does not involve interpersonal comparisons of welfare.

But there is a problem. The ethical appeal of resource egalitarianism derives from the intuition that, once people are equipped equally with resources, how much welfare they manage to achieve is their own affair and not a matter for society to try to equalize. But outcomes also depend on physical and intellectual abilities, which are just as arbitrary as are material resources. Merely equalizing external alienable resources does not go far enough. Equalizing wealth leaves the handicapped with fewer resources. Either abilities should also be treated as resources or some compensation for their inequality must be devised.

If one counts abilities as resources, how can one then equalize resources? One approach is to say that total internal and external resources are equal whenever people have equal amounts of goods and equal amounts of leisure. If everyone has the same tastes, this conforms to Varian's definition (1974, 1985) of a fair distribution – it is Pareto optimal and envy free. Unfortunately, if people's tastes differ, this outcome will generally not be efficient, and the competitive equilibrium resulting from trade from this equal division starting point will not be envy free. Starting with equal endowments of leisure and goods, a highly talented individual will be able to convert leisure time into additional goods at a much better rate than will a less talented individual. In competitive equilibrium, the less talented will wish they could swap their goods–leisure bundles for those of the more talented (Pazner and Schmeidler 1974, Varian 1985). Hence, this way of extending the definition of resource egalitarianism to cover the case of internal resources doesn't have the nice property that competitive market exchange preserves equality. This difficulty has led economists to put forward two alternative definitions of equal resources, whose envy-freeness will not be disrupted by trade.

The first of these is the notion of a "contribution-fair" (Baumol 1986) or "wealth-fair" (Varian 1974, 1975) distribution. Imagine equalizing people's external resources but allowing them to retain the fruits of their differential talents. The resulting competitive equilibrium will not be envy-free, since, as we just noted, those with more talent will tend to have consumption–leisure bundles that others envy. The equilibrium is, however, envy-free in a different sense. Suppose one asks individuals whether they prefer to consume what others do *and* also to make the same contribution to production. Those with few talents may prefer the consumption of the talented, but given how hard it would be for them to contribute as much to production as do the very talented, they will not envy the whole consumption–production package. That is, no agent will want to trade places with another where trading places entails getting the other's consumption bundle but also producing as much as the other person. Contribution fairness essentially leaves talents or internal resources out of the package of things to be equalized, and accepts inequalities due to competitive rewards for talent as fair. This falls short of what many people would think of as equality of resources.

Alternatively, one can define an "income-fair" distribution (Varian 1974, 1975; Pazner and Schmeidler 1974; Baumol 1986). Suppose everyone owned equal partial shares in the labor power (and hence the talents) of everyone. These shares and all external resources are divided equally. So if people do not buy back any of the shares of their labor power (which means that they work almost all the time), then everyone has equal resources and, if tastes are the same, everyone is equally well off. But tastes are not all the same, and people cannot work all the time, so people will want to trade some of their initial resources, and they will want to buy back shares in their labor power so that they can have some leisure. If we define people's "full income" to include the market value of their leisure, the resulting competitive equilibrium will equalize full incomes – hence the name "income-fair." Because the labor-time of the talented is a high-priced commodity, it will thus cost a talented person more to obtain any given amount of free time than it will cost others. If tastes are constant across the community, the talented, who have equal full incomes and more expensive leisure, wind up worse off – equality of resources in this sense winds up overcompensating the untalented in terms of equality of welfare. Ronald Dworkin calls this the "slavery" of the talented (1981b, p. 312), because unlike those whose leisure is cheap, the talented will have no choice but to work long hours.

Ronald Dworkin defends a third alternative. Rather than attempting to equalize ownership of internal resources, he defines equality of resources in terms of a hypothetical insurance scheme to guard against the misfortune of low productive abilities (1981b, pp. 292–323). Dworkin's thought is that if it were possible before birth to purchase insurance against handicaps, individuals would be willing to pay a premium to compensate themselves in the event of the bad luck of being handicapped. Taxation to improve the life prospects of those who are less well-endowed with internal resources can be conceived of as implementing such hypothetical insurance rather than as attempting directly to equalize internal and external resources. As it turns out, economists have criticized Dworkin's analysis of such a hypothetical insurance market (Varian 1985, Roemer 1985). Indeed John Roemer argues that implementing Dworkin's ideas can have the perverse result of making those who are handicapped *worse* off than they would be than if no attempt were made to equalize internal resources (but see Alexander and Schwarzschild 1987, p. 103).

If resources can include internal qualities such as talents, why stop there? Dworkin argues for redistribution of the fruits of unequal talent, but finds inequalities resulting from unequal ambition acceptable. Yet, as John Roemer suggests (1985), a person's willingness to expend effort, like the person's talents, may ultimately be traceable to their biological and personal histories. Why not then treat the capacity to be ambitious as a resource? For that matter, some people may possess enzymes that allow them to extract more nutrition from a meal, or more satisfaction from a movie. Might we not think of these differences too as hidden resources? It is easy to see that, following this route, one might argue that any difference in achieved welfare levels resulting from apparently equal resources really is the product of hidden differences in resources. Roemer (1985, 1986a, b, 1987) has proved that the only distribution meeting several reasonable-looking requirements for a resource equalizing mechanism is equality of welfare (but see Scanlon 1986).

Roemer rightly presents this result not as a proof that equality of welfare is the only proper standard, but as raising two kinds of issues involved in distinguishing resourcist from welfarist views. One concerns the gap between ideal reasoning about just distribution and practical reasoning that takes into account limits on information and problems with incentives. If one attempted to equalize welfare, one would need detailed knowledge of people's preferences, and they would have powerful incentives to misrepresent what their preferences were. Given these problems, some simplified version of resource egalitarianism may be a suitable compromise. The second issue is that one needs a theory of persons and of individual responsibility to decide which internal differences justify compensation and which do not. We may wish to compensate people for being born blind, but not for being born without ambition. We may regard it as appropriate to compensate a person for being stuck with an affliction that brings constant pain, but not appropriate to compensate people for being stuck with religious beliefs that induce them to starve themselves. As Scanlon (1986, pp. 116–17) notes, an ascetic could hardly view his own suffering as a compensatable liability. Articulating and defending these distinctions in a coherent way is a large and unfinished project. It clearly won't do to say that individuals have no control over their handicaps, while their preferences and motives are up to them, for our characters are to a considerable extent beyond our control. G. A. Cohen argues that it is a mistake to draw a line between abilities and preferences. In Cohen's view, the extent to which a disadvantage justifies compensation should depend on the extent to which its acquisition and retention are voluntary (1989, pp. 920–34). The purpose of egalitarianism "is to eliminate *involuntary disadvantage*" (Cohen 1989, p. 916). "The Principle of Equality . . . claims that it is bad if, through no fault of theirs, some people are worse off than others" (Parfit 1984, p. 26; see also Arneson 1990, p. 177).

Cohen's compensation criterion is problematic. It would, as noted, surely be inappropriate to compensate someone for holding involuntary religious beliefs that demand suffering. Cohen concedes the point and revises his account to rule out compensation not only for disadvantages resulting from choice but also for disadvantages that are so intrinsically connected to their bearers that their bearers would not choose to be without them (1989, p. 937). Ronald Dworkin draws the line differently:

> The distinction required by equality of resources is the distinction between those beliefs and attitudes that define what a successful life would be like, which the ideal assigns to the person, and those features of body or mind or personality that provide means or impediments to that success, which the ideal assigns to the person's circumstances. (1981b, p. 303)

In Dworkin's view the distinction does not center around whether the features of the person were acquired or retained voluntarily. The "beliefs and attitudes that define what a successful life would be like" may not be voluntary, while the "features of body or mind or personality that provide means or impediments to that success" may depend on an individual's choices. Regardless of the causal history, "it would be incoherent for me to regard some ethical conviction I have – that the only important thing to do with my life is to create religious monuments, for example – as a limitation on the goodness of the life I can lead" (1990, p. 108). The point of egalitarianism for Dworkin is to show equal respect, not to eliminate involuntary disadvantage. Compensating individuals for their preferences and values does not show equal respect.

Resource egalitarianism derives largely from the value of equal respect. If one can draw the line between resources and what people should be held responsible for, then the resourcist standard will respect individual differences and responsibility. Rawls also stresses that, in making distribution insensitive to individual preferences, this standard achieves fairness toward different notions of the good. It is questionable whether equality of resources promotes fraternity or a desirable sense of community.

10.2.3 Equality of opportunity for welfare

Like Cohen, Richard Arneson draws the line between those traits of an individual that demand compensation and those that don't in terms of the possibility of choice. For Arneson, someone with involuntary expensive tastes may be as deserving of compensation as is someone who is handicapped. "If we put aside practical difficulties about information-gathering and measurement of hypothetical rational preferences, what further good reasons could there be for treating involuntary expensive preferences due to handicaps differently than involuntary expensive preferences due to tastes?" (1990, p. 190). This thought seems fatal to resource egalitarianism, because it is implausible to maintain that one individual possesses fewer resources than another merely because the first has more expensive tastes. Furthermore, admitting that involuntary expensive tastes should be of concern to an egalitarian aggravates the measurement problems involved in comparing the resources of different individuals.

Arneson proposes that egalitarians should aim to equalize *opportunities for welfare* rather than equalizing resources. "For equal opportunity for welfare to obtain among a number of persons, each must face an array of options that is equivalent to every other person's in terms of the prospect for preference satisfaction it offers" (1989, p. 85). Involuntary expensive tastes, like handicaps, limit opportunities for welfare. Spelling this view out in detail leads to surprising complications, and there may not be much practical difference between equal opportunity for welfare and equalizing resources. Arneson supports his proposal by arguing that focusing on opportunities for *welfare* enables one to explain why resources matter and gives one a principled method for weighting their importance. Yet the reference to welfare has its costs, too. Although Arneson specifies that welfare is the satisfaction of "ideally considered" self-interested preferences (rather than the satisfaction of actual preferences), he still faces many of the difficulties with preference-satisfaction views of welfare discussed above in chapter 6.

If respecting individuals involves respecting their (ideally considered and self-interested) preferences, then equality of opportunity for welfare should be judged superior to resource egalitarianism in honoring the value of equal respect. Whether it is fair that differences in what gives people satisfaction should lead to differences in the shares they get of society's resources is more problematic.

10.2.4 Equality of capabilities

Equalizing welfare seems to equalize too much. Some welfare differences are the responsibility of individuals and should not be equalized. Equalizing external resources seems to equalize too little. There are internal differences between individuals, such as handicaps, which are not the responsibility of individuals and which should be equalized. Rather than assimilating handicaps and talents to resources, one might instead attempt to equalize what Cohen calls "access to advantage." Egalitarians ought to look at what is "in between resources and welfare." Resources and internal features of the individual determine the range of outcomes from which the individual chooses. Cohen argues that egalitarians should try to equalize this range of outcomes, or, in other words "access to advantage." This is similar to Sen's proposal that egalitarians seek equality of capabilities (discussed above in section 6.5).

We find Sen's and Cohen's proposals attractive, even though they face many of the problems encountered by Dworkin and Arneson. One still needs to distinguish between those features of an individual that affect capabilities and those that determine what use individuals make of their capabilities. Furthermore, the access to advantage or capabilities approach faces the measurement difficulties involved in specifying when different capabilities are in the relevant sense "equal." Dworkin at least provides the no-envy test and the story about hypothetical insurance, and Arneson reduces the problem to comparing the expected welfare of different life-paths. In addition, given the measurement difficulties, it may be that the only way to implement Sen's or Cohen's proposals would be to focus on resources.

Yet one might argue that the fact that the capabilities or access to advantage approach is "open" on the question of how to weight the relative importance of different capabilities is a strength rather than a weakness. For as Scanlon (1975, 1986) has argued, the valuation of resources, capabilities, or primary goods should be objects of public moral deliberation concerning their importance in facilitating a range of good lives. Whatever one concludes on this matter, it is clear that the main appeal of Sen's and Cohen's proposals is to fairness and equal respect. These proposals appeal especially to the argument from fairness for improving the life chances of those who suffer from handicaps.

10.2.5 An alternative approach: Walzer's complex equality

There is another way of thinking about equality that is less a competitor than a complement to the above arguments concerning what egalitarians should seek to equalize. Although an egalitarian, Michael Walzer denies that there is a single right answer to the question of what should be equalized. Instead he points out that the principles governing disparate aspects of social life appear to be strikingly different. Fathers and mothers are supposed to be trusting, caring, altruistic, and partial. Entrepreneurs are supposed to be self-interested, distrustful, competitive, and acquisitive. Professionals such as doctors and nurses are supposed to be motivated by a concern for the well-being of those to whom they attend. Citizens are supposed to be equal, impartial, and motivated by their views of the collective good.

Many economists are, of course, inclined to regard individuals as basically acquisitive and self-interested in all domains of social interaction. But whether or not people's motives are always the same, the *principles* governing their interactions are still varied. Resources within families are not distributed as wages, profits, and rents. Licenses to practice medicine are not sold to the highest bidder. Political life is governed by principles designed to protect equal rights. Political rights are free, and they are not distributed as rewards or, except in the case of convicted felons, removed as penalties. They are not distributed on the basis of desert, and they cannot be bought or sold (Okun 1975, pp. 6–10). Inequalities from economic life do, of course, spill over into political life. But this is widely thought to be undesirable, and nations erect barriers to limit the extent to which wealth leads to political power.

Walzer maintains that there is no reason to expect the same distributive standards to prevail in different "spheres" of social life. Even within areas of activity that are recognizably economic, one should resist the supposition that they should all be governed by a single underlying standard.

Thus, for example, the social significance of employment in modern industrial societies argues strongly, in Walzer's view, for equal opportunity in
that area. Yet there is no reason to suppose that our society should under-
write a similar commitment to equality of opportunity in consumption.

Walzer's egalitarianism does not rule out economic inequalities,
inequalities in authority within particular institutions, or even political
inequalities that arise from differing abilities to persuade, organize, and
lead. These inequalities are acceptable so long as there are equal political
rights and liberties, and so long as the inequalities in one domain do not
spill over into others. What's wrong with the economic inequalities in our
society is that they lead to inequalities in status, in employment opportunities, in political power, even in health. Although Walzer argues that there is
no reason to *eliminate* economic inequalities completely, he nevertheless
provides good reason to *reduce* them. Furthermore, Walzer argues that
some ostensibly "economic" inequalities, such as those involved in the
authoritarian structure of economic corporations, are actually political in
nature and are as inconsistent with equality in rights and liberties as are
towns that are owned and controlled by corporations (1983, ch. 12).

Walzer's complex equality seems to follow naturally from concerns with
self-respect, equal respect, and fraternity. Indeed, the quotations from
Tawney that we used to illustrate the concerns for fraternity and equal
respect are in very much the same spirit as Walzer's account. Notice that
Walzer's more eclectic approach is not incompatible with inquiries into
conceptions of economic inequality, such as those reviewed in the preceding sections. Since Walzer defends limitations on the permissible degree
of economic inequality, his work would be complemented by clarification
of the moral significance of inequalities within this individual "sphere."
But Walzer's approach points in interestingly different directions from the
work of those who have been struggling over definitions of equality.
Walzer's outlook, in stressing the relativity of conceptions of equality and
justice to the practices of particular societies, is more historically situated
than are the more abstract efforts to clarify notions of equality of
resources, welfare, and the like. While the abstract "equality of what?"
debate points toward reflection on conceptions of individual responsibility
and personhood, Walzer's approach focuses attention on the social meanings of goods and on the influence of economic arrangements on the
broader political and social relationships in a society. These two
approaches are better seen as complements than as alternatives.

Looking to the moral justification for a concern with equality does
not quickly resolve the question of what should be equal. All of the
contenders except for equality of welfare are plausible, and none
is without its difficulties. We believe that egalitarians should support

something like Walzer's complex equality and that they should adopt something like Sen's or Cohen's construal of the nature of inequalities within particular social spheres. However, as noted above, there may be little practical difference among policies intended to decrease inequalities in resources, to equalize opportunity for welfare, or to increase equality of capabilities.

10.3 How important is equality?

Given some sense of *what* one might want to equalize and why, one must then say something about how *important* equality is. Arthur Okun makes this question vivid by means of an analogy to a leaky bucket (1975, pp. 91ff). Suppose that one carries goods from the rich to the poor in a leaky bucket. How much leakage should one accept before deciding that efforts at redistribution are too costly? Redistribution has administrative costs, effects on incentives, and effects on attitudes toward work and care of oneself. When there are trade-offs between equality and efficiency, which Okun stresses, or between equality and freedom, which libertarians emphasize, how much weight should be placed on equality?

These are difficult questions that require a comprehensive ethical theory for an answer. Clearly the extent of trade-offs will be sensitive to the conception of equality that is under examination and will vary from society to society depending on the degree of inequality in a society relative to the level of welfare or freedom there.

Most egalitarians have contended that the inequalities of resources, opportunities, and welfare in modern industrial societies could be greatly diminished without serious loss of efficiency or freedom and without violating anyone's rights. It is plausible that equalizing educational opportunity in the United States would *increase* rather than diminish both efficiency and freedom, and economies such as Japan, Austria, and Sweden demonstrate that inequalities in wealth and income that are small relative to those in the United States are compatible with freedom and economic growth. Some observers might argue that the increase in inequality observed in many countries in the 1980s is evidence that the trade-offs are worsening, but this is not obvious. Indeed, it appears that increasing inequality in the 1980s has often been accompanied by disappointing economic performance.

The extent of these trade-offs between equality and economic growth is ultimately an empirical question. What goes into the scales, however, is a matter of values. For economists to contribute most effectively to social deliberation about how to make difficult choices involving trade-offs between equality and other values, they should understand the conceptions of equality and the values that lend these conceptions moral importance.

Suggestions for further reading

The central texts in the contemporary egalitarian debate are Arneson (1989, 1990), Cohen (1989, 1993), G. Dworkin (1988), R. Dworkin (1981a, 1990), Rawls (1971), Roemer (1985a, 1987, 1988), Scanlon (1986), Sen (1992a), and Williams (1962).

Philippe van Parijs (1989), developing suggestions of Bruce Ackerman (1981), has put forward a weaker egalitarian notion of "undominated diversity of resources," designed to allow for the fact that different people may rank alternative bundles of resources differently. Arguing from a commitment to undominated diversity and other moral principles, van Parijs has made a persistent case for an unconditional grant to be paid to every adult citizen (1989, 1990, 1991).

For a recent challenge to the direction in which the discussion of egalitarianism has gone, see Fleurbaey (1995).

11 Justice and contractualism

The questions of justice that are important to economists concern the distribution of benefits and burdens among members of a community. What claims can persons legitimately make upon one another or upon the state? What burdens can the state place on its citizens or can individuals place on one another? As the "jealous virtue," justice deals with conflicts of interest among people in society.

Economists cannot decide what principles of justice to rely on merely by consulting public opinion or "common sense," because people are committed to many principles of justice, which are at differing levels of generality, and which are often ambiguous and conflicting. Even when there is a social consensus on a principle of justice, economists may still not find much guidance. Consider, for example, equality of opportunity. There's little controversy that it's a good thing, but that's partly because there's so much disagreement about what it is. Does equality of opportunity require that more resources be devoted to the education of the relatively disadvantaged? Does equality of opportunity require steeper inheritance taxes? Questions about the extent to which economic policies contribute to equality of opportunity can scarcely be broached until the concept itself is clarified. Economic evaluation presupposes well-defined principles of justice.

Some economists might deny that economic evaluation should rely on any principles of justice. Not only are these principles controversial, but some economists might question whether it is any more appropriate to raise questions about the justice of wages than to ask whether it is just that lobster is more expensive than cod or that London is cloudier than Rome. But it is plain that people do make moral judgments about economic arrangements and that they want policies to be responsive to such concerns. A repudiation of this kind of moral evaluation itself rests on substantive views concerning justice, and these require a defense.

We doubt that economists can avoid issues of justice. Suppose, for example, an economist is called upon to comment on the economic consequences of alternative policies affecting families. Although some have

150

argued that the family is an institution "beyond justice" (Sandel 1982), marriages involve both conflicts of interests and benefits from cooperation (see Sen 1990). For example, changes in divorce law in the United States in the direction of "no fault" divorce have reduced the need for the partner who wants to get out of a marriage to bargain with the other partner. These changes have contributed to the current state of affairs in which divorce frequently leads to a dramatic drop in the living standards of women and children and a dramatic increase in the living standards of men. (According to Lenore Weitzman [1985] the standard of living of divorced women and their children in California between 1968 and 1977 dropped on average by 73 percent during the first year after divorce, while the standard of living of men increased on average by 42 percent!) These facts about divorce in turn affect the relative bargaining power of married men and women. Evaluating the economic consequences of family law requires principles of justice. It is unlikely that relatively unreflective every-day principles of justice will suffice because they so often conflict, and because their rationale is not clear. In addition, as illustrated by the case of equal opportunity, accepted principles may pose such large problems of interpretation that they provide little guidance. So it seems that economists have to look to moral philosophy.

Libertarian and utilitarian moral theories, the subjects of chapters 8 and 9, imply theories of justice. For libertarians, justice is simply respect-ing the rights that libertarians recognize. For utilitarians, principles of justice are utility-maximizing general rules that facilitate cooperation and regulate conflicts of interest. Yet it is also natural to use the language of agreement, promise, negotiation, and *contract* to talk about the issues of cooperation and conflict, which are central to justice. This chapter describes the resurgent interest among economists and philosophers in theories of justice that build upon the idea of a "social contract."

11.1 The social contract idea

Social interactions are to some extent voluntary. They involve conflicts of interest, but they are on the whole mutually beneficial. People would be in desperate straits without the companionship and assistance of others. Circumstances like these, falling between complete harmony, which would make justice superfluous, and war of all against all, which would render it hopeless, are called by Hume and by Rawls "the circumstances of justice." It is tempting to think of the normative principles governing individual interactions as human contrivances to adjudicate conflicts of interest and to secure the benefits of cooperation. Norms might thus be regarded as arising from some sort of "social contract." The idea is already clearly developed in Plato's *Republic* (though Plato denies that the principles to which individuals would agree in order to facilitate living together are truly principles of justice). In the seventeenth and eighteenth centuries, following the collapse of a vision of society as naturally hierarchical, political philosophers revived the notion of a social contract as the source of political obligation and social norms, including principles of justice.

The basic notion of social contract theories is that one can judge principles and institutions by asking whether people would agree to them in a "state of nature" in which they were not already bound by social obligations, but were governed only by enlightened rational self-interest (which seventeenth- and eighteenth-century philosophers called the "law of nature"). Not all philosophers have found contractualist reasoning valuable – David Hume, for example, famously complained that no contract can explain or justify the duty to keep contracts. Advocates of contractualism, however, find the contract notion attractive because it links justice to *consent* and to *rationality*. Showing that a certain principle would be agreed to by people acting reasonably in the right circumstances increases its claim to guide people's actions, and showing that people in a state of nature would find it *rational* to agree to abide by certain principles supports the claim that the principles themselves are rational. All contract theories test moral principles by asking whether rational agents would agree to them under properly defined circumstances, but they differ in the interpretation of the hypothetical circumstances of choice, in their characterization of the agents' rationality and motivation, and in their view of *what* is to be chosen. These differences lead to large variations among contract theories.

Brian Barry (1989) has helpfully distinguished two broad categories of contract theory, especially as applied to theories of justice. The first, exemplified by Hobbes and Hume, links rationality to self-interest and agreement to the outcome of bargaining, leading to a view of justice as *mutual advantage*. The social contract is a compromise that enables individuals to pursue their separate aims more harmoniously and successfully. The second, exemplified by Kant and Rousseau, links rationality to the autonomous pursuit of ends (which need not be self-interested) and agreement to consensus, leading to a view of justice as *impartiality*. The social contract determines what principles governing interactions would be endorsed by impartial agents. John Rawls, whose theory we will examine in more detail below, regards his own view as representative of a third standpoint of *reciprocity*. Impartiality, argues Rawls, suggests an unconditional commitment to promoting the common good, while reciprocity implies a willingness to do one's part in a cooperative scheme provided that others also do theirs. Like impartiality, and unlike mutual advantage, reciprocity may sometimes entail acting against one's own interest, but only in circumstances where others, if necessary, are disposed to do the same. We shall not, however, distinguish between impartiality and reciprocity interpretations of contract theories.

Unlike utilitarians, who characterize equal respect as counting everyone's interests equally, or libertarians, who characterize equal respect in terms of equal rights, contractarians interpret equal respect as the equal moral status of the parties to the social contract. Thomas Scanlon maintains that a contractarianism based on impartiality requires one to "justify one's actions to others on grounds that they could not reasonably reject – reasonably, that is, given the desire to find principles which others similarly motivated could not reasonably reject" (1982, p. 116). What inspires such a contractualist view of ethics is the vision that moral principles must be rationally acceptable to every agent who is willing to take up a perspective that recognizes the common need for agreement. Scanlon's formulation highlights a feature common to most writing in a contractualist vein: the interest not only in identifying defensible moral principles, but also in giving a good account of why people should feel bound by those principles. Since theorists of mutual advantage adhere closely to a view of rationality as self-interest, a major challenge for their views is to explain why rational persons would ever agree to restrain their pursuit of their interests and why they would adhere to agreements once made. Those who see contractualism as determining what is impartially best instead assert that people may be moved by a desire to regulate their conduct by principles that are morally acceptable from a suitably detached perspective. On the one hand, this assumption makes it easier to explain how moral considerations succeed in moving people; on the other hand, this assumption is less psychologically abstemious than the self-interest assumption favored by theorists of mutual advantage.

11.2 Justice as reciprocity: Rawls' theory of justice

The most influential work in modern moral and political philosophy is John Rawls' *A theory of justice* (1971), an epic exposition of a contractual moral theory adapted to contemporary circumstances. It is worth explaining Rawls' views at some length not only because of their pivotal role in contemporary philosophical discourse but also because Rawls draws on economics and offers a great deal to economists. The derivation of his principles of justice relies heavily on an analysis of rational self-interested choice in a special hypothetical situation that Rawls calls "the Original Position," and Rawls applies his principles of justice to political-economic institutions. Rawls sees the practical implications of his theory as of interest in their own right, and also as an important way of testing his theory. In his view, his theory is only acceptable if it has implications that his readers can, on reflection, endorse.

The contractualist element in Rawls' theory derives from the claim that just principles are those that would be chosen by rational actors in "the original position." One should suppose that one is choosing principles that would shape the basic institutions of one's society while behind a "veil of ignorance" that deprives one of knowledge of what role one would occupy in that society. This "veil of ignorance," which extends to one's social position, one's race, one's sex,[1] one's occupation, and even one's preferences, forces the choosers to be impartial. One cannot craft principles that will be to one's particular advantage because one has no idea of what one's particular advantage is. The veil of ignorance makes vivid the notion that arguments for principles of justice must not rely on such arbitrary factors. Because Rawls is in search of principles that rational individuals who are concerned to advance their interests would accept, he assumes that behind the veil of ignorance agents are neither altruistic nor envious. They are also ignorant of the range of possible social positions and of the relative size of different groups. Thus the decision situation is one of radical uncertainty, rather than calculable risk. This thought experiment is a method of determining what principles of justice should govern the basic institutions of society, which define people's rights and expectations. Rawls does not think that the veil of ignorance offers an appropriate method for deciding all ethical questions. If one is deciding, for example, whether P ought to pay Q some money, one needs to know what the rights and entitlements are. One cannot suppose that they are still to be determined.

Rawls' framework borrows heavily from one developed independently by John Harsanyi and by William Vickrey to defend utilitarianism. They argued that, faced with uncertainty about one's social role, the rational thing to do would be to maximize the expected value of one's utility, averaging over all the possibilities. The proper social principle would be to maximize the average utility of everyone in society. Rawls objects that the principle of average utility is too risky to choose in this special situation. Because the choice involved governs one's prospects over an entire life, there is grave risk if maximizing utility for the whole society involves sacrificing the interests of some particular group. Furthermore, the situation of

---

[1] In *A theory of justice*, Rawls takes individuals behind the veil of ignorance to be heads of households. Okin (1989) argues that, like most theorists of justice, Rawls ignores the problems of justice within the family and the problems of justice posed by children and other dependents. Okin's book is a sustained effort to develop a theory of just relations among men and women through reliance on a Rawlsian framework with explicit attention to gender issues

uncertainty as Rawls defines it makes the calculation of expected utility irresponsible if not virtually meaningless – with no knowledge of the range of possible social groups or of the relative size of groups, one is pushed toward approaches to choice under uncertainty that don't require probability calculations. Finally, it is puzzling how one could choose without knowing what one's preferences are.

Rawls argues that in the special circumstances of choosing principles of justice behind the veil of ignorance it is rational to minimize the costs of winding up at the bottom of the heap. More specifically, Rawls argues that for societies which are at least moderately well-off, rational choosers would seek first to safeguard their basic political and personal liberties and then they would judge basic social and economic institutions according to their tendency to promote the interests of those in the least well-off social group. No one would find their basic liberties threatened, and social and economic institutions would be designed to advance maximally the interests of the worst-off group. It is important to note that how "well-off" individuals are is to be judged not by the subjective standard of preference satisfaction but by the more objective notion of amounts of primary social goods, which individuals deprived of knowledge of their own view of the good will agree on as a standard for assessing basic institutions. (See chapter 6 above.)

In their full elaboration, Rawls' principles of justice are:

First, each person is to have an equal right to the most extensive basic liberty compatible with a similar liberty for others. (1971, p. 60)
[Second] Social and economic inequalities are to be arranged so that they are both (a) to the greatest benefit of the least advantaged and (b) attached to offices and positions open to all under conditions of fair equality of opportunity. (1971, p. 83)

In addition, Rawls specifies that the first principle is, for any society with enough resources to provide the basic liberties for all, lexically prior to the second. That is to say, basic political and civil liberties are never to be traded-off for economic advantage. Moreover, part (b) of the second principle is lexically prior to part (a) – the interests of the least well-off are not to be advanced at the sacrifice of the principle of equal opportunity. Rawls calls part (a) of the second principle "the difference principle."

The "priority of liberty," as the first principle is sometimes labeled, is not easy to capture in economic models, and the lexicographic ranking of this principle, which rejects the notion of trading-off liberty for other valued ends, is not the sort of thing economists find easy to swallow (but see Cooter 1989). Rawls' view is that after one attains a basic minimum of resources, further means to pursue one's goals are valueless unless one preserves the liberties that permit these goals to be effectively pursued. Not to secure the priority of liberty and thus to gamble liberties against resources betrays a failure to understand what it is to hold a conception of a good life.

Economists have also had doubts about the difference principle – that society should maximize the primary goods of the least advantaged – but they have been able to seize upon its formal interpretation as a "maximin" standard. If one simplifies and takes the difference principle as applying to welfare rather than primary goods, it implies that (subject to the first principle and part (b) of the second principle) society should maximize the well-being of the least well-off. This "maximin" rule is as simple as the familiar utilitarian rule "maximize average well-being," and there has been interesting work investigating implications of these two ideals (see, for example, Phelps 1973, Alexander 1974, and Musgrave 1974).

There are serious disadvantages in reinterpreting the difference principle in terms of utility. Doing so makes Rawls' references to "representative individuals" or, in other words, *groups*, puzzling, and it leads to a view of justice that, like utilitarianism, is strictly "patterned." On such a view, if anybody at the bottom could be made better off, then the social institutions are unjust. Rawls' view in contrast is that how well individuals fare does not depend only on their shares of social goods and the rules of social interaction, which are the subject of a theory of justice. A theory of justice that attempts to determine what justice demands as an outcome for each individual is not only unworkable, but it fails to recognize that outcomes also depend on individual choices. The application of his two principles determines a framework of rights and institutions that will insure maximal equal liberty and, insofar as is possible, fair equality of opportunity. If social and economic inequalities benefit the least well-off group, as they may if they encourage effort and risk-taking, then such inequalities will be permitted, but they will be arranged so that the life prospects of those in the worst-off group provide the highest level of primary goods possible. A good deal thus turns on how one defines the worst-off group, and Rawls does not defend any specific definition. He does, however, stipulate that the worst-off group consists of individuals who are not ill or handicapped, and he does not intend his theory of justice to address the moral problems raised by handicaps. Provided that the rights and institutions satisfy Rawls' principles, the results are just, regardless of their details. The assessment of individual outcomes involves "pure procedural justice," just like the assessment of the results of a lottery. Provided that the rules were followed, the results are automatically just because there is no other criterion by which to judge the justice of the outcomes.

In translating Rawls' difference principle into the view that justice involves maximizing the minimum utility level of individuals, economists may thus have missed what is of the greatest potential value in Rawls' theory of justice. Although redistributions may be justified by particular injustices, concerns about justice should not be conceived as fundamentally redistributive. Rawls' views should lead economists instead to think about the design of institutions that will minimize the need for redistributive efforts, and it should lead them to focus on the means out of which individuals construct their own goods rather than directly on satisfying preferences.

Rawls' contribution holds special interest for economists. As we have already indicated, the argument from behind the veil of ignorance makes effective use of notions of rational choice, decision-making under uncertainty, and maximization subject to constraints – all theoretical ideas with which economists are comfortable. His conception of individual distribution as a matter of pure procedural justice and his emphasis on primary goods suggest a new way to address problems of justice and a different set of units in which to talk about how groups are faring.

In addition, Rawls works out implications of his view both to address practical questions and to determine whether his principles yield results that, on reflection, informed observers find reasonable. Rawls investigates implications of his theory for the provision of public goods, the role of redistributive taxation, justice in saving and capital accumulation, the role of competition, and macroeconomic policy toward unemployment. Rawls also considers the issue of whether capitalism or socialism is more compatible with justice, and concludes that under the right circumstances either type of property arrangement can be just.

As one might expect from a theory that focuses on the least well-off group, the institutional implications of Rawls' theory are egalitarian. He favors equalizing educational opportunities for persons of similar capacities, and supports policies discouraging the accumulation of hereditary fortunes and blocking the influence of wealth on political decision. Rawls' ideal society would, however, rely only minimally on redistributive taxes and transfers as an equalizing measure. On grounds of efficiency, liberty, and opportunity, Rawls emphasizes efforts to equalize the starting points of members of successive generations in preference to redistributing unequal outcomes.

The final feature of Rawls' work that should be of interest to economists derives from his concern to investigate the "stability" of societies. Would a society that conformed to the principles of justice as fairness cause people to behave in such a way that those principles would continue to be upheld over time? The answer will depend on how psychological, sociological, and economic forces work themselves out over time. Will children raised under just institutions tend to embrace the principles of justice and regulate their lives properly by them when they become adults? Can institutions be created, compatible with the basic liberties, that will ensure that inequalities do not cumulate over generations so as to undermine the principles of justice over time? Rawls offers interesting answers to these questions, but the interest lies at least as much in the fact that Rawls frames the questions explicitly and highlights their importance for assessing theories of justice. Rawls' views on some of these issues have undergone significant modification, and in his book, *Political liberalism* (1993), he is less concerned to argue that his principles of justice are the correct implementation of the ideal of reciprocity and more concerned to defend his principles of justice as appropriate to an irreducibly pluralistic society in which little substantial agreement concerning what makes for a good life is possible.

Some major features of Rawls' work are more closely tied to his contractualist commitments than are others. In particular, one might find the Original Position framework helpful without being persuaded by the conclusion that Rawls' specific principles of justice would be chosen; conversely, the substantive principles may be appealing to people who would find justifications for them that don't depend on the Original Position argument more persuasive.

11.3 Justice as mutual advantage: David Gauthier

Theorists of justice as mutual advantage reject the features of the Rawlsian contractualist framework that limit the role of self-interest in contractarian reasoning. Thus David Gauthier, perhaps the most prominent of contemporary philosophers in this tradition, denies that agreements reached behind a veil of ignorance are rationally or morally binding. The challenge for a contractualist, in Gauthier's view, is to solve the problem Hobbes formulated: Why is it actually rational for a self-interested actor to conform his or her behavior to moral rules? According to Gauthier, one has to consider what would be the result of bargaining among expected utility maximizers with full common knowledge of everyone's capabilities, endowments, and preferences. Unlike Rawls' original position, where mutual ignorance of differences eliminates the possibility of conflicting interests, Gauthier's framework leads us to conceive of the contractual interaction as *bargaining*.

No actor in Gauthier's setting will agree to accept less than he could get in the absence of agreement. Those who are advantaged initially will emerge with advantages from the bargain. Gauthier proposes that, in the absence of means to make interpersonal utility comparisons, agents in this situation would agree to distribute the gains from cooperation in accordance with a principle of "minimax relative concession." The largest relative concession anyone has to make should be as small as possible. Let u_{max} be the maximum utility the agent can get. Let u be the utility of the bargain, and let u_{na} be the agent's utility at the non-agreement point. An agent's relative concession is then $(u_{max} - u)$ divided by $(u_{max} - u_{na})$. To define these ratios, the preferences of individuals must be represented by cardinal utility functions, but since a comparison of relative concessions is a comparison of ratios, not utilities, there is no need to make interpersonal utility comparisons. In the technical literature on bargaining theory, which we discuss in chapter 13, this is similar to the Kalai and Smorodinsky bargaining solution (see below, p. 192). In most circumstances, minimax relative concession coincides with equal relative concession. Minimax relative concession implies that those who are worse off without agreement will have to give up more to gain agreement. Gauthier argues that this principle would distribute the gains from social interaction fairly relative to the situation that would prevail in the absence of agreement. In Gauthier's view, this non-agreement point would reflect substantial inequalities, which are largely preserved in the just society (else it would not be in everyone's interest). Consequently, the scope for defending equality-promoting institutions and policies is substantially less than on Rawlsian or utilitarian views.

An important goal in developing theories of justice as mutual advantage is to show that a commitment to obey principles of justice is rational, even though rational actors are assumed to lack any independent desire to be just. Actors who are rational in this sense would not, for example, be moved by Scanlon's principle of grounding one's behavior on rules that could not be reasonably rejected by others. The reconciliation between morality and self-interest that mutual advantage theorists seek is hard to achieve, since the presence of rules of justice creates a classic prisoner's dilemma: even if you and I jointly benefit from the rules, I will do still better if you obey them and I allow myself to violate them when it suits me. Gauthier argues that it may be in my rational self-interest to cultivate the kind of character that will lead me to obey the rules of justice, even if having that kind of character sometimes robs me of opportunities to free-ride. It is crucial to this solution that other members of society are reasonably good at determining what kind of character I have, and are able to reward or punish me suitably in terms of their willingness to interact with me, depending on what they discern. The issue here – of when it may be in one's interest to cultivate dispositions that interfere with acting with explicitly self-interested motives – has received valuable treatment from economists (Akerlof 1983, Frank 1988).

11.4 Other contractualist views

James Buchanan and his colleagues argue that, as an empirical matter, self-interested agents who are concerned about "constitutional" choices – choices involved in setting the general rules of the game – face so many uncertainties that they might as well be behind a veil of ignorance. Since the gains from constitutional design may be very large, self-interested agents should be concerned about the rules of the game, and they have reason to step behind "the veil of uncertainty" (as Brennan and Buchanan [1985] style it). Even though the motivational assumptions in this constitutionalist view are more self-interested than in Rawls', the element of impartiality introduced by not knowing how alternatives will affect one's own situation provides a strong common element between the views.

In Buchanan's view, rational agents behind the veil of uncertainty will be more cautious about promoting equality through government action than Rawls' reasoning implies, because they will model both economic and political behavior as self-interested. Rawls is explicit in departing from this assumption: "ideal legislators do not vote their interests" (1971, p. 284). Brennan and Buchanan argue that agents behind the veil of uncertainty will disagree with Rawls partly on grounds of realism and partly on the Humean grounds that in designing constitutions "every man ought to be supposed a knave" (quoted in Brennan and Buchanan 1985, p. 59). One way of expressing this point is to say that the different assumptions Rawls and Buchanan make about people's psychology leads them to different conclusions about the relative stability of societies organized according to various principles of justice. Thus, even supposing that generous provision for the poor is desirable, it is not obvious that political institutions such as majoritarian democracy will produce such an outcome (Brennan and Buchanan 1985). Buchanan argues that individuals adopting a constitutional perspective would not want to leave redistribution to the discretion of self-interested politicians. If they favor measures to equalize resources, they would prefer to embed particular distributive rules, say a negative income tax financed by a flat rate tax, directly into the constitution. Such constitutional distributive rules (like the institutions mandated by Rawls' principles of justice) should not in fact be considered redistributive, since they would figure into the underlying definition of property rights (see also Buchanan 1975).

The general idea that moral principles or social norms can be usefully interpreted as the outcome of self-interested bargains – that is, the research program suggested by the notion of justice as mutual advantage – is receiving wide attention. This sort of contractualism makes heavy use of the tools of game theory (see chapter 13 below), and its findings may have both explanatory and normative force. In assessing the explorations of mutual advantage models, and in comparing their findings to contractualist work that emphasizes reciprocity or impartiality, it is important not to lose sight of the substantial difference in the starting points. What people would agree to if they were motivated as Scanlon assumes is a different matter from what self-interested people would agree to. Which approach is more fruitful depends on understandings about the nature and point of reasoning about justice, which are not themselves answered from within either of these standpoints.

11.5 Conclusion: social contract reasoning and economics

Problems of justice can be addressed from many different perspectives, and the general moral theories we have already discussed – libertarianism and utilitarianism – imply theories of justice. Libertarianism should appeal to economists because many economists share its devotion to the value of freedom. Utilitarianism should appeal to economists because they share its focus on individual well-being. Contractualist approaches may have a harder time getting a hearing. But there is, we contend, good reason why students of economics should take them seriously.

All forms of contractualist reasoning are concerned with rational agreement. In an earlier formulation, Rawls went so far as to say that his approach made the theory of justice a branch of the theory of rational choice. Most contract theorists are also concerned to draw conclusions that concern matters of great interest to normative economics: the justification of property rights, the legitimacy of redistribution, and so on. Finally, forms of contract theory reflect well worked-out and more or less comprehensive alternatives to "welfarist" theories of normative economics. At the same time, it is important for economists who rely on or contribute to work in contract theory to remember that the interpretation of particular bits of contractualist reasoning depends on philosophical understandings of the controversial reasons for adopting a contractualist point of view. The reawakening of interest in theories of the social contract has been an important stimulus to economists' interest in normative theory, and we hope that its influence will grow.

Suggestions for further reading

Historical texts on social contract are especially important for appreciating its purposes and significance. Landmark texts include Hobbes (1651), Locke (1690), Rousseau (1762), and Kant (1785).

The literature on Rawls is exceptionally large and rich. The anthology edited by Norman Daniels (1976) and the books by Wolff (1977), Barry (1973), Pogge (1989), and Kukathas and Pettit (1990) are good starting points. Rawls' economic framework was heavily influenced by James Meade's classic (1964).

As noted in the text, there has recently been an explosion of contractualist writing in the "mutual benefit" vein. Along with Gauthier and Buchanan, Kavka (1986) and Hampton (1986) have outlined general theories of justice that adopt this Hobbesian starting point. Schotter (1981), Sugden (1986), and Taylor (1987) consider the recurrent problems of coordination and conflict individuals face and the sorts of institutions and conventions they will come to accept to resolve them. Binmore (1994) begins a large-scale game-theoretic argument for something like Rawls' conclusions.

Part IV

Moral mathematics

At first glance morality and mathematics seem as unrelated as martyrdom and MTV. But it is possible to characterize moral notions formally and to prove theorems. Doing so does not banish all controversy or replace all verbal argument concerning moral matters, because the abstract mathematical characterizations of moral notions are themselves subject to dispute. Just as there are disagreements concerning the formal definitions of rationality, so there are controversies about formal definitions of moral notions.

Over the last half-century economists and decision theorists have made exciting progress not just in representing individual rationality, but also in characterizing features of human interactions. This work is linked to moral philosophy. Formal models of rationality and game-theoretic studies of incentives hold out the hope of superseding the ancient puzzles concerning the relations between morality, rationality, and self-interest discussed above in chapter 5. Concepts of "fair" or envy-free allocations, discussed in chapter 10, facilitate the articulation of egalitarianism. "Solution" concepts in game theory may enrich the contractarian perspective, discussed in chapter 11, that morality can be justified in terms of agreement. Theorems in social choice theory test the consistency of traditional principles concerning how social policies should respond to individual interests. We face an embarrassment of riches, and we can only comment on how a few of these developments link up with moral philosophy.

12 Social choice theory

As we saw in chapter 7, contemporary "Paretian" welfare economics is of surprisingly little help in evaluating economic institutions and outcomes. Economists espouse "the Pareto principle" (that, other things being equal, A is better than B if somebody prefers A to B and nobody prefers B to A), but it's a rare day when there's this sort of unanimity. Some economists would say that A is better than B when A is only a *potential* Pareto improvement, but this view is dubious. Economists need a better basis for evaluating economic outcomes and institutions. To guide policy, economists need to have something to say when Pareto improvements cannot be made.

12.1 The social welfare function and Arrow's theorem

Social choice theory evolved out of an effort to construct better tools for evaluation. Following Bergson (1938) and Samuelson (1947), let us call any ranking of social states a "social welfare function." Normative principles can be regarded as constraints on social welfare functions. For example, resource egalitarianism rules out social welfare functions unless they favor egalitarian resource distributions. Nazi principles of "racial purity" narrow the set of acceptable social welfare functions to those that give a low ranking to states of affairs in which Jews prosper. Hedonistic utilitarianism picks out social welfare functions that rank states of affairs in terms of total happiness.

The point of discussing social welfare functions is to provide a framework to explore normative principles. Although the framework could in principle be applied to a very broad range of evaluative principles, including highly non-individualistic ones, in practice economists have focused on social welfare functions whose arguments are individual preferences. The Pareto principle, for example, can be characterized in social welfare function terms as picking out those social welfare functions that rank R over S if somebody prefers R to S and nobody prefers S to R. "Welfarism" limits the inputs to social welfare functions to facts about the extent to which individual preferences are satisfied. The formal characterization of Paretian social welfare functions has helped to establish the basic theorems of welfare economics and to clarify the normative claims underpinning cost-benefit analysis (see chapters 4 and 7 above).

In the early days of investigating social welfare functions, it was hoped that thinking in terms of social welfare functions could assist economists to identify additional plausible normative principles that, like the Pareto principle, relate individual and social welfare. If these principles had precise mathematical formulations, then economists would be able to deduce their precise implications. In this way, economists could carry out a sort of moral mathematics. Much of the work in social choice theory has not, however, taken this form because the basic perspective is quite limited, and because of some surprising results of early efforts to carry out such moral mathematics. One problem with the framework is that it is relentlessly consequentialist. All that matters are outcomes, states of the world. Procedural matters such as fairness or due process apparently count only instrumentally. To extend the framework to embed procedures in the descriptions of states of affairs makes it unappealingly complex and indeterminate.

A more specific obstacle to development of the social welfare function framework derives from a remarkable theorem proved by Kenneth Arrow in 1951. Rather than arguing for strong substantive ethical principles, as moral philosophers have, Arrow put forward a set of apparently weak "procedural" principles that constrain acceptable relationships between individual values and social values. Arrow's aim was to identify a set of principles which would be consistent with the usual normative standpoint of economists and which would have widespread ethical appeal in their own right. What Arrow discovered, however, was that in trying to identify a relatively short list of seemingly innocuous constraints, rather than whittling down the acceptable social welfare functions to a more manageable set, he whittled it down to nothing! Arrow proved that no social welfare function could meet the conditions for acceptability he laid down.

What are the conditions Arrow imposed (see Arrow 1967)? First, there is a weak version of the Pareto principle:

(P) If everybody prefers A to B, then A is better than B (weak Pareto).

As we noted before in section 7.2, the Pareto principle is not as uncontroversial as it may appear, but it is obviously plausible and would certainly appeal to economists.

A second principle, which seems to us genuinely uncontroversial, is the following:

(D) Whether A is better than B should not depend on the preferences of a single individual only, regardless of what everybody else prefers (non-dictatorship).

Speaking of dictatorship suggests issues about how to make social choices rather than issues about how to evaluate alternatives, and, as we shall see below, all of these conditions can be interpreted as constraints on decision-making methods rather than as determining the value of alternatives. But on either interpretation, it seems unobjectionable to stipulate that evaluations of all alternatives should not depend on a single person's preferences only.

The third condition is fundamental:

(I) Whether A is better than B should depend on how individuals rank A and B and on nothing else (independence of irrelevant alternatives).

This principle gets its name because it says that the comparison of A and B should not depend on the presence or absence of other "irrelevant" alternatives. But the name is misleading. This version of the principle says that the goodness of alternatives depends on how the alternatives stand in individual preference rankings, and that the goodness of alternatives depends on nothing else. (I) is not as intuitively appealing as the Pareto principle, because it is hard to believe that all other things besides preference rankings are irrelevant to the social evaluation of A compared to B. In actual political systems the choice between A and B may depend on precedent and constitutional provision, the extent to which A and B serve *needs*, or on the intensity of preferences. All of these factors are ruled out by (I). Like some leading social choice theorists, such as Amartya Sen, we believe that (I) is unacceptable.

(I) is more attractive to economists, because they are accustomed to focusing exclusively on welfare interpreted as the satisfaction of ordinal preferences. Furthermore, in its defense, one might argue that (I) should be interpreted as a principle for comparing outcomes *other things being equal*, not as a principle for making overall comparisons. One can interpret (I) as saying only how one should assess outcomes along one important moral dimension, not as denying that there are other important moral dimensions.

Arrow also includes two formal principles that constrain social welfare functions:

(U) No matter what the preferences of individuals may be, the social welfare function must always be able to rank alternatives (universal domain).

(CR) The social ranking of alternatives must be complete and transitive (collective rationality).

These two conditions together are often called "collective rationality." (CR) is of course analogous to the completeness and transitivity of individual preferences. Transitivity of social rankings seems as compelling as transitivity of individual preferences, while completeness of social rankings seems as questionable as completeness of individual preferences – at least if the social welfare function is interpreted as a way of *evaluating* alternatives. The rationale behind the universal domain condition is that the method of evaluating social alternatives should not collapse when there are strange arrays of individual preferences. If the social welfare function is interpreted as a method of collective decision-making rather than as a means of evaluating alternatives, then the universal domain condition seems obvious: a method of decision-making must have some output or other.

Arrow proved that attempting to satisfy these five conditions leads to a contradiction. The only complete and transitive social welfare function that satisfies the Pareto principle and independence of irrelevant alternatives for all profiles of individual preferences is the dictatorial one where the evaluation of alternatives matches the preferences of a single individual! However intuitively appealing these five conditions might appear to be, one cannot consistently endorse them all. At least one of them has to be abandoned. Mathematics here leads morality by the hand and gives it a rude shaking. Regardless of the force of moral intuition or the strength of ethical conviction, these five conditions are not mutually consistent, and they cannot all be right.

12.2 Social choice theory after Arrow

Arrow's staggering theorem has shaped the field of social choice theory, and it has had a major impact on contemporary moral philosophy as well as on the way economists conceive of normative problems. The interpretation of theorems in social choice and even the definition of the subject remain, however, elusive and controversial. Sen (1986) suggests that social choice theory can be defined either by its approaches or by its subject matter. Sen describes its subject matter as follows: "Social choice problems arise in aggregating the interests, or preferences, or judgments, or views, of different persons (or groups) in a particular society" (1986, p. 214). Since aggregating interests and resolving conflicts is central to moral philosophy, a large part of the subject matter of social choice theory *is* moral philosophy.

The methods of social choice theory are distinctively formal and axiomatic. Works in social choice theory are devoted to proving theorems. Although one might regard social choice theory, as Sen suggests, as anything employing its approach *or* concerned with its subject matter, what people think of as social choice theory is in fact the combination of both – that is, the proof and interpretation of theorems concerning the social aggregation of preferences, judgments, and interests. The relevance of social choice theorems to morality depends on exactly *what* is being aggregated, and *for what purpose*.

Sen has helpfully distinguished two broad purposes of aggregation, namely *deciding* and *evaluating*. For example, one might want an aggregation mechanism (1) to decide which movie a group will see and (2) to determine which, among a set of movies the group had seen, was best. The criteria for judging choice mechanisms might be very different from the criteria for judging evaluation methods. Decision-making and evaluating are related, but they are not the same task. The best decision rule is not necessarily to choose the best alternative according to the given evaluative standard. There can be more than one evaluative standard, and decision rules may have procedural virtues. For example, majority rule is more attractive as a decision-making method than as a way of making aesthetic judgments. Since a ranking of x and y cannot express the judgment that x is better than y unless it is transitive, it seems more imperative for social evaluations than for social decisions to be transitive. On the other hand, it is not obvious that a social evaluation has to respect the preferences or evaluations of individuals, so the Pareto principle is more compelling for social decisions than for evaluations (see Broome 1989).

As the movie example suggests, *what* is being aggregated also differs among cases. Sen distinguishes among "interests, preferences, judgments, and views" as things we might want to "add up." This list could be extended to other items, including capabilities, resource endowments, and so on. Any of these properties of individuals might be aggregated either for purposes of social decision-making or evaluation. Arrow's theorem and the conditions specified above are typical of the social choice literature in treating the items to be aggregated as preferences, though as a formal structure, Arrow's theorem applies to other possible inputs to social decision-making.

As illustrated in figure 12.1, we thus have at least four possible interpretations of work relating individual preferences or judgments to social decisions or evaluations. A social welfare function of type 1 – that is, one that attempts to provide a social evaluation based on profiles of individual welfare – is a branch of moral philosophy, and its theorems can reveal to moral philosophers ambiguities or hidden implications of accepted principles. A simple illustration of an interest-aggregation mechanism based on a normative principle – of a type 1 theory – is a utilitarian social welfare function, which defines the socially best outcome as that which

	Purposes	
	----------	-------------
Inputs	Evaluation	Decision-making
Preferences	**Type 1** preference-based evaluation	**Type 2** preference-driven decision-making
Judgments	**Type 3** judgment-based evaluation	**Type 4** judgment-driven decision-making

Figure 12.1 Interpretations of social choice theories

maximizes the sum of individual utilities (where the appropriate measure of individual utility may differ among different versions of utilitarianism). It is important to be clear on the point that what is involved in classical utilitarianism is *not* an attempt to aggregate individual normative *judgments* about what is socially best into a social judgment. Utilitarianism has not been espoused as a type 3 theory. Utilitarians instead judge that the best state is that which maximizes aggregate utility, and they reject all conflicting judgments. There may thus be tensions within utilitarianism to the extent that people's happiness and preference satisfaction depend upon their commitment to non-utilitarian moral principles. Notice, by the way, that a utilitarian social welfare function satisfies four of the five conditions that give rise to Arrow's theorem (the Pareto principle, non-dictatorship, universal domain, and collective rationality). It violates independence of irrelevant alternatives since utilitarian social evaluations depend on interpersonal comparisons, rather than merely on preference rankings.

12.3 Social choice theory and moral philosophy

Social choice theorems raise moral questions. The most obvious concern the axioms. Do they express plausible normative principles? But one may also ask questions about subtler features of a formal set-up. For example, treating the relationship between profiles of individual preferences and a specific social choice as literally a *function* implies the uniqueness of social choice, which may be doubted. Furthermore, one can question whether a particular aggregation mechanism as a whole is morally justifiable, even when one cannot pinpoint the source of one's objections. For example, one may object to a process for aggregating interests for purposes of decision-making (a type 2 theory) as *unfair*, perhaps because of the way it responds to minority interests. Or one may object to a process for aggregating individual normative judgments into a collective judgment (a type 3 theory) because it is *unwise*, in that it fails to respond to the quality of the arguments supporting a particular judgment. Finally, one may ask moral questions about the interests, preferences, and judgments upon which the collective decisions or evaluations depend. We reviewed earlier in chapter 6 the likelihood that individual preferences may need to be "laundered" before they should be granted moral weight, and similar processes might be applied on moral grounds to interests, views, or judgments. One might, for example, want to make sure that the informational basis of these items was adequate.

If the axioms and formal set-up pass preliminary scrutiny, one can then argue from the results of social choice theory to moral conclusions. Proofs are after all valid arguments, and if one accepts the axioms, then one must accept the conclusions. Axiomatic arguments of this kind have been proposed for ethical conclusions as different as utilitarianism, a utility analogue of Rawls' difference principle, and welfare egalitarianism (Roemer 1988). For example, in addition to making a veil-of-ignorance argument for utilitarianism, John Harsanyi demonstrates that if (1) personal and moral preferences satisfy the axioms of expected utility theory and (2) the Pareto principle is satisfied, then the social value of an alternative is a linear function of individual utilities (1955). Harsanyi interprets this theorem as an argument for utilitarianism. Others, such as Amartya Sen (1976b) and John Weymark (1991), have questioned this interpretation of the result on the grounds that Harsanyi has not shown why the cardinal representation of individual and social preferences is the right one to use for ethical comparisons.

Although a good deal of social choice theory looks as if it consisted of formal arguments for moral conclusions, we doubt that this is the best way to appreciate this work. Logically valid arguments only show that one cannot both accept all their premises and reject any of their conclusions. If one is convinced of the correctness of their premises, valid arguments can persuade one to accept their conclusions, but if one is convinced of the incorrectness of the conclusions, then it is equally true that one will have reason to doubt the premises. In general, our confidence in the axioms will derive both from how reasonable they seem to be in their own right and from how reasonable are the conclusions they entail. If the axioms entail a disturbing moral conclusion, we will be motivated to scrutinize them more closely, as well as to reflect on whether our negative reaction is justified.

We suspect that the most important role of theorems in social choice theory has been to reveal the ambiguities and difficulties in apparently plausible moral principles. These ambiguities and difficulties have been highlighted most conclusively by demonstrations that sets of plausible principles may be logically inconsistent. Arrow's theorem is the most famous of these demonstrations. But it is not easy to say exactly what moral lessons should be drawn, because the theorem can be read in at least the four different ways detailed above (see figure 12.1), depending on how the individual *rankings* are interpreted and on whether the point is to evaluate or to choose. In our formulation of the theorem, we supposed that the rankings specify individual preferences, and that the point of the aggregation was evaluation. On this preference-based evaluation reading, Arrow demonstrates that individual welfare (as ordinal preference satisfaction) cannot provide an acceptable basis for evaluating alternatives. If one sticks to the interpretation of individual rankings as preferences but regards the social welfare function as a decision-making method, then one can read Arrow's theorem as showing that there is no acceptable method for reconciling conflicts among individual interests. But as Sen has observed, these results may not be terribly disturbing, since individual ordinal rankings provide little information concerning the relative importance of different interests. If interpersonal comparisons of preference intensity or non-preference data (say, on comparative income or resource levels) are permitted, the impossibility result may no longer hold (Sen 1970a, chs. 7, 8).

One might instead interpret the individual rankings as (moral) *judgments* about what is best for society to do. If the point of the aggegation is evaluation, then Arrow's theorem tells us that no acceptable scheme for aggregating individual moral judgments will produce a consistent evaluation. If the point of the aggregation is social decision-making, then Arrow's theorem implies that no rational decision-making method respects individual moral judgments. It does not seem appropriate to avoid these impossibility results by comparing the intensity with which individuals hold their views of which alternatives are best for the society. Yet one can take some of the sting out of the impossibility results when one remembers that one of Arrows's conditions – universal domain – requires that an aggregation scheme work for all possible preference profiles. The Arrow conditions do not allow any sets of moral rankings to be ruled out as improper, and they do not allow for any modification of individual moral views in response to discussion. When constraints are imposed on preference profiles, the impossibility results may no longer hold (though it takes great optimism about the power of reason to be confident that they won't). Arrow's theorem need not, then, undercut practices such as weighing the importance of competing interests or deliberating over the persuasiveness of arguments (and Arrow has never suggested otherwise).

12.4 The paradox of the Paretian liberal

Amartya Sen has established a paradoxical result that arguably has even more bearing on moral issues than Arrow's impossibility result. Sen demonstrates a conflict between "liberalism" and the Pareto principle.

One crucial element in liberalism is the view that individuals should have a "private sphere" in which they can do as they please without social constraint. However unwise it may be not to brush one's teeth, the decision should be up to the individual. It is difficult to translate this aspect of liberalism fully into the formalism of social choice theory, but Sen formulates a weak necessary condition, which he calls "minimal liberalism." Minimal liberalism states that there must be at least two individuals, each of whom is "decisive" over a pair of alternatives. Minimal liberalism would be satisfied if, for example, (1) Hausman got to decide between two alternatives that differed only in regard to whether Hausman brushed his teeth, (2) McPherson were similarly decisive over a single pair of alternatives that differed only with respect to whether McPherson brushed his teeth, and (3) no one else were decisive over any other pairs. So minimal liberalism is indeed minimal!

Minimal liberalism and the Pareto principle are not *by themselves* inconsistent. For example, if Hausman is indifferent about whether McPherson brushes his teeth and McPherson is indifferent about whether Hausman brushes his teeth, then (in a two-person society) both minimal liberalism and the Pareto principle will favor states of affairs in which Hausman and McPherson brush their teeth whenever they want to. Only certain patterns of preferences lead to a conflict. Strictly speaking, Sen demonstrated that one cannot consistently espouse (1) the Pareto principle, (2) minimal liberalism, (3) unrestricted domain, and (4) a variant of collective rationality (Sen 1970b).

Sen's motivating example involves two individuals, "Lewd" and "Prude" and a copy of D. H. Lawrence's novel, *Lady Chatterley's lover*. Lewd most prefers that both he and Prude read *Lady Chatterley's lover*. If only one should read it, however, Lewd wishes it to be his prudish friend, since it would loosen him up. Prude would most prefer the book not be read at all, but would rather read it himself than further his friend's corruption. So their preferences are as in figure 12.2

Given minimal liberalism, Lewd should be decisive between either (b,p) or (l,n) and Prude should be decisive between either (n,p) or (l,b). Suppose Lewd is decisive over (b,p) and Prude is decisive over (l,b). Since Lewd is decisive between b and p and prefers b to p, b should be socially preferred to p. Since Prude is decisive between l and b and prefers l to b, l should be socially preferred to b. So if social choice respects minimal liberalism, the

Lewd		Prude	
(*b*)	both read the book	(*n*)	neither reads the book
(*p*)	only Prude reads it	(*p*)	only Prude reads it
(*l*)	only Lewd reads it	(*l*)	only Lewd read it
(*n*)	neither reads it	(*b*)	both read it

Figure 12.2 Lewd's and Prude's preferences

outcome should be *l* – that only Lewd reads the book. But both prefer *p* – that Prude read the book – to *l*, and the Pareto principle consequently implies that *p* should be socially preferred to *l*. If one respects both minimal liberalism and the Pareto principle, then there is a cycle, and collective rationality is violated.

Allan Gibbard pointed out that if one strengthens Sen's minimal liberty condition to permit two individuals to be decisive over *all* pairs of alternatives that only differ with respect to purely personal matters, then certain combinations of preferences will rule out the possibility of any social choice, regardless of questions of Pareto optimality. In Gibbard's example of the non-conformist and Mrs. Grundy (1974, p. 389), the non-conformist wants his bedroom walls to be a different color from Mrs. Grundy's, while she wants her bedroom walls to be the same color as the non-conformist's. If each is decisive over social alternatives that differ only with regard to the color of his or her bedroom walls, every possible outcome will be vetoed by somebody.

Sen's example and his theorem are mainly concerned with personal liberty over "private" matters (Riley 1989, 1990). One essential feature that generates the paradox is the fact that people are assumed to have preferences over outcomes that properly – according to the liberty principle – belong in someone else's "private sphere." Indeed, Julian Blau (1975) shows that Sen's paradox does not arise in the two-person case unless at least one person has "meddlesome" preferences in a technically defined sense. The Pareto principle, as applied in this context, treats these preferences on a par with personally oriented ones.

Work by Gibbard (1974), Nozick (1974), Gärdenfors (1981), and Sugden (1985) suggests the possibility that the paradox arises from a misconstrual of rights. To take rights as implying decisiveness points to the conclusion that Prude's and Lewd's rights must be violated if Prude reads *Lady Chatterley's lover* and Lewd does not. For Lewd is decisive between *p* and *b* and prefers *b*. But there is no violation of their rights if they voluntarily reach an agreement whereby Prude promises to read the book and Lewd promises not to read it. In that case the decision whether to read the book or not would still be up to each of the individuals. So Prude and Lewd can improve on the suboptimal outcome where only Lewd reads the book. In the view of Sen's critics, there appears to be a conflict between rights and the Pareto principle only because rights have been mischaracterized in terms of "decisiveness." Rights should instead be modeled as sets of strategies in suitable "game forms." What this means, roughly, is that an individual has a right to read or not to read a book if the choice is up to the individual.

This game-form "dissolution" of the paradox faces two serious problems. First, as Riley has shown (1989; see also Basu 1984), in games corresponding to the social choice problems in which there is a clash between rights and Pareto optimality, the Pareto optimal outcomes will not be "Nash equilibria" (see p. 188 below). Each agent has an incentive unilaterally to break his or her promise. So Lewd's and Prude's promises would give rise to enforcement problems, and enforcing them would require illiberal interference in the private affairs of individuals. As Sen notes, it is thus questionable whether such contracts or their enforcement are morally desirable. Second, as Sen (1992b) argues, the game-form interpretation of rights seems too weak. On the game-form interpretation of rights, Hausman has the right not to brush his teeth even if his dentist will shoot him if he doesn't. Sen argues that it is hard to see how any system of rights that provided genuine protection to individual liberty could fail to satisfy his minimal liberty condition – to make at least two individuals decisive over a single separate pair of social alternatives. So the paradox is real. In Sen's view, its moral is that normative social policy cannot be based only on preferences.

One may try to resolve the liberal paradox through relaxing the Pareto principle. Why should preferences regarding other people's private activities be accorded the same moral importance as those regarding one's own activities or public matters? Indeed, acknowledgment of a private sphere of activity for a person creates a presumption that nosy preferences should receive less weight. Other moral arguments have been offered for discounting other-regarding preferences in making public decisions (Dworkin 1977, ch. 12). Sen's paradox underscores the importance of permitting other things besides preferences to count. In particular, one may want to examine the *reasons* behind preferences in deciding on the role they should play in social decisions and moral judgments – a point we have noted elsewhere in this book.

12.5 Non-welfarist social choice theory

Before concluding this brief discussion of social choice theory, we would like to give one example of work in social choice theory that is not concerned with aggregating preferences or judgments. John Roemer (1988, pp. 160–72) offers a plausible set of axioms that together imply equality of welfare. Roemer invites us to consider the distributional principles that should govern a hypothetical economic environment in which there is a single output (corn), which is produced and consumed by two individuals, Able and Infirm, who have the same preferences for bundles of corn and labor, but very different skills. Able can produce much more corn per hour of labor than can Infirm. If egalitarians want to compensate Infirm yet remain fair to Able, what overall egalitarian principle should they follow? Just as economists in their attempts to define a social welfare function sought conditions relating individual and social welfare, so Roemer proposes moral principles governing the allocation of corn to Able and Infirm. His conditions are the following:

1. (Pareto optimality) The corn allocation should be Pareto optimal.
2. (Land monotonicity) If the amount of land increases, neither individual should be made worse off.
3. (Technological monotonicity) If it becomes possible to produce more corn with the same inputs of land and labor, neither individual should be made worse off.
4. (Limited self-ownership) Able should not be worse off than Infirm.
5. (Protection of Infirm) Infirm should be at least as well-off as he or she would be if Able had no more skills than Infirm has.

These moral principles seem attractive. Greater productivity should not harm either individual. Able should not do worse than Infirm. Infirm should not lose in absolute terms from Able's greater skills. And the allocation of corn should be Pareto optimal. Yet Roemer proves that *the only method of allocating corn that satisfies these five rules is to equalize Able's and Infirm's utility*! The weak egalitarianism that makes rules such as protection of Infirm or the monotonicity conditions attractive, when combined with limited self-ownership and the Pareto principle, implies an incredibly strong egalitarian conclusion. One reaction would be to go back to chapter 10 and rethink the arguments against equalizing welfare. Perhaps the criticisms described there were premature, and equalizing welfare is after all an appropriate ideal. Alternatively, one can reconsider Roemer's rules and their role in the proof of his theorem.

The point of discussing this example is not to reopen the discussion of egalitarianism. Instead our object has been to show how the techniques of social choice theory can be employed with different inputs and for different purposes. Although Roemer's principles are concerned in part with preferences, the issue here is not aggregating preferences, and allocations are supposed to depend on facts about technology, resources, and skills as well as on preferences. The techniques of social choice theory may apply to many kinds of moral issues.

12.6 Conclusions

What do examples such as Arrow's impossibility theorem, Sen's paradox, Roemer's surprising demonstration, and other proofs of moral systems from sets of axioms tell us about the fruitfulness of social choice theory in illuminating moral issues? Its typical subject matter – especially the problem of assembling individual judgments or interests into social evaluations – is of undeniable moral importance. But we are ambivalent about the value of its axiomatic approach.

We are not ambivalent about the value of precision and rigor. There is no doubt that the formal approach can lead to important clarifications and can stimulate a new awareness of the depth of problems – as the literature on the liberal paradox shows. At the same time, the abstractness of these methods has pitfalls. To quote Sen: "Arrow was undoubtedly right in saying that 'one of the great advantages of abstract postulational methods is the fact that the same system may be given several different interpretations, permitting a considerable saving of time' (Arrow 1951, p. 87). But *that* probably is *also* one of the great disadvantages of these methods" (Sen 1977b, p. 190). Considerable confusion has been generated, particularly in discussions of Arrow's theorem, by a failure to distinguish among alternative interpretations of the *objects* being aggregated and the *purposes* of aggregation.

It is difficult to spend much time with the social choice literature without becoming aware of the disparity between the large amount of attention lavished on the derivation of theorems and the small amount devoted to their interpretation. Unless guided by ethical sophistication, social choice theory can degenerate into empty formal exercises. But it would be unfair to single out economists for blame. Moral philosophers ought to be more involved with this work. If formalizations of plausible moral principles lead to inconsistencies or to unacceptable conclusions, then philosophers and economists need to understand what has gone wrong. It may be that the formalizations fail to express the informal principles they attempted to restate, or it may be that there are ambiguities or problems within those principles themselves. Only careful interpretation of both the informal moral principles and their formal restatements enables one to appreciate the significance of the particular theorem. Social choice theorists have left lots of philosophical work to be done!

Suggestions for further reading

One of the best general introductions to social choice theory is still Sen (1970a). Arrow's theorem was first presented in Arrow (1951), a classic.

For an interesting book-length philosophical discussion see MacKay (1980). A range of critical and constructive essays on social choice is presented in Elster and Hylland (1986).

Sen first presented his paradox in 1970. For some of the major discussions, see Sen (1976a, 1983, 1986, 1992b), Gibbard (1974), Nozick (1974), Gärdenfors (1981), Riley (1989, 1990), and Gaertner *et al.* (1992).

For axiomatic arguments for utilitarianism, see Fleming (1952), Harsanyi (1955), and Vickrey (1945, 1960). A reinterpreted and spruced up contemporary version of something like Harsanyi's argument can be found in Broome (1991b). Harsanyi's interpretation of his theorem as an argument for utilitarianism is challenged in Sen (1976b) and Weymark (1991).

For axiomatic arguments for a utility analogue to Rawls' difference principle, see Strasnick (1976), d'Aspremont and Gevers (1977), and Hammond (1976).

13 Game theory

Game theory arose as an attempt to understand strategic interactions among individuals, and its main applications still lie in this domain. But game theory is less wedded to a particular set of questions than is social choice theory, and it has applications to such disparate phenomena as computer programming and biological evolution. Game theory might be regarded as a branch of mathematics rather than as specifically a theory of interactive decision-making. In this chapter, however, we will focus exclusively on applications of game theory to strategic interactions among individuals. An interaction among individuals is strategic if the payoffs of some individuals depend on the choices of others.

13.1 What is a game?

Game theory represents strategic interactions in two main ways. The first is called the "extensive form" of a game. Consider the following simple example. An American quarter is flipped and both J and K observe whether it comes up heads or tails. J conceals the coin in one of her hands, and K then taps one of J's hands. If the coin landed heads and K taps the hand with the coin, then K gets to keep it. If the coin landed tails and K taps the hand that is empty, then K again gets it. Otherwise J gets the coin. Figure 13.1 is an extensive form represention of this game.

An extensive form representation of a game is a sideways "tree" beginning with a single "node" on the left and ending on the right with a set of nodes labeled with the payoffs to the players. The first number is J's payoff, and the second is K's. For the sake of simplicity, the payoffs are given here in dollars, but they are usually specified in units of utility, which may or may not be interpersonally comparable. Each node that determines the path of play is either a chance node (which we indicated with a square) or is labeled with the initial of the decision-maker and a number indicating the information available at that decision node. In this example, information state "1" contains the information that the coin landed heads, while

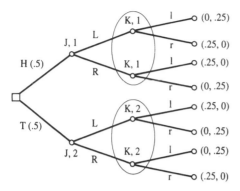

Figure 13.1 An extensive form of a game

information state "2" contains the information that the coin landed tails. Dotted lines are drawn around the two nodes labeled "*K*,1" and the two nodes labeled "*K*,2" because *K* cannot tell which of the *K*,1 nodes he is at, and he cannot tell which of the *K*,2 nodes he is at. The dotted lines thus surround a single information state. Each branch in the tree is labeled with the action taken at the previous decision node or with the outcome of a chance node. The outcomes of a chance node are mutually exclusive and exhaustive, so that their probabilities add up to one. In this example each node has two branches emerging from it, but this is only a peculiarity of the particular example.

The games with which we will be concerned involve players who are rational and intelligent, who have perfect recall of earlier moves in the game, and who possess "common knowledge" of the extensive form of the game and of their common rationality, intelligence, and memories. Game theorists usually take rationality to be expected utility maximizing. The players are "intelligent" in the sense that they can figure out anything about the game that the game theorist can. The players possess common knowledge in the sense that they all know the extensive form and that they are rational, intelligent, and have perfect memories, and they all know that the others know this and that the others know that they know this and so forth.

A player's strategy consists of the choices he or she makes. A strategy is complete: it records what choice the player will make at every possible decision point to which the game can lead. Note also that a player's strategy may have random elements: the choice a player makes at a given node may be chosen to depend on the result of a random process. The outcome of a game depends on the strategies of the players and on what happens at chance nodes. One can represent a game more compactly in "strategic" or

K J	lh, lt	lh, rt	rh, lt	rh, rt
Lh, Lt	(.125, .125)	(0, .25)	(.25, 0)	(.125, .125)
Lh, Rt	(0, .25)	(.125, .125)	(.125, .125)	(.25, 0)
Rh, Lt	(.25, 0)	(.125, .125)	(.125, .125)	(0, .25)
Rh, Rt	(.125, .125)	(.25, 0)	(0, .25)	(.125, .125)

Figure 13.2 A strategic form of a game

"normal" form by listing the strategies and their joint outcomes. For example, figure 13.2 represents the above game in strategic form, where the first number again states J's payoff and the second K's. "Lh,Lt" here is J's strategy of putting the coin in her left hand however it lands. "Lh,Rt" is J's strategy of putting the coin in her left hand if it lands heads and in her right hand if it lands tails, and so forth. "lh,lt" is K's strategy of tapping J's left hand regardless of how the coin lands. "lh,rt" is K's strategy of tapping J's left hand if the coin lands heads and of tapping J's right hand if the coin lands tails, and so forth. The numbers are calculated as follows. Suppose J plays "Lh,Lt" and K plays "lh,lt," then if the coin lands heads K wins and if the coin lands tails J wins. Since the probability of the coin landing heads or tails is one half, both J's and K's expected payoffs are one half of a quarter or $0.125. If, on the other hand, J plays Lh,Rt and K plays "lh,lt" then K wins the coin regardless of whether it comes up heads or tails, and J loses regardless.

The strategic form contains all information concerning possible strategies and their payoffs, but it is silent about the order of play. Game theorists are concerned with the "solution" to different kinds of games. That is, they seek to determine what are the best strategies for players to employ and consequently what the outcomes of games for rational and intelligent players will be.

13.2 Moral philosophy and some simple games

Much of game theory is not concerned with moral questions, and moral philosophy bears less directly on many games than on social choice theorems. But the subject matter of the game theory with which we are

K J	A	B
A	3, 3	0, 4
B	4, 0	2, 2

Figure 13.3 The prisoner's dilemma

concerned – problems of human interactions – is also the subject matter of much of ethics, and the problems faced by players are often moral problems. So game theory and moral philosophy have a good deal to do with one another.

Human flourishing requires social cooperation but, as philosophers have long recognized, social cooperation is problematic. In Hobbes' state of nature, where there is little cooperation, "the life of man [is] solitary, poor, nasty, brutish, and short" (1651, p. 107). The theory of games is particularly relevant to moral philosophy in its revelation of the sorts of interaction problems with which moral principles have to deal. For example, Russell Hardin (1988) argues that attention to strategic interactions complicates both applications and criticisms of utilitarianism. A sophisticated utilitarianism that recognizes these factors may be able to defend rights assignments as devices to simplify strategic interactions and to avoid suboptimal outcomes. Kantian moral philosophy may similarly profit from game-theoretic analyses of the consistency of everyone following the same rule (Elster 1989a, Schelling 1978).

Problems of social cooperation (or social cooperation "games") are often complicated and it can be enlightening to think about recurring patterns. Consider a game in which the two players J and K each have a choice of two actions, A and B. The normal form representation of the game is depicted in figure 13.3. The numbers represent J's and K's *utilities* (so 4 is best and 0 worst). In the game in figure 13.3, J and K both have "dominant" strategies: to play B. No matter what K does, J does better playing B, and no matter what J does, K does better playing B. Yet the result seems paradoxical, for if there were some way for J and K to cooperate and to play A, both would be better off.

The game in figure 13.3 is called "the prisoner's dilemma" because of a story that goes with it. J and K are two prisoners, A is the action of not-confessing, and B is confessing. The district attorney offers each separately the choice between confessing and not-confessing. The best outcome for J occurs if J confesses and K does not. Second best is if both refuse to confess. Third best is if both confess. Worst for J is if K confesses and J does not. So each pursuing his/her own interests winds up confessing. Rational self-interest leads to a suboptimal outcome.

Prisoner's dilemmas vividly represent problems of social cooperation, free-riding, and public-goods provision. Individuals deciding whether to contribute to the production of a public good seem like players in an n-person prisoner's dilemma game. "Free-riding" – that is, enjoying the public good but not contributing to its provision – is best of all. Second best is enjoying the public good and contributing one's share. Third best is doing without the public good. Worst is having others free-ride on one's contribution. Whether public-goods provision is best modeled as a prisoner's dilemma is, however, controversial (Hampton 1987). There are two main grounds for doubt. First, doing without the public good may be worse than having others free-ride on one's contribution, in which case one has a game of "chicken" rather than a prisoner's dilemma (see figure 13.4d). Second, problems involving public-goods provision arise in a context of continuing social interactions, and it may be misleading to model them as "one-shot" or "single-play" games. The "super-game" consisting of a sequence of moves that by themselves would be prisoner's dilemmas does not itself have a prisoner's dilemma structure.

Prisoner's dilemmas can also model problems of moral cooperation (Parfit 1979). For example, each mother trying to save her own child from drowning in a beach accident may do less well than all would do if they cooperated in saving all the children. The collectively self-defeating character of moral commitments that are subject to this problem is disturbing, and one might want to require that acceptable moral views not be collectively self-defeating. But many familiar moral maxims seem to fail in just this way.

Not all problems of social interaction have the structure of a prisoner's dilemma. There are also pure-coordination problems (Lewis 1969, Schelling 1978), such as determining which side of the road to drive on. It does not matter whether everybody drives on the right or whether everybody drives on the left, but it matters a great deal whether everybody drives on the same side of the road! A normal form of a pure-coordination problem is given in figure 13.4a. Pure-coordination problems are "easier" in the sense that they may have self-enforcing solutions, which can arise spontaneously. Once a custom becomes established, everybody has an incentive to adhere to it. But pure-coordination problems also have less bearing on moral problems in which there are conflicts of interest to resolve.

Closely related to pure-coordination games, but of more relevance to moral philosophy, are games with the structure illustrated in figure 13.4b. Games with the structure illustrated in figure 13.4b are called "battle of the sexes" games because of a story that goes with them. A man and a

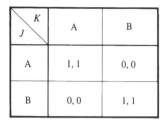

J \ K	A	B
A	1, 1	0, 0
B	0, 0	1, 1

a A pure-coordination game

J \ K	A	B
A	2, 1	0, 0
B	0, 0	1, 2

b A battle of the sexes game

J \ K	A	B
A	4, 4	0, 2
B	2, 0	1, 1

c An assurance game

J \ K	A	B
A	3, 3	2, 4
B	4, 2	0, 0

d A game of chicken

Figure 13.4 Some simple games

woman want to go out together for an evening, and they face a choice of what to do. Both would prefer to be together at either activity than splitting up, but they disagree on what they would most want to do. Many conflicts of interest resemble battle of the sexes games, and these games are much easier to solve than are prisoner's dilemmas.

As illustrated by battle of the sexes games, conflicts of interest are not always prisoner's dilemmas (Taylor 1987, ch. 2; Hampton 1987; Hardin 1982). Consider the rather different game in figure 13.4c. *J* and *K* might both want to do their part toward providing some collective good that requires both their efforts. It is best for each to cooperate if the other cooperates, but worst to cooperate if the other does not. All it takes to make cooperation individually optimal is "assurance" that others will cooperate. Hence this is called the "assurance problem" (Sen 1967). In assurance problems the obstacles in the way of social cooperation are slighter than in a prisoner's dilemma and the prospects for reconciling individual rationality and social optimality are brighter. One strategy for coping with prisoner's dilemmas is to convert them into assurance problems by changing either incentives or personal motivations.

Suppose instead that one faces the problem in figure 13.4d. As in the assurance game, *J* and *K* have no dominant strategy, but now each prefers to play *A* if and only if the other plays *B*. This game of "chicken" can arise when failing to provide a public good is worse than having others free-ride on one's contribution or when conflicts over possessions are costly. For example, both *J* and *K* might prefer to have a fishing ground all to themselves. *A* is a pacifist strategy and *B* is a fighting strategy. Best for *J* is to fight if *K* doesn't, but worst of all is for both to fight. In such games, cooperation may be individually rational, or, as Robert Sugden (1986) has argued, if the positions of the interactors are not fully symmetrical, conventions can arise directing those who occupy different positions to play different strategies. Property rights might be regarded as such conventions, although they have also been shaped by explicit legislation.

As we hinted above, even a structure of interactions resembling a prisoner's dilemma need not prevent self-interested rational agents from cooperating if the interactions are repeated. Suppose that players in what would be a prisoner's dilemma game if it were played only once are likely to play again. The game has then changed; in such "iterated prisoner's dilemmas," defection is no longer a dominant strategy since "cooperative" moves can elicit like cooperative moves from others. Though the formal analysis of repeated games is complex (Taylor 1987, chs. 3, 4), simple strategies such as "tit-for-tat" (cooperate on the first move, then do whatever one's opponent did on the previous move) do well against a wide range of alternatives (Axelrod 1984). A strategy that does strictly better against itself than does any other strategy is called "an evolutionarily stable strategy" (Maynard Smith 1982). The biological terminology is not merely metaphor. Animal traits and behavior can be regarded as strategies, and game theory can be applied to the study of evolution. Tit-for-tat is not an evolutionary stable strategy in an iterated prisoner's dilemma, since other strategies, such as the strategy of always cooperating, do as well against tit-for-tat as tit-for-tat does when played against itself. But it can be proved that when the probability of repeated play is high enough, tit-for-tat is "absolutely (collectively) stable" – that is, that it does no worse when played against itself than does any other strategy (Axelrod 1984, pp. 59, 207–9). When the probability of repeated play is high enough, a group of individuals who play tit-for-tat can "invade" a population of players who defect on every move and, if "survival" depends on success, eventually drive those who always defect to extinction. So cooperation can evolve among rational self-interested agents, and one might be tempted to regard much of morality as the conventional outcome of repeated games.

13.3 Paradoxes and difficulties

But game theory does not always have such reasonable results, and one may question how useful it is for the purposes of moral philosophy.

Suppose two players are playing a one-hundred-move game, where the payoffs for each move are those of the prisoner's dilemma game in figure 13.3. If they both play conditionally cooperative strategies such as tit-for-tat, the outcome for both will be 300. If they both defect, the outcome for both will be only 200. Surely they should be able to find a way to cooperate in at least some of the one hundred moves. Yet there is an argument that apparently shows that if the number of repetitions is known, then "defection" (refusing to cooperate) on every move is the only rational strategy! The argument begins by noting that the 100th repetition is just like the one-shot game. Cooperating in order to elicit further cooperation from the other player is senseless, because there will be no further repetitions. So defection is the only rational action. Consider then the 99th repetition. Since cooperation is rationally excluded on the 100th repetition, cooperation on the 99th round cannot elicit later cooperation, and defection cannot be "punished." So defection is the only rational course in the 99th repetition, too. Proceeding one move at a time, this so-called "backwards-induction" argument yields the conclusion that the only rational strategy is to defect on every move.

But this conclusion seems hard to accept, and it seems that ordinary people have the last laugh on game theorists, for they manage to cooperate quite a lot and consequently do a great deal better in their interactions than rational game theorists with common knowledge of their rationality. The practical irrelevance of the backward-induction argument may conceivably be explained by uncertainty about the number of plays parties will be engaged in. But experiments show that if individuals are permitted to form personal connections (which do not, however, involve any promises or contractual arrangements concerning their play), then they typically cooperate even in a one-shot prisoner's dilemma game (Dawes *et al.* 1990)!

Furthermore, the argument itself runs into paradoxical difficulties. Suppose player *J* fully accepts the backward-induction argument and defects in the first game in the series. But for some reason or other, *K* cooperates. What is poor rational *J* to do on the next move? *K*'s first move decisively refutes *J*'s view of the game. It demonstrates that *K* is not rational (or does not understand the game) or that *K* does not believe that *J* is rational (or understands the game) or that *K* does not believe that *J* believes that *K* is rational or . . . Moreover, *K* knows that making a cooperative move is going to pose this perplexing problem for *J* and that such a move may thus induce *J* to cooperate in order to take advantage of *K*'s apparent "irrationality"! Is it then obviously irrational after all to cooperate for some of the moves of a one-hundred repetition prisoner's dilemma? It is hard to tell a convincing story of how a player should work out a suitable strategic response to contingencies that ought only arise if the other player is irrational.

Ethical applications of game theory are bound to be precarious because game theory is in turmoil. If controversy simmers in the theory of rational choice in circumstances of uncertainty, it boils in game theory. Not only are there the problems involved in incorporating imperfect knowledge and imperfect rationality, but there is disagreement about what "solution concepts" are appropriate, even in circumstances of perfect knowledge and rationality. The traditional solution concept for non-cooperative game theory is the Nash equilibrium. A set of strategies is a Nash equilibrium if each strategy is a best reply to the others – that is, if no one can benefit by playing some other strategy given the strategies of others. For example, mutual defection is a Nash equilibrium in a prisoner's dilemma, while everybody driving on the left and everybody driving on the right are two Nash equilibria in a pure-coordination game. Most game theorists would hold that it is a reasonable necessary condition that solutions should be Nash equilibria. But it is not a sufficient condition: not all Nash equilibria are rational solutions.

Consider the game whose extensive form is shown in figure 13.5. If X plays *down*, the game is over and the payoff is 1 to X and 3 to Y. If X plays *up*, the payoffs are $(0,0)$ or $(2,2)$ depending on whether Y plays *left* or *right*. There are two Nash equilibria here (*down*, *left*) and (*up*, *right*). One can verify that these are the Nash equilibria as follows. If Y plays *left*, then *down* is X's best response. If Y plays *right*, then *up* is X's best response. If X plays *down*, then it does not matter what Y plays, but if Y had had the chance to play and played *right*, then *down* would not have been X's best response so (*down*, *right*) is not a Nash equilibria. If X plays *up*, then *right* is Y's best response. So (*down*, *left*) and (*up*, *right*) are the two Nash equilibria. But if X is rational, X will never play *down*. For given that X has played *up* (and X gets to move first), the only rational move for Y is to play *right*. Y's threat to play *left* is empty. (Notice that the order of play, which is left out of the strategic representation, is crucial in the denial that (*down*, *left*) is a rational solution.) There may be two Nash equilibria, but there is only one rational solution to the game. (*up*, *right*), unlike (*down*, *left*) is what is called a "perfect equilibrium" (Selten 1975). Solution concepts that are stronger than the notion of a Nash equilibrium are needed, but there is no agreement on what they should be. Most of game theory is currently too controversial to permit drawing ethical implications with any confidence.

Even if game theory were not wracked by controversy and paradox, there would be grounds to hesitate before employing it to address ethical questions. First, there are qualms about its "welfarism" – that is, its

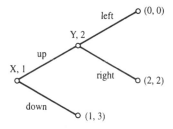

Figure 13.5 An unreasonable Nash equilibrium

reliance on nothing but information about the utilities of outcomes. Game theory is not strictly welfarist, for non-preference information determines what the possible strategies are and what their utility consequences will be. But one might reasonably say that it is quasi-welfarist, for other ethically relevant factors – rights, capabilities, needs, and reasons – make no explicit appearance and their role is heavily truncated (Roemer 1986a). For example, if the strategic problem is to distribute some set of commodities, then the solution will be the same regardless of what the commodities are, if the feasible allocations and utility functions are the same. But people's judgments about just distributions do not depend only on information about preferences or welfare; they also depend on what the goods to be distributed are. As we shall see below, the outcomes reached in experimental tests of bargaining theory depend on non-welfarist information. Indeed Yaari and Bar-Hillel (1984) have shown that people have different ethical views about how to distribute avocados and grapefruits depending on *what* the fruits are wanted for, not just on how much the fruits are wanted. Many people would insist that justice requires a more egalitarian distribution if the fruits are wanted for their vitamins than if they are wanted for their taste.

Not only does most game theory specify the values and choices of agents in terms of preference satisfaction, but game-theoretic analyses of social interactions implicitly assume that the only (and hence the proper) perspective for individuals to adopt in their social interactions is individual maximization. This assumption begs some of the deepest questions in social and political philosophy. It does not rule out altruism or sympathy, and it need not in principle rule out "commitment" (p. 63 above), but it does rule out a collective perspective – a perspective that considers what *we* should do and what the consequences will be for *us*. And it has been argued that such a collective perspective is essential to the very notion of social interaction (Gilbert 1990) and to the explanation for why real individuals play simple games so differently than game theory would prescribe and predict (Dawes *et al.* 1990; see also Hurley 1989, p. 145; Regan 1980, ch. 8). What better explanation is there for the fact that experimental sub-jects are much more likely to cooperate when they have an opportunity to talk with one another on irrelevant subjects? We do not conclude that game theory is useless for ethical purposes. Our view is that its application to moral philosophy remains controversial, and the suitability of its assumptions must be addressed explicitly in each application.

13.4 Bargaining theory and the social contract

To clarify the difficulties involved in applying game theory to moral phi-losophy, let us focus on some game theory that has actually been applied to ethical issues: two-person cooperative bargaining theory. In John Nash's classic analysis, the two parties are supposed to have cardinal util-ities that are not interpersonally comparable. The bargaining problem is to select a distribution of utility, u^* to the first party and v^* to the second party, from a closed convex set, S, of possible utility outcomes. (A set is closed if it includes its boundaries, and it is convex if, for any two points x, y in the set, it includes every point on the straight line segment between x and y.) The set of possible outcomes, S, contains a "threat point," $d = (u_d, v_d)$, consisting of the utilities the two individuals receive if no bargain is reached. Rational individuals will, of course, not settle for less than they can get if no bargain is made. So $u^* \geq u_d$ and $v^* \geq v_d$. Nash proved that if the solution to the bargaining problem satisfies four further explicit condi-tions, then the solution maximizes the product of the utility gains from bargaining. That is, (u^*, v^*) is the Nash solution when $(u^* - u_d).(v^* - v_d) > (u - u_d).(v - v_d)$ for all points (u,v) in S other than (u^*, v^*) itself (Nash 1950). Nash's four conditions are the following:

1. (Pareto optimality) There is no point (u,v) in S other than (u^*, v^*) such that $u \geq u^*$ and $v \geq v^*$.
2. (Invariance) Suppose (u^*, v^*) is the solution to the original bargaining problem in which the agents have utility functions U and V. Suppose then that the bargaining problem is changed so that U' and V', which are positive linear transformations of U and V, represent the two agents' utility functions. Then the solution to the transformed bargain-ing problem is found by applying the same positive linear transforma-tions to the original solution. That is to say, if $U' = aU + b$ and $V' = cV + d$, where a,b,c, and d are real numbers and a and c are positive, then $(au^* + b, cv^* + d)$ is the solution to the transformed bargaining problem.
3. (Symmetry) If $u_d = v_d$, and (v,u) is in S whenever (u,v) is in S, then $u^* = v^*$. If the agents are in symmetrical positions, then the bargaining solu-tion must also be symmetrical.

4. (Independence of irrelevant alternatives) Suppose that S' is a subset of S and that both the threat point (u_d, v_d) and the solution (u^*, v^*) to the bargaining over the larger set S are also in the smaller set S'. Then the solution to the bargaining game restricted to S' should also be (u^*, v^*). (Notice that this is quite different from Arrow's independence of irrelevant alternatives axiom, discussed in chapter 12.)

These conditions seem plausible, and the Nash solution has many defenders. Yet it has awkward consequences, for if the feasible set of utility outcomes expands in person A's favor, the result may be that person A will get *less* than before (Kalai and Smorodinsky 1975, p. 515). The Nash solution may also be morally objectionable in the extent to which it disadvantages both the poor (whose u_d will be low) and the risk averse (whose utilities increase more slowly as a function of their physical shares).

A further problem is that, in empirical studies, the bargains that individuals reach systematically diverge from the Nash solution, even when both individuals have perfect knowledge of their utility functions. In so-called "binary lottery" games, individuals bargain over the distribution of lottery tickets which give them a chance of winning separate prizes. Since their utility functions are not interpersonally comparable, one can stipulate that each individual's utility is zero when he or she has no tickets – that is, no probability of winning – and that the utility for each of having all the tickets – that is, of winning his or her prize for sure – is 1. The utility of each player then equals the percentage of the lottery tickets each has. The Nash solution is a fifty-fifty split of the lottery tickets.

The Nash solution follows regardless of what prizes the individuals can win. If both A and B will win \$5 if they win their separate lotteries, then the Nash solution, a fifty-fifty split of the lottery tickets, seems reasonable. If A's lottery pays off \$5, while B's lottery pays off \$20, then the Nash solution of a fifty-fifty split of the lottery tickets no longer seems so obviously right. When the prizes differ, the actual experimental outcomes of the bargaining games are "bimodal," with both the Nash solution and the solution that equalizes monetary returns as the two modes (Roth and Malouf 1979). Roth, Malouf, and Murnighan (1981) argue persuasively that *moral norms* concerning just distributions affect the bargaining solutions. The person who stands to win the larger prize is seen as having a weaker moral claim on lottery tickets than the less advantaged person. Yet recent experimental work by Binmore *et al.* suggests that people's moral views are fragile and depend on their experience in bargaining. It seems that even purely positive bargaining theory must take cognizance of the moral commitments of the bargainers, and it is by no means obvious how this is to be accomplished formally (Gibbard 1990, esp. p. 262; Pettit 1990).

An alternative to the Nash solution developed by Kalai and Smorodinsky (1975) forms the basis from which David Gauthier constructs his contractarian derivation of justice from rational choice (1986). Kalai and Smorodinsky conceive of the bargaining problem much as Nash does, and they accept Nash's first three assumptions. But in place of Nash's fourth condition, his independence of irrelevant alternatives constraint, Kalai and Smorodinsky impose a "monotonicity" requirement. This monotonicity condition says that if the maximum utility available to one of the parties increases, then the utility that party gets in the bargaining solution must not decrease.

With the monotonicity condition in place of independence of irrelevant alternatives, Kalai and Smorodinsky derive for the two-person case an "equal relative concession" solution. Recall that the "relative concession" of each bargainer is $(u_{max} - u)/(u_{max} - u_d)$, where u_{max} is the largest feasible utility attainable by the individual, u is the utility if a given bargain were made, and u_d is the utility at the threat point. Because there may be no Pareto-optimal equal relative concession solution with more than two bargainers, Gauthier substitutes "minimax relative concession" – the solution that minimizes the largest concession anybody has to make. If equal relative concession is Pareto optimal, then equal relative concession coincides with minimax relative concession. Although this extension of the Kalai and Smorodinsky solution avoids some of the awkward implications of the Nash solution, it still disadvantages the poor and risk averse, and it is equally inconsistent with the experimental evidence concerning bargaining over shares of lottery tickets.

Gauthier argues that rational individuals who are aware of their own rationality and the rationality of others and who are aware of the utility consequences of their bargaining will accept the minimax relative concession solution (1986, ch. 5). In Gauthier's view this argument suffices to establish that such a solution is just, although Gauthier also maintains that this solution satisfies conditions that have been thought reasonable to impose on conceptions of justice, such as impartiality (1986, ch. 8). Gauthier argues further that it is individually rational to adhere to such bargains (1986, ch. 6).

Gauthier's argument has been strongly contested, and its difficulties highlight the complex interconnections between game theory and moral philosophy. The characterization of individual rationality that Gauthier relies on is controversial, the relevance of solutions to a two-person bargaining problem under conditions of complete information is questionable, the particular solution concept is dubious, and the limitation to quasi-welfarist information is objectionable. This list of difficulties is not intended as a criticism of Gauthier's path-breaking efforts or as an argument against employing game theory to tackle moral problems. Indeed, it is only through Gauthier's efforts that these dimensions of a contractualist argument for principles of justice could be clearly seen.

This example illustrates the present relations between game theory and moral philosophy. Game theory cannot now solve moral problems, because of difficulties with its notions of rationality, its solution concepts, and its strong knowledge assumptions. Yet game theory has already provided a valuable and influential conceptual framework in which to think about moral problems, and as it continues to develop, it may yet help to solve them, too.

Suggestions for further reading

There are many introductions to game theory. Luce and Raiffa (1957) is a classic and is still very helpful. Harsanyi (1977b) is also very accessible, although it defends some controversial positions. Two recent good texts are Gibbons (1992) and Binmore (1992). Most authors accept the view that solutions to non-cooperative games should be Nash equilibrium, but some such as Bonnano (1991) disagree.

The prisoner's dilemma has been discussed in hundreds of books and essays. Axclrod (1984) and Parfit (1984, ch. 2) contain particularly helpful discussions. Frolich et al. (1975), Hardin (1982), Taylor and Ward (1982), and Hampton (1987) all question whether problems of collective goods provision are always best understood as prisoner's dilemma. For Sen's discussion of the assurance game see Sen (1967, pp. 112–24). There are other kinds of mixed coordination/conflict games than those described here. For excellent discussions of how coordination can arise in various circumstances, particularly when there are asymmetries in the positions of different players, see Schotter (1981) and Sugden (1986).

For discussions of the backwards-induction argument and its difficulties, see Kreps et al. (1982), Kreps and Wilson (1982), Binmore (1988, 1989), Bicchieri (1988, 1990), Pettit and Sugden (1989), and Bonnano (1991).

A wonderful introduction to bargaining theory and its applications to moral philosophy is Barry (1989). Other useful discussions can be found in Luce and Raiffa (1957, pp. 124–37) and Thomson and Lensberg (1989). Binmore (1994) is an important recent application of game theory to moral philosophy.

Critical discussion of Gauthier's theory can be found in Roemer (1986a), Kraus and Coleman (1987), Nelson (1988), Paul et al. (1988) and Sugden (1990). See also Gauthier (1990), which is a collection of his essays.

Conclusion

14 Conclusion

We opened this volume with a look at the controversial memorandum Lawrence Summers wrote exploring the advantages of exporting pollution to LDCs (less developed countries). The memo served both to illustrate how sound economic reasoning can lead to shocking moral conclusions and to motivate our investigation of moral concepts and frameworks. In this concluding chapter we return to Summers' example to see what we have learned. It is not our purpose to defend an answer to the question whether it would be a good thing to export pollution to LDCs, though we shall express our view later. Our main purpose is instead to illustrate the value of the wider menu of moral conceptions and principles described in this book. These concepts and principles clarify the moral issues at stake in difficult practical problems, identify relevant factual questions, and focus moral disagreements.

Summers' argument in favor of compensated transfers of pollution to poor countries ran in standard efficiency terms. Given the great inequality in incomes, wages, and environmental quality between rich and poor countries, and the fact that pollution damage (or, in positive terms, environmental quality) is not a marketable good, there are unexploited opportunities for Pareto-improving trades between rich and poor countries: citizens of rich countries will be willing to offer amounts of compensation to citizens of poor countries for accepting pollution damage which the citizens of poor countries will be willing to accept. Thus, welfare-enhancing trade between rich and poor countries in pollution (or in the location of polluting industries) should be possible and the transfer of pollution should be encouraged. Uncompensated transfer of pollution to LDCs cannot be justified in this way, for it would not be beneficial to all parties. Yet even uncompensated pollution transfers would apparently represent a potential Pareto improvement and would be viewed favorably from the perspective of cost-benefit analysis discussed in section 7.4.

We went on to suggest three objections to this argument. The first was technical: relocating polluting industries to poor countries might increase the total amount of pollution in the world sufficiently that, even if the distribution were more efficient, the overall effect might be harmful. The other two objections were aimed more directly at the moral basis of Summers' argument. One was that the exchange in question, even if it was mutually beneficial, was *unfair* given the gross disparity in bargaining position of the rich and poor countries. The other objection was that the measure of welfare on which the Summers' argument relies is flawed, and that more adequate measures would not lead to the conclusion that moving pollution to poor countries would be welfare enhancing.

The latter two objections point toward alternative frameworks for conducting a moral assessment of the Summers proposal. Concerns about fairness might profitably be considered from the standpoint of social contract theories, the subject of chapter 11. Furthermore, one might think through the issue of exporting pollution from the perspective of freedom and rights presented in chapter 9, and from that of equality discussed in chapter 10. The problem of alternative welfare standards has occupied us at several points. Let us approach this issue both from the standpoint of utilitarianism, which permits the interpersonal comparisons of welfare that are ruled out in the Pareto efficiency framework, and from the standpoint of "objective" measures of welfare considered as alternatives to the preference-satisfaction view of welfare that is implicit in Summers' memorandum.

14.1 Do transfers of pollution make people better off?

Summers reduces the question of whether LDCs are "underpolluted" to the question of whether the welfare consequences of shifting more pollution to the LDCs would be favorable. To make this argument, one must say something about how the welfare consequences of pollution should be measured. If one takes welfare to be the satisfaction of preferences, then one might attempt to measure the extent to which people prefer to avoid various kinds of pollution. This method, which is implicit in standard cost-benefit analysis, is problematic, since the extent to which people prefer to avoid pollutants depends on their beliefs concerning the consequences of the pollutants, which may be mistaken. Summers' memorandum avoids these problems, because he focuses on the actual effects of additional pollution. Regardless of what people in LDCs believe about the effects of pollution, its welfare costs will in fact be less there. But "welfare" for Summers, as for most economists, is still preference satisfaction. The "cost" of the consequences of pollution is thus the amount by which people's preferences are less well satisfied. And Summers' measure of this is essentially "willingness-to-pay." A permanent injury to a child lowers the welfare of the child's family much more if the family happens to live in a rich country, because the cost of the child's care, the extent to which the child's prospective earnings are diminished, and the amount which the family would be willing to pay to avoid the injury are all much greater in rich countries than in poor.

Measuring preference satisfaction this way seems morally unacceptable. It is just as morally important to avoid crippling a poor child as to avoid crippling a rich one. As we will note below, a careful formulation of Summers' argument for compensated pollution transfers may avoid wealth bias in the measure of preference satisfaction. Yet, even then, he is still shaping his treatment of the general issue by taking welfare to be the satisfaction of preferences. In chapter 6 we considered two objective conceptions of welfare, Sen's notion of capabilities and Rawls' notion of primary goods. Let us consider whether the argument for transferring pollution on the grounds of its consequences for welfare would still go through if one were to measure welfare in terms of some index of capabilities or primary goods.

In order to address the question, we need to say something about how pollution affects capabilities and primary goods. The costs of pollution are diverse and hard to analyze. To simplify, let us focus only on the negative health consequences. The capabilities affected by pollution would include the capability to breathe freely (or to continue breathing at all!), the ability to see well, and so on. Although Rawls himself does not include health among the primary goods on the grounds that it is a natural rather than a social good, many have argued that health is heavily and increasingly influenced by social factors and that health should be included among the primary goods. We agree. So, at least for the purposes of argument, let us include health among the primary goods. Pollution would then have direct consequences on primary goods.

In some cases a given exposure to a pollutant will diminish the capabilities or primary goods of people in LDCs less than it will diminish the capabilities or primary goods of people in rich countries. If, to use Summers' own example, a pollutant increases the risk of prostate cancer, which is a disease of elderly men, then the pollutant will not increase risk of suffering or death as much if one is likely to die young from other causes. Furthermore, a given dose of a particular pollutant may have fewer negative health consequences if there is already very little pollution, than if there is a great deal. On the other hand, the interaction between pollution effects and the generally worse health status of people in poor countries might render some of these effects more serious. Similarly, the numbers of people affected by pollution might sometimes be higher and sometimes lower in poor countries. There seems to be no justified presumption that *uncompensated* transfers of pollution toward poor countries would result in a net increase in primary goods or capabilities in the world.

Analysis of the objective welfare consequences of *compensated* transfers is more complicated. The Pareto efficiency argument in favor of compensated transfers doesn't require any comparison of the welfare effects of pollution in rich and poor countries and in this sense it avoids the direct wealth bias noted earlier in the argument for uncompensated transfers. The argument instead is that the valuation consumers place on pollution reduction relative to other goods is larger in rich than in poor countries – asserting, in other words, that environmental quality is a good with a high income elasticity of demand. People in poor countries are willing to give up environmental quality in exchange for items like food and basic health-care on terms that people in rich countries find attractive. As we pointed out on page 97 above, however, even an actual Pareto improvement given a particular distribution does not imply that the policy contemplated (compensated pollution transfers in this case) would result in a Pareto improvement given a different distribution of income. We will have more to say about this in the next section.

There is yet a further problem here that we did not mention in chapter 2. The idea of compensating a *country* is a cheat: the Paretian argument requires that every individual in each country is made subjectively better off. Even in its own terms the argument may be in trouble here, because the compensation may fail to reach the individuals who are harmed by the pollution. One advantage of reverting to an objective standard that permits interpersonal comparisons is that one can make sense of the idea of compensating a country without requiring the heroic assumption that every individual can be compensated. Consider for example a case in which a country accepted a polluting industry and was compensated through improved health care. One might meaningfully be able to say that the *average* health status of the country improved as a result of this deal, and conclude that the welfare effect was positive (although there might be important issues of fairness if different people were affected by the health-care improvements and the pollution damage).

There remains the question whether policies that are truly Pareto optimal, as judged by a subjective welfare standard, are also welfare promoting according to objective welfare criteria. As long as subjective judgments are well informed, there is some presumption that this should be so. Objective welfare criteria aim to measure central human concerns that will also show up in subjective evaluations. Still, the presumption is clearly rebuttable, especially in cases like this one in which circumstances and preferences are changing rapidly and in which so many of those affected are children.

14.2 Utilitarianism

Consider how a utilitarian analysis might differ from the efficiency analysis provided by Summers. Utilitarians, as we saw in chapter 8, differ among themselves in how they would measure utility. Some might endorse objective welfare standards such as those we have just discussed. Here, however, we want to focus specifically on the difference it makes to analyzing the Summers proposal that utilitarians are willing to make interpersonal comparisons of utility. For simplicity of comparison, assume that the utilitarian agrees that welfare is the satisfaction of preferences. Granting Summers' empirical assumptions, a compensated transfer of polluting industries to poor countries would enable the citizens of all countries to satisfy their preferences better and thus would increase utility overall. In this sense, utilitarians who endorsed Summers' empirical assumptions and accepted his view of welfare would agree that compensated transfers of polluting industries to poor countries are an improvement on the status quo.

But it does not follow that a preference utilitarian would support the pollution exchange policy. For there are more than two alternatives. In addition to the status quo and to compensated transfers of pollution, one might consider the alternative of simply redistributing wealth. On plausible utilitarian assumptions, the marginal utility of income is much lower in rich than in poor countries. Transferring income or resources from rich to poor countries will, then, be welfare-enhancing in utilitarian terms, for the gains in utility to persons in poor countries will outweigh the losses to those in the rich countries. (Utilitarians recognize that one needs to consider the long-run consequences and that it would probably be better to provide technical and educational aid rather than just money, but these complications are not germane to the argument we are making here.) Are such one-way transfers of resources from rich to poor countries more or less effective in promoting world welfare than are exchanges like the one Summers contemplates?

Imagine breaking the compensated transfer of pollution into two parts. Part 1 is the transfer of compensation (jobs, medical facilities, etc.) from rich to poor countries. Part 2 is the transfer of pollution toward poor countries (or the transfer of environmental quality from poor to rich countries). Part 1 is clearly, on standard utilitarian assumptions, welfare-enhancing for the reasons just discussed. However, there is no general reason to believe that Part 2, the movement of pollution toward poor countries, is welfare-enhancing. Clean air is worth more in dollar terms in rich countries, but it is far from obvious that clean air is worth more in *utility* terms in rich countries. As we saw above when discussing the comparative health consequences of pollution in rich versus poor nations, the consequences are sometimes better if the pollution occurs in the poor nation, sometimes better if it occurs in the rich nation, and sometimes just the same regardless of where it occurs.

We can take this a step further in a way that clarifies the relationship between preference utilitarian and Paretian views. It's clear that the best utilitarian outcome will be a Pareto optimum, for if it were possible to satisfy somebody's preferences better without lessening the preference satisfaction of someone else, then one would not have maximized utility. Given the present disparities in resources between rich and poor countries, the kinds of Pareto-improving transfers between rich and poor countries contemplated by Summers would produce small gains in total utility compared to the large gains that could be expected by wealth transfers from rich toward poor countries. However, if through transfers or other means, these inequalities in standards of living were greatly reduced, the question of getting further gains in welfare by redistributing pollution would surface. It is striking, however, that at that point it would no longer be obvious that movements of pollution toward LDCs would be welfare enhancing since the principal force pushing in that direction – namely the very low incomes and wages in poor countries – would no longer be operating.

14.3 Other modes of evaluation

We noted in chapter 2 that one objection to the Summers proposal is its *unfairness* – the way in which it permits rich countries to take advantage of the vulnerabilities of poor countries. We did not, however, say anything about rights or liberty. Off-hand, one might think that there would be no freedom or rights-based objection to the argument for compensated pollution transfers. One might argue that since these are mutually beneficial and would be agreed to voluntarily by both parties if there were no barriers to such exchanges, they respect rights and freedom. But there is a very great difference between, on the one hand, a voluntary exchange between two individuals who have a right to what they are exchanging and, on the other hand, a policy that brings about the same result. What is at stake here are not voluntary agreements among individuals in different countries to accept pollutants for compensation, but rather efforts by governments to enforce transfers that would approximate the results of such voluntary exchange. As Nozick stresses, the libertarian is much less concerned with outcomes than with how they came about. One does not respect freedom by forcing people to do what they would have chosen to do, and one does not respect rights by forcing on people risks that they would voluntarily have chosen to impose upon themselves. When one adds to these observations the important point that compensated transfers of pollution are not genuine Pareto improvements, because those who incur the costs of the additional pollution will not necessarily receive the compensation, one can begin to appreciate just how problematic Summers' proposal is from a perspective that values rights and freedom most of all. Libertarians like Nozick are prepared to reject the entire welfare-improving perspective of welfare economics and to restrict policies to the protection of individual rights. Those who value both freedom and welfare and who have a more expansive view of rights would take a more nuanced view. To pursue the issue further from this perspective would, however, lead to enormous complications, because the problems of pollution raise serious problems about the appropriate specification of rights.

We should also consider briefly how issues of equality bear on assessing the pollution transfer proposal. The central point is that according to any of the conceptions of equality discussed in chapter 10, the proposed transfer takes place against a background of very great inequality. Uncompensated transfer of pollution to poor countries, which might be recommended on cost-benefit grounds, would worsen these inequalities. One might suppose that compensated transfers would be roughly neutral with regard to inequality of welfare, resources, or capabilities. This simply confirms the point that efficiency-oriented policy analysis takes as given the status quo distribution of resources.

Suppose instead that one were to take a position of equality as the starting point. In noting that poor countries may be greatly "underpolluted," Summers invites us to think of environmental quality as a resource that is unequally distributed under current arrangements, and to notice the advantages of distributing it more equally. Representatives of LDCs might jump at the chance to adopt this perspective more generally and to contemplate equalization of various resources across nations. One could readily argue that, just as LDCs are "underpolluted," so are they "undercapitalized" and "undereducated." In this spirit, one might consider an analysis which begins by assuming that every country owns an equal per capita share of all currently existing external resources, including environmental quality, land, natural resources, machinery and equipment, and so on. Trade in these shares from this egalitarian starting point would result in Pareto improvements, and in principle one should reach what we described in chapter 10 as a "contribution-fair" or "wealth-fair" distribution (see p. 141). It is quite plausible that in such an equilibrium, as in the one which would result from the Summers proposal, environmental quality would be lower in some poor countries than it is now. But per capita ownership of other resources would be much higher and the final distribution would not reflect (or magnify) initial inequalities.

If one looks to the values underlying a concern with equality – especially equal respect, solidarity, and fairness – then one can see how objectionable Summers' proposal and his arguments are from an egalitarian point of view. Showing equal respect precludes assigning greater values to the lives, health, and comfort of those who are richer. Solidarity points toward protecting those who are least well-off and toward sharing the burdens of technological advances rather than making good use of the poverty characteristic of the LDCs. And we have already questioned whether Summers' proposal was fair.

For further consideration of the fairness objection, consider how one might apply social contract views to Summers' proposal. Some contractarian theorists, notably John Rawls, have been cautious about extending their theories to international settings, and the problems in working out a contractarian view in those settings are formidable (see Beitz 1979). However, it is possible cautiously to examine the issues at stake from the perspectives of impartiality and of mutual advantage that underlie different contractarian views.

If one emphasizes impartiality, one will want to ask the following sort of question. Would representative citizens, deprived of knowledge of whether their countries were rich or poor, endorse principles that would justify the compensated transfer of pollution? Or, to revert to Scanlon's more general formulation, would it be reasonable for people in poor countries to reject such principles, given an interest in coming to an agreement on principles? It's immediately clear that one can't get very far with this kind of question when considering a single policy in isolation. In considering the justice of the particular policy, one cannot suppose that the determination of fundamental rights and duties is up for grabs, as it is in deciding on the principles of justice to govern basic social institutions. On the contrary, one needs a prior specification of rights and general moral principles. The reasonableness of a particular policy will depend on the whole fabric of the relationship between the parties.

Still it may be helpful to think about alternative principles that might govern the location of polluting industries. A principle that would justify Summers' proposal is this: locate polluting industries so as to minimize economic costs. Let us call this "the cost-minimizing principle." What are some plausible alternatives? A second might be: locate polluting industries where they will produce the least human suffering. Let us call this "the pain-minimizing principle." A third might be: locate polluting industries so that those who derive the largest benefits from the industries endure most of the pollution costs. Let us call this "the pay-your-way principle."

These principles are too crude to underpin real policies, and are only intended to suggest a range of alternatives. One might try to decide which might reasonably be rejected by parties seeking a fair agreement, or how they might be ranked from behind a veil of ignorance. The result is unfavorable to the cost-minimizing principle. This principle concludes that suffering should be concentrated in LDCs because suffering is cheaper there than in rich countries. One would not choose such a principle behind a veil of ignorance, not knowing whether one will live in a rich or a poor country. Such a principle could certainly be reasonably rejected. Choosing between the pain-minimizing and the pay-your-way principles is less simple. If it turns out that additional pollution causes relatively less pain if it is concentrated in LDCs, then advocates of the pain-minimizing principle face the tough problem of explaining why it is reasonable for people in poor countries to endure the costs of industries which mainly benefit those in rich countries. The pay-your-way principle, on the other hand, provides some assurance that costs cannot be inflicted by one group upon another. It also has attractive incentive features. (It resembles in this regard the semi-facetious proposal of those concerned about the safety of workers in chemical plants to circulate air from the shop-floor through corporate offices.)

As with our discussion of utilitarianism, an optimal policy would take another step beyond the simple principles formulated above. From an impartial perspective, one would want to work out a whole scheme of distributive and allocative principles governing relations between rich and poor countries. In that context, which presumably would include various kinds of protections for the welfare of persons in poor countries, schemes for trading pollution rights might well enter.

Mutual benefit contract theories might come closer to endorsing something like the Summers proposal. Theories in this vein constrain principles of justice by the requirement that they be in the rational self-interest of all parties from the standpoint of their situations prior to agreement, and such theories allow inequalities in the pre-agreement situation to influence the outcome of the rational bargain that yields principles of justice. Whether one should accept the large existing inequalities between rich and poor countries as pre-agreement "data" for working out principles of international justice is a big question for those who adopt the mutual benefit approach. If one goes back only a few hundred years, those inequalities were much less, and much of the interaction between rich and poor countries in the intervening years would not meet any plausible standard of mutual benefit.

Suppose, though, that we put that aside and ask simply what kinds of bargains between rich and poor countries might be just, given the huge existing disparities in incomes and living standards. If just agreements are defined by the rational self-interest of all concerned, it may be that compensated pollution transfers would be just. Even on this view, however, there is one important caveat concerning the distribution of costs and compensation within poor countries. It is easy to imagine agreements in which one segment of the population of a poor country benefits from a deal to import polluting industries, while other segments suffer. In order for the mutual benefit standard to be upheld, compensation would have to extend to those within the country who are losers on the deal, and not simply to the country as a whole.

14.4 The overlapping generations example

In chapter 2 we also considered Paul Samuelson's influential article on interest rates in an economy where saving was driven by the need to provide for retirement. Our argument was that much of the interest in that article, as well as the lively controversy it immediately spawned, derived from its relevance to normative issues. It is helpful to return to this example briefly to see what more can be said about it following our journey through moral philosophy and economics.

Samuelson's article made some theoretical points that might by themselves be regarded as without any ethical content. He showed that in a barter economy, of the kind that underpins much economic modeling, market competition would lead to an inefficient profile of overconsumption in the first period of life followed by penury in the second and third periods. To overcome this market imperfection, the economy required an institutional structure that relied on *trust* – the necessary institution being either a "social contract" in which younger generations acknowledged an obligation to support the elderly, or "fiat" money whose value was taken on faith by the members of the community. Yet, as Abba Lerner points out, the pattern of savings and consumption that results from this trust is also open to ethical objection. In a growing economy, it results (if one permits interpersonal comparisons) in a smaller average utility in every period than a pattern that equalizes consumption across the periods of one's life. The first two points were made by Samuelson and the third by Lerner with regard to a highly stylized and abstract formulation of an economy; their application to practical problems would plainly require much careful work.

We find this abstract theorizing instructive in three regards. First, although the above points can all be regarded as "positive economics," their interest and the way they are presented and debated depends on their relevance to normative issues. Samuelson is himself intrigued by his model because it presents a case in which perfectly competitive markets are inefficient. Since economists regard perfect competition as an ideal (other things being equal), this was a striking result, which brought an immediate response from William Meckling. Furthermore, the model obviously has some relevance to the issue of whether one should conceive of social security as a savings program or as a transfer program. Without an appreciation of the normative relevance of the abstract models, one would have a hard time understanding why Samuelson presents the model as he does, and why he is challenged by Lerner and Meckling. At the same time, Samuelson's model also shows how much economists have to contribute to understanding of normative issues. There are few moral philosophers with the command of the technical apparatus of economics required to produce a formulation like Samuelson's. As a result of their specialized training and their knowledge of relevant facts and techniques, economists can help resolve issues of moral importance. Third, and less positively, we noted in chapter 2 that Samuelson was in fact quite oblique in making the normative points we have highlighted, and indeed his critics did not initially formulate their objections directly in ethical terms, but instead in the guise of analytical disputes. It is our belief that progress on both normative and positive issues would be more sustained if economists recognized and scrutinized the normative dimensions of their work. One main hope for this book is that it will make available concepts and tools that will make that process easier.

14.5 Conclusion

Our discussion of the proposal to export polluting industries to poor countries is meant to illustrate the way in which standard economic analyses narrow evaluative questions and some of the ways in which they may be broadened without the discussion becoming formless, ill-disciplined or irrational. This discussion is not meant to be a contribution to any current policy debate, for pollution transfers are not a major subject of current policy debate, and in any case we did not express our own views on the subject. As it happens, our view is that such transfers would be very bad policy. We believe that serious worldwide environmental problems would be aggravated if pollution could be more readily exported. LDCs have fewer resources for monitoring and controlling pollutants, and those which benefit from polluting industries would no longer have to bear as many of the costs. Exporting pollution would be morally objectionable not only because of these bad consequences but also because it is unfair and it callously fails to show equal concern for people who happen to be born in poor countries. Furthermore, because of its unfairness and callousness, it would undermine global cooperation, which is needed in order to protect the environment. Regardless of your attitude toward relocating polluting industries to LDCs, we hope this book has made it obvious that such policy suggestions should not be made without more explicit and serious moral reflection.

After working through the arguments and analytical perspectives reviewed in this volume, different readers might arrive at different judgments about practical policy options such as exporting polluting industries to poor countries. We have not defended any single view of ethics, and we have not attempted to weight the differing considerations. Furthermore, policy conclusions also depend on judgments concerning the likely consequences of alternatives, and there are many disagreements concerning these matters. But we hope that this discussion encourages our readers to reflect on this question: Should one rest content with evaluating policies solely according to their consequences for satisfying people's preferences (with perhaps a few *ad hoc* adjustments to allow for equity concerns), or should one strive to include in one's evaluation the consequences for freedom, equality, justice, and indicators of quality of life that go beyond preference satisfaction? Although the former path may keep economics neater and perhaps in appearance more "scientific," the latter will, we contend, make it more useful and sensible.

Finally, as we have stressed repeatedly, and as our example of the overlapping generations model illustrates, ethics is not only relevant in the context of evaluating policy. Ethics enters directly into the development of social welfare theory and game theory. It is needed in order to formulate relevant questions for "positive" research. It is implicit in the standard theory of rationality that lies at the core of contemporary economics. It is implicit in theories of how labor markets work and of how social cooperation in general is possible. Economics is not just a wayward branch of moral philosophy, but it's not unrelated to moral philosophy either. One enriches both economics and moral philosophy by acknowledging their interdependence.

Appendix

How could ethics matter to economics?

We hope in this book to have shown how a better understanding of moral philosophy can improve economic analysis. The most persuasive way to make this case is the one we pursued in the main text: by describing important aspects of moral philosophy and showing their bearing on economics. But many economists are inclined on principle to deny that moral philosophy has anything to do with economics. Why? In this appendix, we shall explore the two main reasons and reaffirm the conclusion of this book – that ethics *is* relevant to economics.

A.1 Objection 1: Economists are just like engineers

Economists who deny that ethics is relevant to economics concede that economics is relevant to policy-making. But it is, they maintain, relevant to policy in the same way that civil engineering is. Owing to a need for electric power, policy-makers might consider building a dam. Civil engineering does not say whether this is a worthy objective. Civil engineers instead provide information about how difficult it is to build dams in different locations, how much electricity the dams can generate, how much land they will flood, and so forth. Civil engineers thereby provide answers to some of the "What if . . .?" questions that policy-makers need to answer when they are trying to decide whether and where to build a dam. To accomplish anything, one needs knowledge of cause and effect. Engineering is one source of such knowledge. The first objection asserts that the role of economics is just the same. Ethics determines the ends that policy-makers pursue, and it constrains the means that may be employed. Economics clarifies the consequences of alternative policies. Both economics and ethics are crucial to policy-making, but neither has anything to do with the other.

The following very simple schema might help clarify this view:
1. Our policy should achieve goal G and satisfy constraint C.
2. X satisfies C and achieves G.
3. Thus our policy should be to do X.

In this oversimplified schema, premise 1 comes from ethics or political philosophy, while premise 2 comes from economics and other relevant bodies
of empirical knowledge. The conclusion is a moral judgment, and it
requires both the moral premise 1 and the technical premise 2. The first
objection maintains that premises 1 and 2 have nothing to do with one
another and that ethics has nothing to contribute to economics.

This schema may be useful as a caricature, but it is too simple. X may
have other desirable or undesirable features, and there may be better alternatives. The following schema is more defensible:

1. Our policy should be governed by the moral or social ranking R.
2. The consequences of X rank higher in R than do the consequences of
   any other policy.
3. Thus our policy should be to do X.

The moral part of policy-making, represented by premise 1, requires not
just a specification of a particular goal and constraint, but a complete
determination of the relative moral importance of the various consequences different policies may have. For example, in the case of a proposed
law prohibiting arbitrary firings, R would specify the moral importance of
arbitrary firings, of intimidation of workers on the job, of unemployment
among the lowest strata of workers, of difficulties for firms in firing
workers, of overall productivity, and so forth. The economist's job is then
to determine all the relevant consequences of the alternative policies. Once
all the consequences are known, the policies can be ranked in terms of
their consequences. If one does not know for sure what the consequences
of policies will be, but can estimate the probabilities of outcomes, then one
can rank policies by weighting the moral values of their outcomes by the
probabilities that they will obtain. As in the simpler schema, the policy
conclusion depends on both moral and technical premises that are independent of one another.

The second schema, unlike the first, is not too simple. Its drawback is
that it is too demanding. No moral system is refined enough to provide the
needed first premise, and economics is not up to the challenge of providing
the second. Although the sharp separation between economics and ethics
thus cannot be sustained, there is some truth to this picture of the economist as an engineer – a purveyor of purely technical information. It is a
useful caricature. It fits some economic activities – for example, work
devoted to estimating how much revenue would result from changing
income-tax rates. But reflection on values is unavoidable if economists are
to understand what policy-makers want to know and if they are to know
what questions to ask.

As Fritz Machlup (1969) recognized, applying the second schema to the
activities economists undertake is often impossible. Machlup made the

telling observation that the political process rarely formulates its economic problems clearly. When economists are called on to give "purely technical" advice about how to accomplish certain ends, they are rarely given purely technical problems. Just think about the tasks of economists who are asked to advise governments on how to transform formerly "socialist" command economies into market economies. Is it not inevitable that their own values will influence what alternatives they consider and what weights they place on the comparative advantages and costs? Could policy-makers in Bulgaria or Latvia possibly provide their economic advisors with a full list of all the relevant goals and constraints with precise weights and priorities specified for each? To give advice, economists need to know all of the objectives policy-makers have and how to weight them. At some point, economists will have to rely on their own values to fill in the gaps. Economists may not think systematically about ethics, and they may not want to think about ethics at all. But they are not going to be able to understand what policy-makers want or to translate policy problems into technical problems of economic analysis without some moral understanding.

Similar problems arise when economists select problems to investigate. Economists want to solve problems that matter to people's lives. They want to solve theoretical puzzles in ways that do not conflict with their moral commitments. So long as economic processes and outcomes remain so important to human interests, evaluative commitments are bound to be crucial to the choice of problems to investigate. In stressing the evaluative roots of economic research, we intend no criticism of this research. We doubt whether there is any alternative, and we are confident that it would be a bad thing if the moral commitments of economists did *not* inspire their research. Economics is not only devoted to pure research and puzzle solving, it is also relevant to the pressing practical problems we humans face. If economists refuse to muck about with messy moral matters, they will not know what questions are important. Economists are not value-free social engineers. In deciding what to study and in thinking about how to apply economics to practical problems, economists *must* think about ethical matters. They need not do so systematically, self-consciously, or well, but they cannot avoid ethics altogether.

A.2 Objection 2: Positive economics is value-free

Economists cannot avoid ethical questions if they want to understand the terms of policy debate, to contribute to determining public policies, or to select problems to study. But many economists would argue that the above answer to the first objection does not preclude the possibility of a science of economics within which ethics has no role. These economists would grant that ethics has a role in determining what problems to study. They would point out that it is hardly surprising that ethics is relevant to normative economics. But they would insist that the role of ethics ends there. Ethics may pose the economist's questions, but it cannot contribute to their answers. Ethics has nothing to contribute to *positive* economic analysis itself. The second objection maintains that there is a "positive" economic science which is value-free. Let us call this position "the standard view." Some further clarification is in order.

A.2.1 Positive and normative economics

Most people can readily distinguish questions concerning (non-moral) facts from questions concerning what is good or bad or what ought or ought not to be done. This is the so-called "fact/value distinction." It is difficult to make it precise. There are many hard cases. (In stating, "That was a kind thing to do," is one describing or appraising?) And some philosophers argue that the fact/value distinction breaks down altogether. But let us suppose that it is possible roughly to classify questions as either factual or evaluative. Ethics is then taken to be concerned with questions of value, while the sciences (or at least the natural sciences) are taken to be concerned with questions of fact.

The standard view maintains that questions of fact and questions of value are not only distinguishable, but *independent*. No question concerning values is supposed to be settled by the facts alone, and no question concerning facts is supposed to be settled by values. On the standard view, it is accordingly possible for there to be "value-free" inquiries into matters of fact.

To speak of a "value-free" inquiry may be misleading. It suggests that the *conduct* of the inquiry is value-free. But the conduct of inquiry cannot possibly be value-free. Inquiring involves action, and action is motivated by values. As we have already seen, values influence choices of what to study. Values also influence choices of what methods to employ and consequently of what hypotheses to discard or to pursue. It is because of their *moral* identification with the goals of science that economists resist "cooking" their data. It is because of their personal morality that economists rarely shoot those who disagree with them or even try to get them fired. The standard view does not deny that values influence the conduct of inquiry. What is meant by a "value-free" inquiry is instead (a) an inquiry into a question of fact and (b) one in which the answers are not influenced by any values apart from those which are part of science itself.

Investigations of matters of fact are called "positive" investigations. The standard view concedes that the results of positive inquiries may be relevant to policy, because they may show that policies facilitate or frustrate the attainment of valued objectives. But without some prior evaluative commitment, the findings of positive science settle no questions of policy or value. According to the standard view, positive science can be value-free, positive science ought to be value-free, and, apart from lapses, positive science is in fact value-free. Thus the study of "ideology" and of the values of economists is irrelevant to understanding economics or economic methodology, though it may help one to understand the scientific failings or motivations of particular individuals.

On the standard view, "normative science," which is contrasted to positive science, consists of inquiries into matters of policy or values. Normative economics consists of the application of positive economics to explore questions that are of immediate evaluative relevance. Notice that sharply distinguishing between facts and values and between positive and normative science does not commit one to the extreme views, which have unfortunately been popular among economists, that evaluative claims cannot be true or false and that conflicts concerning fundamental values cannot be settled by rational argument. Nothing is settled concerning the status of questions of value when one insists on their independence from questions of fact. Indeed, as Samuel Weston (1994) points out, the possibility of distinguishing between positive and normative economics does not imply that they should be pursued separately.

A.2.2 On the independence of ethics and economics

On the standard view, our response to the first objection is unfair. Economics consists of many different activities. No one would maintain that ethics has no relevance to *any* of these activities. Some parts of "economics" are not at all like engineering. The standard view does not deny that normative work exists. No one denies that economists are human beings with human interests and that they are accordingly deeply concerned with ethics and economic policy. So parts of economics are necessarily highly evaluative. But it does not follow from this that ethics is relevant to all of economics. In particular it does not follow that ethics is relevant to positive economics, to that part of economics that is concerned to represent, explain, and predict how economic systems function.

So those who hold the standard view can readily concede Machlup's point that economists need to understand some ethics to appreciate the objectives of policy-makers. Only with reference to such moral understanding will economists be able to formulate clear and relevant technical problems. Economists who hope that their work will be relevant to policy questions need to know ethics. But once precise technical questions have been formulated, there is no reason to believe that knowing ethics has anything to contribute to answering them. On the contrary, according to the standard view, there is a categorical difference between questions concerning facts and questions concerning values, and ethics will not be relevant to the answers to technical questions. Some of those who have espoused the standard view have denigrated normative work. Milton Friedman, for example, maintains that with respect to disagreements about fundamental values "men can ultimately only fight" (1953, p. 5). But as we saw above, the standard view leaves the status of value judgments open, and, in any case, the possibility of rational argument concerning values is not what is at issue.

It may well be impossible to be a good *economist* without knowing some ethics, because ethics is so important in formulating research problems and applying the solutions. But on the standard view there is still a *body of knowledge* – namely, positive economics – to which ethics has no relevance.

A.3 How positive economics involves morality

Before appraising this second objection, it is important to recognize how much it concedes. It confesses that economists may need to understand the concepts and the criteria that guide the evaluation of economic outcomes and processes, and it concedes that ethics has an important part to play in economics. It concedes that it may be difficult to be a good economist without knowing some ethics. All the standard view maintains is that positive economics, considered as a body of knowledge, is independent of ethics. We could thus grant this objection without abandoning our project of showing how much ethics has to contribute to doing economics. Just as it is important for economists to know some topology and some statistics even though there are important parts of economics to which these have nothing to contribute, so we might argue that it is important for economists to know some ethics, even if it is not relevant to everything economists do.

We have no wish to deny that there is some truth to the standard view. Some work in economics is largely independent of all ethical concepts and theories. Consider all the work that goes into estimating demand elasticities. Yet, as examples in this book suggest, a good deal of positive economics is unavoidably penetrated with ethical concerns. Ethics has a role within positive economics because ethical commitments affect individual choices and hence economic outcomes, because economic institutions and policies affect ethical commitments, and because the terms in which economists conceptualize and explain individual choices have moral implications.

A.3.1 Institutions, morality, and economic outcomes: the case of blood donation

Ethical commitments are among the causal factors that influence people's economic behavior, and consequently they are among the factors with which economists need to be concerned. If people did not generally tell the truth and keep their promises, economic life would grind to a halt. As theorists who study labor markets have noted, employees and employers have moral beliefs that affect the wage and employment bargains they make. People's moral dispositions affect economic outcomes.

A defender of a value-free economics might respond, "People's beliefs and preferences, including their moral beliefs and preferences obviously have economic consequences. But so do facts about their physiology or about the climate. Why then need economists pay any more attention to morality than to biology or physics?"

This dismissal of the importance of knowing something of ethics cannot be sustained, however, because ethical commitments are not just givens: they depend on economic institutions and outcomes. An example will help clarify this claim. In 1971 Richard Titmuss published *The gift relationship: from human blood to social policy*. In this book Titmuss compared different systems by which human blood is collected for the purposes of transfusion. He was particularly concerned to contrast the system in Britain, in which all blood was obtained by voluntary donations, with the system in the United States, in which some blood was donated and some blood was purchased. He found that blood shortages were more severe in the United States and that the incidence of hepatitis and other blood-borne diseases was higher. The monetary costs in the United States were also much higher. In some intuitive sense of the word "efficient," the system in the United States appeared to be much less efficient.

This much was established pretty firmly by the statistical data. But Titmuss went on to offer a striking causal explanation for these data. He argued that the existence of a market in human blood undermined people's willingness to supply blood, which in turn caused the mediocre outcome. In short, Titmuss argued that the existence of the market *caused* the efficiency loss.

The comparison between Britain and the United States was not Titmuss' only evidence for this striking, and, for most economists, paradoxical claim. Titmuss also pointed out that in Japan prior to World War II, there was a voluntary blood donation system with outcomes similar to those in Britain. After World War II a commercial system was instituted, and the outcomes then resembled those in the United States. Blood donations dropped precipitously. The evidence from Japan is particularly striking not only because it shows blood shortages developing after the institution of a commercial system for acquiring blood, but also because Japan, unlike the United States, is a homogeneous nation with a great deal of social solidarity. In addition to the statistical evidence, Titmuss pointed to statements people make about *why* they donated blood. Donors repeatedly said that they were giving "the gift of life." Implicit in Titmuss' discussion and explicit in Peter Singer's later (1977) defense of Titmuss from Kenneth Arrow's criticisms was the thought that when a pint of blood can be purchased for $50, donors may *reasonably* feel that instead of giving something priceless, the gift of life itself, they are giving the equivalent of $50. Hence people might be less willing to donate blood when blood is also obtained commercially. The moral commitment depends on the institutions and is not just a given.

The bad consequences – higher costs, shortages, and more hepatitis can then be explained. Since fresh blood is perishable, supplies must be regular, and blood cannot be stockpiled to accommodate fluctuations in demand. Shortages may result in a commercial system because people are less willing to donate blood and because the amount of blood available from the small part of the population that is willing to sell blood increases and decreases irregularly. The higher costs are obvious. Finally, in commercial systems, unlike systems involving only voluntary donation, people have an incentive to conceal illnesses such as hepatitis.

This is a fascinating case. It illustrates how people's moral beliefs and preferences influence economic outcomes and how economic arrangements (in this case, whether there is a market for human blood) can influence people's moral commitments. We do not know whether Titmuss' explanation for the dramatic differences between the outcomes in the United States and Britain is correct, but there is no way to understand or assess it without attention to the systems of moral beliefs, which, according to Titmuss, explain the choices of individuals.

A.3.2 Do economists need to have an understanding of morality?

Defenders of the standard view may not yet be convinced. For they might maintain that the causal factors just cited are sociological rather than moral. What matters are people's behavioral dispositions and their *beliefs* about what is right and charitable, not what is "in fact" right or charitable. Economists can study the art market without appreciating art, and they can study the wine market without a cultivated palate. In just the same way, they can study the economic causes and consequences of moral beliefs and preferences without any understanding of morality itself. It doesn't matter for the economist's purposes whether people are motivated by vicious Nazi nonsense concerning "Aryan superiority" or by the simple decency of ordinary blood donors. Economists do not need to evaluate moral beliefs. All that matters is whether people have them and what their causes and consequences are.

Economists can of course sometimes invoke moral beliefs and preferences to explain choices without evaluating them. And in general, to understand why people give blood, one does not have to judge whether people's moral beliefs are true or false. But to assess Titmuss' explanation and to assess the impact of instituting a market in blood, one needs to understand the *reasons* why people donate blood. Without some grasp of the moral issues at stake, one will not be able to understand why people give blood, or what impact a market in human blood will have on their continued willingness to supply blood.

Some of Titmuss' data, such as the lower rate of disease, make good economic "sense." But why should the possibility of selling blood *decrease* its supply? In a generally sympathetic review, Kenneth Arrow can make little sense of this. Part of the problem may be in some of Titmuss' specific formulations, as, for example, when he says that markets "deprive men of their freedom to choose to give or not to give." The quotation is puzzling because the option to donate blood still exists, and indeed it seems that the existence of markets can only *increase* freedom by providing an additional alternative. Furthermore, altruism is obviously not unlimited. Perhaps we are better advised not to squander it when it is not needed. As Adam Smith pointed out

But man has almost constant occasion for the help of his brethren, and it is in vain for him to expect it from their benevolence only . . . It is not from the benevolence of the butcher, the brewer, or the baker, that we expect our dinner, but from their regard to their own interest. We address ourselves, not to their humanity but to their self-love and never talk to them of our own necessities but of their advantages. (1776, pp. 26–7)

Why should the blood donor be different from the butcher or the baker? Surely, an economist might claim that it makes sense to call upon limited supplies of altruism only when there is no alternative (Robertson 1956). Apart from the specific problem that results from imperfections in the ability to test blood and the consequent incentive that commercial providers have to lie about their health, markets in blood, like markets in bread, meat, or wine can only be for the good.

But as Arrow recognizes, Titmuss' case cannot be easily dismissed.

Though the goodwill of neighbors, fellow citizens, and fellow humans is limited, it does not follow that the best society minimizes acts of altruism. Acts of altruism are costly. It takes time to donate blood, and sometimes one feels sick or dizzy for a while. It's not very pleasant. But these acts carry rewards, too. People take pride in doing something decent and unselfish. They take pleasure in thinking of the good their blood may do for someone else. They take pleasure in the good opinion others may form of them (though the concern for reputation is parasitic on the act of giving being independently valued). Having given blood once, one may be *more* rather than less likely to give again. If many of one's neighbors donate, one may again be *more*, rather than less, likely to give, even though the need for one's gift is reduced by the larger supply. Altruism is scarce, but it is not in fixed supply, and in some instances, its supply increases with its consumption (Hirschman 1985). To appraise and comprehend Titmuss' explanation, one needs to understand factors such as these. And there is no way to do so, if one has no understanding of morality.

Arrow is puzzled by the claim that people are on average less willing to supply blood when it can be sold as well as donated and he is unwilling to accept it, because he cannot understand *why* it should be true. What's needed to convince Arrow is not statistical data, but an explanation of the structure of people's moral beliefs and of how moral beliefs change. Arrow is not convinced, because Titmuss fails to make clear that people may be more strongly motivated to make more valuable gifts and that commercializing blood diminishes the value of the gift. If one cannot make sense of these claims, Titmuss' story would be an inscrutable story of strange irrationality. We see no reason why there should not be true stories of strange human irrationality. But Titmuss' story is much easier to credit, if one can "make sense" of it – and there is no way to make sense of it without entering into the moral universe of the donors, learning its rules, and learning how it is affected by factors such as whether blood may be sold.

The moral commitments of economic agents are of course sociological and psychological factors, but they differ from other sociological and psychological factors because they are supported by reasons and held to be generally binding. They need not *always* make sense, but it's puzzling when they don't, and one's first reaction will be that one has not understood them correctly. To understand economic phenomena, one will sometimes need to understand the moral commitments of agents, for these may be of great economic importance. And to do so requires some ability to enter into the moral universe of the agents. Furthermore, the consequences of economic institutions and policies will often be mediated by their effects on people's moral commitments. To be able to predict and explain how people's moral beliefs and preferences change in response to economic policies and institutions (and thus to be able to predict economic outcomes) will again require that one know something about morality.

There is no general justification for setting aside questions about the quality of the arguments supporting the moral commitments of economic actors. Economists may be able to advance their work by *appraising* people's moral dispositions as well as by tracing their causal consequences. It is natural, illuminating, and virtually unavoidable for economists to inquire whether people's observed (or alleged) moral commitments "make sense." Understanding moral beliefs cannot be separated from appraising them and hence from understanding ethics. Descriptions of individual motivation and judgment are likely to be evaluations too, and are not less useful for that.

A.3.3 The moral implications of positive economics and of economic institutions

This evaluative element in positive economics is not only unavoidable, it is also itself causally significant; for the moral convictions of economic agents, unlike causal factors such as rainfall, can be influenced by the way in which they are analyzed and described by economists. In virtually all ethical systems, the question of whether an action or principle is morally defensible will depend at least in part on what its consequences are. Learning economic theory may change people's view of consequences and hence their moral principles and conduct. Knowledge of economics may, for example, have contributed to the change in attitude toward "usury" (charging interest on loans of money). So moral commitments are not only causal factors, but they are also influenced by economic theory.

Furthermore, generalizations about what people in fact do, will (unless written in terms of condemnation) influence what people think ought to be done. Even if what ought to be does not follow logically from what is, it often follows psychologically. Saying that human behavior can be modeled as if it were entirely self-interested unavoidably legitimizes and fosters self-interested behavior. Indeed, there is some evidence that learning economics may make people more selfish (Marwell and Ames 1981, Frank et al. 1993). As we argued in section 4.3, the terms of economic explanations, like Willie Sutton's account of why he robbed banks, can easily carry moral implications.

Learning economics has moral consequences because people's moral commitments are malleable. They are most strongly influenced by the moral education provided by parents, churches, and schools, but they change in response to pressures from peers and in response to the normative expectations of the many groups and institutions in which individuals find themselves. A firm with a well-deserved reputation for honesty and decency will not only have an easier time hiring honest and decent employees, but it will lead the employees it hires to become more honest and decent. The moral culture of the firm, the moral standards of the employees it hires, and the moral commitments of its customers, suppliers, and of the community at large all interact to affect the productivity of the employees and the profitability of the firm.

The honesty, trust, and sense of fair play that help economies to function well are not givens that are fortunately abundant or unfortunately scarce. They are not comparable to geological formations or biological necessities. They grow or wither depending on the institutions within which people live and the shared understandings of these institutions. Their content varies widely from individual to individual and from society to society. Economists need to be concerned not only to nurture these vital moral resources, but also to improve them. Better moral principles may enable people to coordinate their behavior better, and they may spread more readily because they command respect and emulation from others.

Economists need to think about the economic role of moral commitments, and they cannot do so intelligently without understanding and appraising the content of those commitments.

hold or now...

Is this true?

A.4 Conclusions

The fact that economists can rarely describe moral commitments without evaluating them and that economists affect what they see by how they describe it, provide even purely positive economists with reason to think about both the morality that is in fact accepted in the society they study and the morality they think should be accepted. As this book has shown, moral reflection has a role in both positive and normative economics.

Glossary

altruism (sections 5.1, 5.3, and 5.5)

Altruism consists of action that aims at the good of someone else. It is not the same thing as morality.

Arrow's theorem (section 12.1)

This theorem proves that there is no way of making social choices or social evaluations that satisfies a small number of apparently reasonable conditions.

backwards-induction argument (section 13.3)

This argument purports to show that the uniquely rational strategy to follow in a finite iterated prisoner's dilemma is to defect on every move.

bargaining theory (section 13.4)

This is a branch of game theory in which individuals can improve upon an initial non-agreement point only if they can reach agreement on some distribution of the gains from cooperation.

Bayesian theory (section 3.2)

Bayesians offer an interpretation of probability as degrees of belief and support the use of expected utility theory in circumstances of uncertainty.

capability (section 6.5)

A feature of a person that enables the person to carry out various activities ("functionings"). Two examples: literacy and the ability to see. Amartya Sen argues that the standard of living should be understood in terms of capabilities.

cardinal utility (section 3.2)

A utility representation in which comparisons of utility differences are not arbitrary.

commitment (section 5.5)

A person P has a commitment to perform action A if and only if P regards doing A as a duty and would perform A in some circumstances even if doing so conflicted with self-interested and sympathetic preferences.

completeness (see section 3.1)

A condition on preferences. A person's preferences are complete if for all objects of preference x and y, either the person prefers x to y or y to x or the person is indifferent.

consequentialism (chapter 8)

A structure of ethical theories in which the rightness of actions and policies depends upon the goodness of their results.

contractualism (chapter 11)

A range of views concerning justification and motivation for moral theories. The main idea of contractualism is that a moral theory is justified it would be agreed to by rational individuals under the right circumstances.

cost-benefit analysis (section 7.4)

Cost-benefit analysis consists of techniques to determine how much those who would benefit from policies would be willing to pay to institute them and how much those who would be harmed by policies would have to be compensated not to object to instituting them. Although the comparison of these benefits and costs may not by itself decide policy questions, practitioners of cost-benefit analysis believe that such information helps.

deontological moral principles (section 8.5)

Deontological moral principles are non-consequentialist principles like the Ten Commandments. In Samuel Scheffler's terminology, deontological (non-consequentialist) ethical theories employ both "agent-centered prerogatives" (they sometimes *permit* agents to act in a way that does not maximize the good) and "agent-centered constraints" (they sometimes *prohibit* agents from acting so as to maximize the good).

efficiency (chapter 7)

In theoretical economics, efficiency is taken to be Pareto efficiency and thus a matter of preference satisfaction. *See* Pareto optimality.

envy-free allocations (sub-section 10.2.2)

An allocation is envy free if nobody prefers anybody else's to his or her own.

equity (chapter 11)

Economists use the term "equity" frequently as a synonym for "justice."

ethics

Although some people treat ethics as more theoretical than morality, we take ethics and morality to be synonymous. *See* morality.

expected utility (section 3.2)

The expected utility of an action is the utility of its possible outcomes multiplied by their probabilities.

extended sympathy judgments (section 7.1)

An extended sympathy judgment is a preference ranking of "extended alternatives" such as (Jill,y). Extended sympathy judgments are supposed to provide a basis for making interpersonal comparisons of the extent to which people's preferences are satisfied.

externality (section 2.2 and 7.2)

An externality is a consequence of an agent's action that cannot be charged to the agent or to others. Those who cause negative externalities by, for example, polluting the air need not take the costs imposed on others into account in their private calculations of economic benefit. Nor can someone who causes a positive externality by, for example, building a lighthouse collect from all those who benefit from it.

fair allocations (sub-section 10.2.2)

A fair allocation is an allocation that is both Pareto optimal and envy free.

folk psychology (section 4.1)

Folk psychology is the view that people's actions are to be explained by their beliefs and their desires. The explanations economists offer of individual choice behavior conform to folk psychology.

freedom (section 9.1)

Freedom is a relation among three things: (1) an agent, (2) obstacles of some kind, and (3) some of the agent's objectives. An agent is free in some regard when there are no obstacles of a particular kind preventing the agent from doing something. The main kinds of freedom concern (1) the absence of intentional interference from others, (2) the range of alternatives open to one, and (3) the extent to which one is autonomous or self-determining.

game theory (chapter 13)

Game theory is a mathematical theory concerning interdependencies with applications in several fields. It arose as an attempt to understand strategic interactions among individuals, and its main applications still lie in this domain.

independence condition (section 3.2)

A condition on preferences. An agent's preferences satisfy the independence condition if the agent's preferences between two lotteries that differ in only one prize match the agent's preferences between the differing prizes.

independence of irrelevant alternatives (section 12.1)

Arrow's independence of irrelevant alternatives condition says that the social ranking of x and y should depend on nothing except individual rankings of x and y.

justice (chapter 11)

Most philosophers take justice to be the most important part of morality. Justice involves respecting people's rights.

libertarianism (section 9.6)

A kind of moral theory that takes freedom to be the most important social value, emphasizes rights to be as unhindered as possible, and takes justice to be a matter of protecting rights.

moral norms (sections 5.2 and 5.3)

Moral norms are distinguished from other norms by their subject matter (interpersonal interaction where significant benefits and harms are at stake), their weight (they typically override other considerations), and the sanctions, both internal (guilt) and external (blame) attached to their violation.

morality

Morality consists of judgments concerning what things are intrinsically good for people, and what actions are permissible, impermissible, and obligatory, and concerning the moral worth of people and their characters.

normative vs. positive theories (section A.3)

Positive theories say what is, while normative theories say what ought to be. Positive theories are concerned with facts, while normative theories are concerned with values. The distinction is not a sharp one.

norms (sections 5.2 and 5.3)

Norms are prescriptive rules regarding behavior which are shared among a group of people and which are partly sustained by the approval and disapproval of others.

ordinal utility (section 3.1)

An ordinal utility function represents the order of an individual's preferences and nothing more.

paradox of the Paretian libertarian (section 12.4)

Amartya Sen's paradox of the Paretian libertarian is the proof of an inconsistency between the Pareto principle and a principle of minimal liberty (given some other technical conditions).

Pareto improvement (sections 4.2 and 7.2)

A state of affairs S is a Pareto improvement over a state of affairs R if nobody prefers R to S and somebody prefers S to R.

Pareto optimality (or Pareto efficiency) (sections 4.2 and 7.2)

A state of affairs S is Pareto optimal or Pareto efficient if no states of affairs are Pareto improvements over S – in other words, a state of affairs in which it is not possible to satisfy anyone's preferences better without frustrating someone else's preferences.

Pareto principle (sections 12.1 and 12.4)

The strong Pareto principle says that if nobody prefers x to y and somebody prefers y to x, then x ought to be socially preferred to y. The weak Pareto principles says that if everybody prefers x to y, then x ought to be socially preferred to y.

perfect competition (section 4.2)

Perfect competition obtains when there are no interdependencies among people's utility functions, there are markets for all goods and services (and thus no externalities), no barriers to entry or exit from any market, and so many traders in every market that no one can influence prices.

positive affine transformation (section 3.2)

$f'(x)$ is a positive affine transformation of $f(x)$ if and only if $f'(x) = af(x) + b$, where a and b are real numbers and $a > 0$.

positive vs. normative theories – see normative vs. positive theories

potential Pareto improvement (section 7.4)

State S is a potential Pareto improvement over state R if it would be possible for those whose preferences are better satisfied in S than in R to compensate those whose preferences are less well satisfied and thereby to bring about a genuine Pareto improvement.

primary goods (section 6.5)

Primary goods are all-purpose means, such as income and education, that contribute to or do not hinder everyone's life plans. This is Rawls' notion, and he argues that primary goods are a better basis for the evaluation of institutions than are utilities.

prisoner's dilemma (section 13.2)

A prisoner's dilemma is a game with a particular pattern of payoffs. All the players have a single dominant strategy, and the result of each employing that dominant strategy is suboptimal. The following is a version of a two-person prisoner's dilemma:

		K's choice	
		A	B
	A	second best for both	best for K worst for J
J's choice			
	B	best for J worst for K	third best for both

probability (section 3.3)

Probabilities are real numbers between zero and one that are attached to states of affairs and which satisfy the axioms of the mathematical theory of probability. There are currently two main interpretations. "Objective probabilities" may be regarded as the limit of the relative frequency of an occurrence, as one-half is the limit of the frequency with which an unbiased coin will land heads. "Subjective probabilities" are degrees of belief.

rationality (Part I)

A controversial term. In its loosest sense rational behavior is behavior based on good reasons. Economists define rational preferences as preferences that are complete and transitive; rational choice is choice that is determined by rational preference.

reasons (sections 4.1 and 4.3)

Reasons are propositions or the contents of mental states that justify actions or other mental states.

revealed-preference theory (section 3.1)

The theory of revealed preference was an attempt to construct preferences out of choice behavior that satisfied consistency conditions. The aim was to avoid referring to preference as a subjective state responsible for choice.

rights (sections 9.2–9.4)

Rights involve freedoms for the right-holder and various duties for others. Legal and conventional rights are established by law and convention. To say that agents have a moral or natural right to X is to say that the agent ought to have a legal or a conventional right to X.

risk (section 3.2)

One is in a circumstance of risk when the outcome of action is not certain, but all the possible outcomes and their probabilities are known.

Sen's paradox – see paradox of the Paretian libertarian

social choice theory (chapter 12)

Social choice theory is the proof and interpretation of theorems concerning the social aggregation of preferences, judgments, and interests.

social welfare function (section 12.1)

A social welfare function is a ranking of social states.

transitivity (section 3.1)

A condition on preferences. An agent's preferences are transitive if the agent prefers x to z whenever the agent prefers x to y and y to z for all objects of preference x, y, and z, and similarly for indifference.

uncertainty (3.2)

One is in a circumstance of uncertainty when some of the possible outcomes of an action or their probabilities are not known. One is usually in circumstances of uncertainty.

universal domain condition (chapter 12)

The universal domain condition says that a method of social evaluation or social decision-making should work for every profile of individual preferences. It is common in social choice theories and figures in both Arrow's theorem and Sen's paradox of the Paretian libertarian.

utilitarian (chapter 8)

A utilitarian is a proponent of utilitarianism. *See* utilitarianism.

utilitarianism (chapter 8)

Utilitarianism is the best-known variety of consequentialism. According to utilitarianism, an action or policy is right if it results in no less happiness or no less preference satisfaction than any alternative.

utility (section 3.1)

Utility is simply a mathematical device for representing features of preference orderings – an index or indicator. It is not a subjective state like pleasure and it is not itself an object of preference or choice.

welfare (section 4.2 and chapter 6)

A person's welfare is how good things are for the person. Economists often take welfare to be the satisfaction of preferences.

References

Ackerman, Bruce 1981. *Social justice in the liberal state*. New Haven: Yale University Press.

Akerlof, George 1982. "Labor contracts as partial gift exchange." *Quarterly Journal of Economics* 84: 488–500.

1983. "Loyalty filters." *American Economic Review* 73: 54–63.

1984. "Gift exchange and efficiency wage theory: four views." *American Economic Review Proceedings* 74: 79–83.

Akerlof, George and Janet Yellen 1986. "Introduction," in George Akerlof and Janet Yellen (eds.), *Efficiency wage models of the labor market*. New York: Cambridge University Press, pp. 1–21.

Alexander, Larry and Maimon Schwarzschild 1987. "Liberalism, neutrality, and equality of welfare vs. equality of resources." *Philosophy and Public Affairs* 16: 85–110.

Alexander, Sidney 1974. "Social evaluation through notional choice." *Quarterly Journal of Economics* 88: 597–624.

Allais, Maurice 1952. "The foundations of a positive theory of choice involving risk and a criticism of the postulates and axioms of the American school," in Allais and Hagen, 1979, pp. 27–145.

Allais, Maurice and Otto Hagen (eds.) 1979. *Expected utility hypotheses and the Allais paradox*. Dordrecht: Reidel.

Arneson, Richard 1989. "Equality and equal opportunity for welfare." *Philosophical Studies* 56: 77–93.

1990. "Liberalism, distributive subjectivism, and equal opportunity for welfare." *Philosophy and Public Affairs* 19: 158–94.

Arrow, Kenneth 1951. *Social choice and individual values*. New York: Wiley, (2nd edn., 1963).

1967. "Values and collective decision making," reproduced in Frank Hahn and Martin Hollis eds. 1979, *Philosophy and economic theory*. Oxford: Oxford University Press, pp. 110–26.

1972. "Gifts and exchanges." *Philosophy and Public Affairs* 1: 343–62.

1973. "Some ordinalist-utilitarian notes on Rawls' theory of justice." *Journal of Philosophy* 70: 245–63.

1974. *The limits of organization* (1st edn.). New York: Norton.

1978. "Extended sympathy and the possibility of social choice." *Philosophia* 7: 223–37.

227

Arrow, Kenneth and Frank Hahn 1971. *General competitive analysis*. San Francisco: Holden Day.

Axelrod, Robert 1984. *The evolution of cooperation*. New York: Basic Books.

Baker, C. 1975. "The ideology of the economic analysis of law." *Philosophy and Public Affairs* 5: 3–48.

Barry, Brian 1973. *The liberal theory of justice*. Oxford: Clarendon Press.

  1989. *Theories of justice. Volume 1 of treatise on social justice*. Berkeley, CA: University of California Press.

Basu, Kaushik 1984. "The right to give up rights." *Economica* 51: 413–22.

Bator, Francis M. 1957. "The simple analytics of welfare maximization." *American Economic Review* 47: 22–59.

Batson, C. Daniel 1993. "Experimental tests for the existence of altruism," in David Hull, Micky Forbes, and Kathleen Okruklik (eds.), *PSA 1992*, vol. 2. East Lansing, MI: Philosophy of Science Association, pp. 69–78.

Baumol, William 1986. *Superfairness: applications and theory*. Cambridge, MA: MIT Press.

Becker, Gary 1981. *A treatise on the family*. Cambridge, MA: Harvard University Press.

Beitz, Charles 1979. *Political theory and international relations*. Princeton: Princeton University Press.

Benn, Stanley 1967. "Egalitarianism and the equal consideration of interests," in Pennock and Chapman, pp. 61–78.

Bentham, Jeremy 1789. *An introduction to the principles of morals and legislation*. (Ed. W. Harrison, Oxford: Basil Blackwell, 1967).

Berg, J., J. Dickhaut, and J. O'Brien 1985. "Preference reversal and arbitrage," in Vernon Smith (ed.), *Research in experimental economics*, vol. 3. Greenwich: JAI Press, pp. 31–72.

Bergson, Abram 1938. "A reformulation of certain aspects of welfare economics." *Quarterly Journal of Economics* 52: 30–4.

Berlin, Isaiah 1969. "Two concepts of liberty," in *Four essays on liberty*. Oxford: Oxford University Press, pp. 118–72.

Bicchieri, Cristina 1988. "Self-refuting theories of strategic interaction: a paradox of common knowledge." *Erkenntnis* 29: 69–85.

  1990. "Paradoxes of rationality." *Midwest Studies in Philosophy* 15: 65–79.

Binmore, Ken 1987. "Modeling rational players: Part I." *Economics and Philosophy* 3: 179–214.

  1988. "Modeling rational players: Part II." *Economics and Philosophy* 4: 9–56.

  1992. *Fun and games*. New York: D. C. Heath.

  1994. *Playing fair: game theory and the social contract*. Cambridge MA: MIT Press.

Binmore, K., J. Swierzsbinski, S. Hsu, and C. Proulx 1993. "Focal points and bargaining." *International Journal of Game Theory* 22: 381–409.

Blackorby, Charles and David Donaldson 1988. "Cash versus kind, self-selection, and efficient transfers." *American Economic Review* 78: 691–700.

Blau, Julian H. 1975. "Liberal values and independence." *Review of Economic Studies* 42: 395–401.

Blinder, Alan and Don Choi 1990. "A shred of evidence on theories of wage stickiness." *Quarterly Journal of Economics* 105: 1003–15.

Block, Walter 1982. "A free market in roads," in Machan, pp. 164–83.

Bonnano, Giacomo 1991. "The logic of rational play in games of perfect information." *Economics and Philosophy* 7: 37–65.

Boulding, Kenneth 1978. *The economy of love and fear; a preface to grants economics*. Belmont, CA: Wadsworth.

Bowles, Samuel 1985. "The production process in a competitive economy: Walrasian, neo-Hobbesian and Marxian models." *American Economic Review* 75: 16–36.

Bowles, Samuel and Herbert Gintis 1993. "A political and economic case for the democratic enterprise." *Economics and Philosophy* 9: 75–100.

Bowles, Samuel, Herbert Gintis, and Bo Gustaffson (eds.) 1993. *Markets and democracy: participation, accountability, and efficiency*. Cambridge: Cambridge University Press.

Brandt, Richard 1979. *A theory of the right and the good*. Oxford: Oxford University Press.

Braybrooke, David 1987. *Meeting needs*. Princeton: Princeton University Press.

Brennan, Geoffrey and James Buchanan 1985. *The reason of rules: constitutional political economy*. New York: Cambridge University Press.

Brennan, Geoffrey and Philip Pettit 1993. "Hands invisible and intangible." *Synthese* 94: 191–225.

Brennan, Timothy 1989. "A methodological assessment of multiple utility frameworks." *Economics and Philosophy* 5: 189–208.

Broome, John 1989. "Should social preferences be consistent?" *Economics and Philosophy* 5: 7–18.

   1991a. "Utility." *Economics and Philosophy* 7: 1–12.

   1991b. *Weighing goods*. Oxford: Basil Blackwell.

Buchanan, Allen E. 1985. *Ethics, efficiency, and the market*. Totowa, NJ: Rowman and Allanheld.

Buchanan, James 1975. *The limits of liberty: between anarchy and leviathan*. Chicago: University of Chicago Press.

Carter, Ian 1995. "Interpersonal comparisons of freedom." *Economics and Philosophy* 11: 1–23.

Christman, John (ed.) 1989. *The inner citadel: essays on individual autonomy*. New York: Oxford University Press.

Chu, Y. and R. Chu 1990. "The subsidence of preference reversals in simplified and marketlike experimental settings: a note." *American Economic Review* 80: 902–11.

Churchland, Paul M. 1989. *A neurocomputational perspective: the nature of mind and the structure of science*. Cambridge, MA: MIT Press.

Coase, Ronald 1960. "The problem of social cost." *Journal of Law and Economics* 3: 1–30.

Cohen, G. A. 1989. "On the currency of egalitarian justice." *Ethics* 99: 906–44.

   1993. "Equality of what? On welfare, goods, and capabilities," in Nussbaum and Sen, pp. 9–30.

Coleman, James 1990. *Foundations of social theory*. Cambridge, MA: Harvard University Press.

Coleman, Jules 1984. "Economics and the law: a critical review of the foundations of the economic approach to law." *Ethics* 94: 649–79.

Coleman, Jules L. and Jody Kraus 1986. "Rethinking the theory of legal rights." *Yale Law Review* 95: 1335–71; reprinted in *Markets, morals and the law*. Cambridge: Cambridge University Press, 1988, pp. 28–63.

Collard, David 1978. *Altruism and economy: a study in non-selfish economics*. New York: Oxford University Press.

Cooter, Robert 1989. "Rawls's lexical orderings are good economics." *Economics and Philosophy* 5: 47–54.

Cowen, Tyler (ed.) 1988. *The theory of market failure: a critical examination*. Fairfax, VA: George Mason University Press.

Daniels, Norman 1976. *Reading Rawls*. New York: Basic Books.

D'Aspremont, Claude and Louis Gevers 1977. "Equity and the informational basis of collective choice." *Review of Economic Studies* 44: 199–209.

Davidson, Donald 1963. "Actions, reasons, and causes." *Journal of Philosophy* 60; reprinted in Davidson 1980, pp. 3–20.

1980. *Essays on actions and events*. New York: Oxford University Press.

1986. "Judging interpersonal interests," in Elster and Hylland, pp. 195–211.

Davies, J. C. 1963. *Human nature in politics*. New York: Wiley.

Dawes, Robyn, Alphons van de Kragt, and John Orbell 1990. "Cooperation for the benefit of us – not me, or my conscience," in Jane Mansbridge (ed.), *Beyond self-interest*. Chicago: University of Chicago Press, pp. 97–111.

Debreu, Gerard 1959. *Theory of value*. New York: Wiley.

Demsetz, Harold 1964. "The exchange and enforcement of property rights." *Journal of Law and Economics* 7; reprinted in Cowen 1988, pp. 127–45.

1967. "Toward a theory of property rights." *American Economic Review* 57: 347–59.

Dennett, Daniel 1987. *The intentional stance*. Cambridge, MA: MIT Press.

Dretske, Fred 1988. *Explaining behavior: reasons in a world of causes*. Cambridge MA: MIT Press.

Dworkin, Gerald 1971. "Paternalism," in Richard Wasserstrom (ed.), *Morality and the law*. Belmont, CA: Wadsworth, pp. 107–36.

1988. *The theory and practice of autonomy*. Cambridge: Cambridge University Press.

Dworkin, Gerald, Gordon Bermant, and Peter Brown (eds.) 1977. *Markets and morals*. Washington: Hemisphere Publishing.

Dworkin, Ronald 1977. *Taking rights seriously*. Cambridge: Harvard University Press.

1981a. "What is equality? Part 1: Equality of welfare." *Philosophy and Public Affairs* 10: 185–246.

1981b. "What is equality? Part 2: Equality of resources." *Philosophy and Public Affairs* 10: 283–345.

1990. "Foundations of liberal equality," in *The Tanner Lectures on Human Values, XI, 1990*. (Ed. Grethe B. Peterson.) Salt Lake City: University of Utah Press, pp. 1–119.

Ellsberg, Daniel 1961. "Risk, ambiguity, and the Savage axioms." *Quarterly Journal of Economics* 75: 643–99.

Elster, Jon 1983. *Sour grapes: studies in the subversion of rationality.* Cambridge: Cambridge University Press.

1989a. *The cement of society: a study of social order.* Cambridge: Cambridge University Press.

1989b. "Social norms and economic theory." *Journal of Economic Perspectives* 3: 99–117.

Elster, Jon and Aanund Hylland (eds.) 1986. *Foundations of social choice theory.* New York: Cambridge University Press.

Elster, Jon and John Roemer (eds.) 1991. *Interpersonal comparisons of well-being.* Cambridge: Cambridge University Press.

Etzioni, Amitai 1986. "The case for a multiple-utility conception." *Economics and Philosophy* 2: 159–84.

1988. *The moral dimension. Toward a new economics.* New York: Macmillan.

Feinberg, Joel 1973. *Social philosophy.* Englewood Cliffs, NJ: Prentice-Hall.

1986. *Harm to self.* Oxford: Oxford University Press, 1986.

Fleming, Marcus 1952. "A cardinal concept of welfare." *Quarterly Journal of Economics* 66: 366–84.

Fleurbaey, Marc 1995. "Equal opportunity or equal social outcome." *Economics and Philosophy* 11: 25–56.

Foley, Duncan 1967. "Resource allocation and the public sector." *Yale Economic Essays*, Spring, pp. 45–102.

Frank, Robert 1988. *Passions within reason: the strategic role of the emotions.* New York: W. W. Norton.

1993. "Melding sociology and economics: James Coleman's *Foundations of social theory.*" *Journal of Economic Literature* 9: 115–64.

n.d. "What price the moral high ground?" unpublished.

Frank, Robert, Thomas Gilovich, and Dennis Regan 1993. "Does studying economics inhibit cooperation?" *Journal of Economic Perspectives* 7: 159–72.

Frankfurt, Harry 1971. "Freedom of will and the concept of a person." *Journal of Philosophy* 68: 5–20.

Friedman, Milton 1953. "The methodology of positive economics," in Milton Friedman (ed.), *Essays in positive economics.* Chicago: University of Chicago Press, pp. 3–43.

1962. *Capitalism and freedom.* Chicago: University of Chicago Press.

Friedman, Milton and Rose Friedman 1980. *Free to choose.* New York: Harcourt Brace Javanovich.

Frolich, Norman, Thomas Hunt, Joe Oppenheimer, and R. Harrison Wagner 1975. "Individual contributions for collective goods: alternative models." *Journal of Conflict Resolution* 19: 310–29.

Gaertner, Wulf, Prasanta Pattanaik, and Kotaro Suzumura 1992. "Individual rights revisited." *Economica* 59: 161–77.

Gambetta, Diego (ed.) 1988. *Trust: making and breaking cooperative relations.* Oxford: Basil Blackwell.

Gärdenfors, Peter 1981. "Rights, games and social choice." *Nous* 15: 341–56.

Gärdenfors, Peter and Nils-Eric Sahlin (eds.) 1988. *Decision, probability, and utility: selected readings*. Cambridge: Cambridge University Press.

Gauthier, David 1986. *Morals by agreement*. Oxford: Oxford University Press.

1990. *Moral dealing: contract, ethics, and reason*. Ithaca: Cornell University Press.

Gibbard, Allan 1974. "A Pareto-consistent libertarian claim." *Journal of Economic Theory* 7: 388–410.

1986. "Interpersonal comparisons: preference, good, and the intrinsic reward of a life," in Elster and Hylland, pp. 165–94.

1990. *Wise choices, apt feelings: a theory of normative judgment*. Cambridge, MA: Harvard University Press.

Gibbons, R. 1992. *Game theory for applied economists*. Princeton: Princeton University Press.

Gilbert, Margaret 1990. "Walking together: a paradigmatic social phenomenon," in Peter French, Theodore Uehling, and Howard Wettstein (eds.), *Midwest Studies in Philosophy* vol. 15, *The philosophy of the human sciences*. Notre Dame, IN: University of Notre Dame Press, pp. 1–14.

Glover, Jonathan 1990. *Causing death and saving lives*. London: Penguin Books.

Graaf, Jon de von 1957. *Theoretical welfare economics*. Cambridge: Cambridge University Press.

Grether, David and Charles Plott 1979. "Economic theory of choice and the preference reversal phenomenon." *American Economic Review* 69: 623–38.

Griffin, James 1986. *Well-being: its meaning, measurement and moral importance*. Oxford: Clarendon Press.

1991. "Against the taste model," in Elster and Roemer, pp. 45–69.

Griffith, William B. and Robert S. Goldfarb 1991. "Amending the economist's 'rational egoist' model to include moral values and norms," in Kenneth J. Koford and Jeffrey B. Miller (eds.), *Social norms and economic institutions*. Ann Arbor: University of Michigan Press, pp. 39–84.

Hamlin, Alan 1986. *Ethics, economics, and the state*. New York: St. Martin's Press.

Hammond, Peter 1976. "Equity, Arrow's conditions and Rawls' difference principle." *Econometrica* 44: 793–804.

1983. "Ex-post optimality as a dynamically consistent objective for collective choice under uncertainty," in Prasanta Pattanaik and Maurice Salles (eds.) *Social choice and welfare*. Amsterdam: North-Holland.

Hampton, Jean 1986. *Hobbes and the social contract tradition*. Cambridge: Cambridge University Press.

1987. "Free-rider problems in the production of collective goods." *Economics and Philosophy* 3: 245–73.

1994. "The failure of expected-utility theory as a theory of reason." *Economics and Philosophy* 10: 195–242.

Harberger, Arnold C. 1978. "On the use of distributional weights in social cost-benefit analysis." *Journal of Political Economy* 86: s 87–120.

Hardin, Russell 1982. *Collective action*. Baltimore: Johns Hopkins University Press.

1988. *Morality within the limits of reason*. Chicago: University of Chicago Press.

Hare, Richard 1981. *Moral thinking: its levels, method, and point.* Oxford: Oxford University Press.

Hargreaves Heap, S., M. Hollis, B. Lyons, R. Sugden, and A. Weale 1992. *The theory of choice: a critical guide.* Oxford: Basil Blackwell.

Harris, Richard and Olewiler, Nancy 1979. "The welfare economics of *ex-post* optimality." *Economica* 46: 137–47.

Harsanyi, John 1955. "Cardinal welfare, individualistic ethics and interpersonal comparisons of utility." *Journal of Political Economy* 63: 309–21.

  1977a. "Morality and the theory of rational behavior." *Social Research* 44: 623–56. (Reprinted in Sen and Williams, 1982, pp. 39–62.)

  1977b. *Rational behavior and bargaining equilibrium in games and social situations.* Cambridge: Cambridge University Press.

Hart, Herbert L. A. 1955. "Are there any natural rights?" *Philosophical Review* 64: 175–91. (Reprinted in Waldron, 1984, pp. 77–90.)

Hausman, Daniel 1992. *The inexact and separate science of economics.* Cambridge: Cambridge University Press.

  1995. "The impossibility of interpersonal utility comparisons." *Mind* 104: 473–90.

Hausman, Daniel and Michael McPherson 1993. "Taking ethics seriously: economics and contemporary moral philosophy." *Journal of Economic Literature* 31: 671–731.

  1994. "Preference, belief, and welfare." *American Economic Review Papers and Proceedings* 84: 396–400

Hayek, Friedrich von 1960. *The constitution of liberty.* Chicago: University of Chicago Press.

  1967. "The moral element in free enterprise," in *Studies in philosophy, politics and economics.* Chicago: University of Chicago Press, pp. 229–36.

  1976. *The mirage of social justice.* Chicago: University of Chicago Press.

Hicks, John 1939. "The foundations of welfare economics." *Economic Journal* 49: 696–712.

Hirsch, Fred 1976. *The social limits to growth.* Cambridge: Harvard University Press.

Hirschman, Albert 1985. "Against parsimony: three easy ways of complicating some categories of economic discourse." *Economics and Philosophy* 1: 7–22.

Hobbes, Thomas 1651. *Leviathan, or the matter, forme and power of a common wealth ecclesiasticall and civil.* (Reprinted New York: Collier Books, 1962.)

Hochman, Harold and James Rodgers 1969. "Pareto optimal redistribution." *American Economic Review* 59: 542–57.

Hohfeld, Wesley 1919. *Fundamental legal conceptions.* New Haven: Yale University Press.

Hornstein, Harvey, Elisha Fisch, and Michael Holmes 1968. "Influence of a model's feelings about his behavior and his relevance as a comparison other on observers' helping behavior." *Journal of Personality and Social Psychology* 10: 220–26.

Hume, David 1738. *A treatise of human nature.* (Reprinted Oxford: Clarendon Press, 1966.)

1748. *An inquiry concerning human understanding*. (Reprinted Indianapolis: Bobbs-Merrill, 1955.)

Hurley, Susan L. 1989. *Natural reasons: personality and polity*. Oxford: Oxford University Press.

Kagan, Shelly 1989. *The limits of morality*. Oxford: Oxford University Press.

Kalai, Ehud and Meir Smorodinsky 1975. "Other solutions to Nash's bargaining problem." *Econometrica* 43: 513–18.

Kaldor, Nicholas 1939. "Welfare propositions of economics and interpersonal comparisons of utility." *Economic Journal* 49: 549–52.

Kamm, Frances M. 1992. "Non-consequentialism, the person as an end-in-itself, and the significance of status." *Philosophy and Public Affairs* 21: 354–89.

Kant, Immanuel 1785. *Groundwork of the metaphysics of morals*. (Trans. H. Paton, New York: Harper & Row, 1948.)

Kavka, Gregory 1986. *Hobbesian moral and political theory*. Princeton: Princeton University Press.

Kelman, Steven 1981. *What price incentives?* Boston, MA: Auburn House.

1986. "A case for in-kind transfers." *Economics and Philosophy* 2: 53–74.

Knight, Frank 1921. *Risk, uncertainty and profit*. Chicago: University of Chicago Press.

1935. "Economics and human action," in *The ethics of competition, and other essays*. New York and London: Harper & Brothers.

Kolm, Serge-Christophe 1972. *Justice et équité*. Paris: Editions du Centre National de la Recherche Scientifique.

Koopmans, Tjalling 1957. *Three essays on the state of economic science*. New York: McGraw-Hill.

Kraus, Jody and Jules Coleman 1987. "Morality and the theory of rational choice." *Ethics* 97: 715–49.

Kreps, David M., Paul Milgrom, John Roberts, and Robert Wilson 1982. "Rational cooperation in the finitely repeated prisoner's dilemma." *Journal of Economic Theory* 27: 245–52.

Kreps, David and Robert Wilson 1982. "Sequential equilibria." *Econometrica* 50: 863–94.

Kukathas, Chandran and Philip Pettit 1990. *A theory of justice and its critics*. Oxford: Blackwell.

Kymlicka, Will 1990. *Contemporary political philosophy: an introduction*. New York: Oxford University Press.

1991. "Rethinking the family." *Philosophy and Public Affairs* 20: 77–97.

Layard, Richard and Stephen Glaister 1994. *Cost-benefit analysis* (2nd edn.). Cambridge: Cambridge University Press.

Lerner, Abba 1959a. "Consumption-loan interest and money." *Journal of Political Economy* 67: 512–18.

1959b. "Rejoinder." *Journal of Political Economy* 67: 523–5.

Levi, Isaac 1980. *The enterprise of knowledge*. Cambridge, MA: MIT Press.

1986. "The paradoxes of Allais and Ellsberg." *Economics and Philosophy* 2: 23–53.

1990. "Pareto unanimity and consensus." *Journal of Philosophy* 89: 481–92.

Lewis, David 1969. *Convention*. Cambridge: Harvard University Press.

Lichtenstein, Sarah and Paul Slovic 1971. "Reversals of preference between bids and choices in gambling decisions." *Journal of Experimental Psychology* 89: 46–55.

Little, Ian 1957. *A critique of welfare economics* (2nd edn.). Oxford: Oxford University Press.

Locke, John 1690. *Second treatise on government*, in Peter Laslett, *Two treatises of government: a critical edition* (2nd edn.). Cambridge: Cambridge University Press.

Lomasky, Loren 1987. *Persons, rights and the moral community*. New York: Oxford University Press.

Luce, Robert Duncan and Howard Raiffa 1957. *Games and decisions*. New York: Wiley.

Lukes, Steven 1977. *Essays in social theory*. New York: Columbia University Press.

MacCallum, Gerald 1967. "Negative and positive freedom." *Philosophical Review* 76: 312–34.

McClennen, Edward 1990. *Rationality and dynamic choice: foundational explorations*. Cambridge: Cambridge University Press.

McDowell, John 1978. "Are moral judgments hypothetical imperatives?" *Proceedings of the Aristotelian Society Supplementary Volume*, pp. 13–29.

Machan, Tibor (ed.) 1982. *The libertarian reader*. Totowa, NJ: Rowman and Littlefield.

Machina, Mark 1987. "Choice under uncertainty: problems solved and unsolved." *Journal of Economic Perspectives* 1: 121–54.

　　1990. "Choice under uncertainty: problems solved and unsolved," in Karen Schweers Cook and Margaret Levi (eds.), *The limits of rationality*. Chicago and London: University of Chicago Press, pp. 90–132.

Machlup, Fritz 1969. "Positive and normative economics," in Robert Heilbroner (ed.), *Economic means and social ends: essays in political economics*. Englewood Cliffs, NJ: Prentice-Hall, pp. 99–124.

MacKay, Alfred 1980. *Arrow's theorem: the paradox of social choice. A case study in the philosophy of economics*. New Haven: Yale University Press.

　　1986. "Extended sympathy and interpersonal utility comparisons." *Journal of Philosophy* 83: 305–22.

McKean, Roland N. 1975. "Economics of trust, altruism, and corporate responsibility," in Edmund Phelps (ed.), *Altruism, morality and economic theory*. New York: Russell Sage Foundation, pp. 29–44.

Mackie, John 1977. *Ethics: inventing right and wrong*. Harmondsworth: Penguin.

McPherson, Michael 1982. "Mill's moral theory and the problem of preference change." *Ethics* 92: 252–73.

　　1983a. "Efficiency and liberty in the productive enterprise: recent work in the economics of work organization." *Philosophy and Public Affairs* 12: 354–68.

　　1983b. "Want formation, morality, and some 'interpretive' aspects of economic inquiry," in Norma Haan, Robert N. Bellah, Paul Rabinow, and William M. Sullivan (eds.), *Social science as moral inquiry*. New York: Columbia University Press, pp. 96–124.

Mansbridge, Jane (ed.) 1990. *Beyond self-interest*. Chicago: University of Chicago Press, pp. 254–63.

Margolis, Howard 1982. *Selfishness, altruism and rationality*. Cambridge: Cambridge University Press.

Martin, Rex 1993. *A system of rights*. Oxford: Clarendon Press.

Marwell, Gerald and Ruth Ames 1981. "Economists free ride. Does anyone else? Experiments on the provision of public goods. IV." *Journal of Public Economics* 15: 295–310.

Maynard Smith, J. 1982. *Evolution and the theory of games*. Cambridge: Cambridge University Press, 1982.

Meade, James E. 1964. *Efficiency, equality, and the ownership of property*. London: G. Allen and Unwin.

Meckling, William 1960a. "An exact consumption-loan model of interest: a comment." *Journal of Political Economy* 68: 72–6.

1960b. "Rejoinder." *Journal of Political Economy* 68: 83–4.

Melden, A. I. 1961. *Free action*. London: Routledge.

Mill, John Stuart 1859. *On liberty*. (Ed. Currin V. Shields, New York: Macmillan, 1985.)

1863. *Utilitarianism*. (Reprinted in Marshall Cohen (ed.), *The Philosophy of John Stuart Mill*. New York: Modern Library, 1961, pp. 321–98.)

Miller, David 1982. "Arguments for equality." *Midwest Studies in Philosophy* 7: 73–88.

Mises, Ludwig von 1949. *Human action. A treatise on economics*. New Haven: Yale University Press.

Mishan, E. 1971. *Cost benefit analysis: an introduction*. New York: Praeger.

1981. *An introduction to normative economics*. Oxford: Oxford University Press.

Mueller, Dennis 1992. "The corporation and the economist." *International Journal of Industrial Organization* 10: 147–70; reprinted and cited from D. Hausman (ed.), *The philosophy of economics: an anthology* (2nd edn.). New York: Cambridge University Press, 1994, pp. 289–314.

Musgrave, Richard 1974. "Maximin, uncertainty, and the leisure trade-off." *Quarterly Journal of Economics* 88: 625–42.

Nagel, Thomas 1970. *The possibility of altruism*. Oxford: Clarendon Press.

1983. "Libertarianism without foundations," in Jeffrey Paul (ed.), *Reading Nozick: essays on anarchy, state and utopia*. Oxford: Basil Blackwell, pp. 191–205.

1986. *The view from nowhere*. New York: Oxford University Press.

Narveson, Jan 1988. *The libertarian idea*. Philadelphia: Temple University Press.

Nash, John 1950. "The bargaining problem." *Econometrica* 18: 155–62.

Nelson, Alan 1988. "Economic rationality and morality." *Philosophy and Public Affairs* 17: 149–66.

Neumann, John von and Oskar Morgenstern 1947. *Theory of games and economic behavior* (2nd edn.). Princeton: Princeton University Press.

Ng, Yew-Kwang 1983. *Welfare economics: introduction and development of basic concepts* (revised edn.). London: Macmillan.

Nielsen, Kai 1985. *Equality and liberty: a defense of radical egalitarianism*. Totowa, NJ: Rowman and Allanheld.

Nozick, Robert 1974. *Anarchy, state and utopia*. New York: Basic Books.

Nussbaum, Martha and Amartya Sen (eds.) 1993. *The quality of life*. Oxford: Clarendon Press.

Okin, Susan Moller 1989. *Justice, gender and the family*. New York: Basic Books.

Okun, Arthur 1975. *Equality and efficiency: the big tradeoff*. Washington, DC: Brookings Institution.

Parfit, Derek 1979. "Prudence, morality and the prisoner's dilemma." *Proceedings of the British Academy*.

  1984. *Reasons and persons*. Oxford: Oxford University Press.

Paul, Ellen, Fred Miller, Jr., Jeffrey Paul, and John Ahrens (eds.) 1988. *The new social contract: essays on Gauthier*. Oxford: Blackwell.

Pazner, Elisha A. and David Schmeidler 1974. "A difficulty in the concept of fairness." *Review of Economic Studies* 41: 441–3.

Pennock, J. Roland and John W. Chapman (eds.) 1967. *Equality*. New York: Atherton Press.

Pettit, Philip 1990. "*Virtus normativa*: rational choice perspectives." *Ethics* 100: 725–55.

Pettit, Philip and Robert Sugden 1989. "The backward induction paradox." *Journal of Philosophy* 86: 169–82.

Phelps, Edmund S. 1973. "Taxation of wage income for economic justice." *Quarterly Journal of Economics* 87: 332–54.

Pitt, Joseph (ed.) 1981. *Philosophy in economics*. Boston: Reidel.

Plamenatz, John 1967. "Diversity of rights and kinds of equality," in Pennock and Chapman, pp. 79–98.

Pogge, Thomas 1989. *Realizing Rawls*. Ithaca: Cornell University Press, 1989.

Posner, R. 1972. *Economic analysis of law*. Boston: Little, Brown & Co.

Putterman, Louis 1984. "On some recent explanations of why capital hires labor." *Economic Inquiry* 22: 171–87.

Railton, Peter 1984. "Alienation, consequentialism, and the demands of morality." *Philosophy and Public Affairs* 13: 134–71.

Ramsey, Frank 1926. "Truth and probability," in R. B. Braithwaite (ed.), *The foundations of mathematics and other logical essays*. London: Routledge and Kegan Paul, pp. 156–98.

Rand, Ayn 1964. *The virtue of selfishness*. New York: Signet Books.

Rawls, John 1955. "Two concepts of rules." *Philosophical Review* 64: 3–33.

  1971. *A theory of justice*. Cambridge, MA: Harvard University Press.

  1982. "Social unity and primary goods," in Sen and Williams, pp. 159–86.

  1993. *Political liberalism*. New York: Columbia University Press.

Raz, Joseph 1986. *The morality of freedom*. Oxford: Oxford University Press.

Reder, Melvin 1979. "The place of ethics in the theory of production," in Michael Boskin (ed.), *Economics and human welfare: essays in honor of Tibor Scitovsky*. New York: Academic Press, pp. 133–46.

Regan, Donald 1980. *Utilitarianism and Cooperation*. Oxford Clarendon Press.

Reich, Michael and James Devine 1981. "The microeconomics of conflict and hierarchy in capitalist production." *Review of Radical Political Economy* 12: 27–45.

Riley, Jonathan 1989. "Rights to liberty in purely private matters, Part I." *Economics and Philosophy* 5: 121–66.

  1990. "Rights to liberty in purely private matters, Part II." *Economics and Philosophy* 6: 27–64.

Robbins, Lionel 1935. *An essay on the nature and significance of economic science* (2nd edn.). London: Macmillan.

Robertson, Dennis 1956. "What does the economist economize?" in *Economic commentaries*. London: Staples Press, pp. 147–55.

Roemer, John 1985. "Equality of talent." *Economics and Philosophy* 1: 151–88.

  1986a. "The mismarriage of bargaining theory and distributive justice." *Ethics* 97: 88–110.

  1986b. "Equality of resources implies equality of welfare." *Quarterly Journal of Economics* 101: 751–84.

  1987. "Egalitarianism, responsibility, and information." *Economics and Philosophy* 3: 215–44.

  1988. *Free to lose*. Cambridge: Harvard University Press.

Rosenberg, Alexander 1976. *Microeconomic laws: a philosophical analysis.* Pittsburgh: University of Pittsburgh Press.

  1988. *Philosophy of social science*. Boulder: Westview Press.

Roth, Alvin and Michael Malouf 1979. "Game theoretical models and the role of information in bargaining." *Psychological Review* 86: 574–94.

Roth, Alvin, Michael Malouf, and J. Keith Murnighan 1981. "Sociological versus strategic factors in bargaining." *Journal of Economic Behavior and Organizations* 2: 153–77.

Rousseau, Jean-Jacques 1762. *The social contract*. (Trans. Maurice Cranston. Harmondsworth: Penguin, 1968.)

Ryan, Alan (ed.) 1979. *The idea of freedom: essays in honour of Isaiah Berlin*. New York: Oxford University Press.

Sagoff, Mark 1986. "Values and preferences." *Ethics* 96: 301–16.

Samuelson, Paul 1947. *Foundations of economic analysis.* Cambridge, MA: Harvard University Press.

  1950. "Evaluation of real national income." *Oxford Economic Papers* NS 2: 1–29.

  1958. "An exact consumption-loan model of interest with or without the social contrivance of money." *Journal of Political Economy* 66: 467–82.

  1959. "Reply." *Journal of Political Economy* 67: 518–22.

  1960. "Infinity, unanimity and singularity: a reply." *Journal of Political Economy* 68: 76–83.

Sandel, Michael 1982. *Liberalism and the limits of justice*. Cambridge: Cambridge University Press.

Savage, Leonard 1972. *The foundations of statistics*. New York: Dover.

Scanlon, Thomas 1975. "Preference and urgency." *Journal of Philosophy* 72: 655–70.

1982. "Contractualism and utilitarianism," in Sen and Williams, pp. 103–28.

1986. "Equality of resources and equality of welfare: a forced marriage?" *Ethics* 97: 11–18.

1991. "The moral basis of interpersonal comparisons," in Elster and Roemer, pp. 17–44.

Scheffler, Samuel 1982. *The rejection of consequentialism: a philosophical investigation of the considerations underlying rival moral conceptions*. Oxford: Clarendon Press.

(ed.) 1988. *Consequentialism and its critics*. Oxford: Oxford University Press.

Schelling, Thomas 1978. *Micromotives and macrobehavior*. New York: Norton.

1984. *Choice and consequence*. Cambridge: Harvard University Press.

Schick, Frederic 1986. "Money pumps and Dutch bookies." *Journal of Philosophy* 83: 112–1981.

Schotter, Andrew 1981. *The economic theory of social institutions*. Cambridge: Cambridge University Press.

Seidenfeld Teddy, Joseph Kadane, and Mark Schervish 1989. "On the shared preferences of two Bayesian decision makers." *Journal of Philosophy* 86: 225–44.

Selten, Reinhart 1975. "Re-examination of the perfectness concept for equilibrium in extensive games." *International Journal of Game Theory* 4: 22–5.

Sen, Amartya 1967. "Isolation, assurance, and the social rate of discount." *Quarterly Journal of Economics* 81: 112–24.

1970a. *Collective welfare and social choice*. San Francisco: Holden-Day.

1970b. "The impossibility of a Paretian liberal." *Journal of Political Economy* 78: 152–7.

1971. "Choice functions and revealed preference." *Review of Economic Studies* 38: 307–17.

1973. "Behaviour and the concept of preference." *Economica* 40: 241–59.

1976a. "Liberty, unanimity and rights." *Economica* 43: 217–45.

1976b. "Welfare inequalities and Rawlsian axiomatics." *Theory and Decision* 7: 243–62.

1977a. "Rational fools." *Philosophy and Public Affairs* 6: 317–44.

1977b. "Social choice theory: a re-examination." *Econometrica* 45: 53–89.

1982a. *Choice, welfare and measurement*. Cambridge, MA: MIT Press.

1982b. "Rights and agency." *Philosophy and Public Affairs* 11: 3–39.

1983. "Liberty and social choice." *Journal of Philosophy* 80: 5–28.

1985a. *Commodities and capabilities. Volume 7 of the Professor Dr. P. Hennipman lectures in economics: theory, institutions, policy*. Amsterdam: North-Holland.

1985b. "Rationality and uncertainty." *Theory and Decision* 81: 109–27.

1986. "Foundations of social choice theory: an epilogue," in Elster and Hylland, pp. 213–48.

1987a. *On ethics and economics*. Oxford: Basil Blackwell.

1987b. "The standard of living. Lecture I: Concepts and critiques," in Sen *et al.*, pp. 1–19.

1987c. "The standard of living. Lecture II: Lives and capabilities," in Sen *et al.*, pp. 20–38.

1990. "Gender and cooperative conflicts," in Irene Tinker (ed.), *Persistent inequalities*. London: Oxford University Press, pp. 123–49.

1992a. *Inequality reexamined*. Cambridge, MA: Harvard University Press.

1992b. "Minimal liberty." *Economica* 59: 139–59.

Sen, Amartya, John Muellbauer, Ravi Kanbur, Keith Hart and Bernard Williams 1987. *The standard of living*. (Ed. Geoffrey Hawthorn.) Cambridge: Cambridge University Press.

Sen, Amartya and Bernard Williams (eds.) 1982. *Utilitarianism and beyond*. Cambridge: Cambridge University Press.

Sidgwick, Henry 1901. *The methods of ethics* (6th edn.). London: Macmillan.

Singer, Peter 1975. *Animal liberation: a new ethics for our treatment of animals*. New York: Random House.

1977. "Freedoms and utilities in the distribution of health care," in Dworkin, Bermant, and Brown, pp. 149–74.

1979. *Practical ethics*. Cambridge: Cambridge University Press.

(ed.) 1986. *Applied ethics*. Oxford: Oxford University Press.

Smart, J. C. C. 1973. "An outline of a system of utilitarian ethics," in J. J. C. Smart and Bernard Williams, *Utilitarianism: for and against*. Cambridge: Cambridge University Press, pp. 1–74.

Smith, Adam 1776. *An inquiry into the nature and causes of the wealth of nations*. (Reprinted New York: Random House, 1937.)

Solow, Robert 1981. "Wage bargaining and unemployment." *American Economic Review* 71: 896–908.

1990. *The labor market as a social institution*. Oxford: Basil Blackwell.

Stewart, Hamish 1995. "A critique of instrumental reason in economics." *Economics and Philosophy* 11: 57–84.

Stich, Steven 1983. *From folk psychology to cognitive science: the case against belief*. Cambridge, MA: MIT Press.

Stone, Christopher 1988. *Earth and other ethics: the case for moral pluralism*. New York: Harper and Row.

Strasnick, Steven 1976. "Social choice and the derivation of Rawls's difference principle." *Journal of Philosophy* 73: 85–99.

Streeten, Paul 1953. "Appendix: recent controversies," in Gunnar Myrdal, *The political element in the development of economic theory*. (Trans. Paul Streeten.) London: Routledge and Kegan Paul, pp. 208–17.

Sugden, Robert 1985. "Liberty, preference and choice." *Economics and Philosophy* 2: 213–31.

1986. *The economics of rights, co-operation and welfare*. New York: Basil Blackwell.

1989. "Spontaneous order." *Journal of Economic Perspectives* 3: 85–97.

1990. "Contractarianism and Norms." *Ethics* 100: 768–86.

Sugden, Robert and Alan Williams 1978. *The principles of practical cost-benefit analysis*. New York: Oxford University Press.

Sumner, L. W. 1987. *The moral foundation of rights*. Oxford: Clarendon Press.

Tawney, R. H. 1931. *Equality*. New York: Harcourt, Brace and Co.

Taylor, Michael C. 1987. *The possibility of cooperation*. New York: Cambridge University Press.

Taylor, Michael and Hugh Ward 1982. "Chickens, whales and lumpy goods: alternative models of public goods provision." *Political Science* 30: 350–70.

Thomson, Garrett 1987. *Needs*. London: Routledge.

Thomson, Judith 1990. *The realm of rights*. Cambridge: Harvard University Press.

Thomson, William and Terje Lensberg 1989. *Axiomatic theory of bargaining with a variable number of agents*. New York: Cambridge University Press, 1989.

Thurow, Lester C. 1977. "Cash vs. in-kind redistribution," in Dworkin, Bermant, and Brown, pp. 85–106.

Titmuss, Richard 1971. *The gift relationship: from human blood to social policy*. New York: Random House.

Tversky, Amos, Paul Slovic, and Daniel Kahneman 1990. "The causes of preference reversal." *American Economic Review* 80: 204–17.

Tversky, Amos and Richard Thaler 1990. "Preference reversals." *Journal of Economic Perspectives* 4: 201–11.

van Parijs, Philippe 1989. "On the ethical foundations of basic income," Working Paper #CMID 32, Institute Supérieur de Philosophie, Université Catholique de Louvain.

1990. "The second marriage of justice and efficiency." *Journal of Social Policy* 19: 1–25.

1991. "Why surfers should be fed: the liberal case for an unconditional basic income." *Philosophy and Public Affairs* 20: 101–31.

Varian, Hal 1974. "Equity, envy and efficiency." *Journal of Economic Theory* 9: 63–91.

1975. "Distributive justice, welfare economics and the theory of fairness." *Philosophy and Public Affairs* 4: 223–47.

1985. "Dworkin on equality of resources." *Economics and Philosophy* 1: 110–27.

Vickrey, William 1945. "Measuring marginal utility by reactions to risk." *Econometrica* 13: 319–33.

1960. "Utility, strategy, and social decision rules." *Quarterly Journal of Economics* 74: 507–35.

Waldron, Jeremy (ed.) 1984. *Theories of rights*. Oxford: Oxford University Press.

1990. *The right to private property*. New York: Oxford University Press.

Walsh, Vivian 1994. "Rationality as self-interest vs. rationality as present aim." *American Economic Review Papers and Proceedings* 84: 401–5.

Walzer, Michael 1983. *Spheres of justice*. New York: Basic Books.

Weibull, Jörgen 1987. "Persistent unemployment as subgame perfect equilibrium." Seminar Paper No. 381 of the Institute for International Economic Studies, Stockholm, May.

Weitzman, Lenore 1985. *The divorce revolution: the unexpected social and economic consequences for women and children in America*. New York: The Free Press.

Wellman, Carl 1985. *A theory of rights: persons under laws, institutions and morals*. Totowa, NJ: Rowman and Allanheld.

Weston, Samuel 1994. "Toward a better understanding of the positive/normative distinction in economics." *Economics and Philosophy* 10: 1–18.

Weymark, John 1991. "A reconsideration of the Harsanyi–Sen debate on utilitarianism," in Elster and Roemer, pp. 255–320.

242   **References**

Williams, Bernard 1962. "The idea of equality," in P. Laslett and W. Runciman (eds.), *Philosophy, politics and society*, New York: Barnes and Noble.
  1973. "A critique of utilitarianism," in J. J. C. Smart and Bernard Williams, *Utilitarianism: for and against*. Cambridge: Cambridge University Press, pp. 77–150.
  1987. "The standard of living: interests and capabilities," in Sen *et al.*, pp. 94–102.
Winch, Peter 1958. *The idea of a social science*. London: Routledge.
Wolff, Robert Paul 1977. *Understanding Rawls: a reconstruction and critique of a theory of justice*. Princeton: Princeton University Press.
Wright, Georg von 1971. *Explanation and understanding*. Ithaca: Cornell University Press.
Yaari, Menachem and Maja Bar-Hillel 1984. "On dividing justly." *Social Choice and Welfare* 1: 1–24.

Index